This book may be kept

FOURTEEN DAYS

A fine of TWO CENTS will be charged for each day
the book is kept over time.

Contents

Illustrations

Preface

FRED LEWIS PATTEE is generally acknowledged to have been the first regularly appointed Professor of *American* Literature. His distinctive contribution to his time was his unrelenting and finally successful battle for the recognition of *American* literature as an entity related to, but separate from, the great traditional body of *English* literature—this in addition to the lasting impress he made on the thousands of students who sat in his classes during the more than 50 years of his active teaching career.

Professor Pattee left the manuscript of his autobiography to The Pennsylvania State College, where the long middle years of his life were spent. To the college he also gave his books and papers, which have an honored place now in the library which bears his name.

Publication of the autobiography was approved by the Board of Trustees of The Pennsylvania State College in January 1953, and President Milton S. Eisenhower named the following committee to supervise preparation and publication of the manuscript: Richard C. Maloney, Administrative Assistant, Office of the President; Louis H. Bell, Director of Public Information; and William L. Werner, Professor of American Literature, whom Professor Pattee had designated as his literary executor. Active cooperation was given by the staffs of the Fred Lewis Pattee Library, the Office of Public Information, the Office of the Comptroller, and the Penn State and Dartmouth Alumni Associations. In addition to an appropriation by the Board of Trustees, funds contributed by friends, former students, and the Dartmouth classmates of Professor Pattee made this publication possible.

My World as in My Time was the title Professor Pattee had given to his life story, but the picture that remains when the book is read is not so much of the world in which he lived, as a self-portrait of the man. And so it seemed fitting for us to substitute the title *Penn State Yankee*. This was the only liberty we took in editing the manuscript. Otherwise, except for minor changes of word-order, corrections of a few errors of fact, and the deletion of some redundancies and repetitions, the autobiography appears as it was written.

Here Professor Pattee is revealed in his own words: his romanticism, his inveterate Yankee-ness, a certain naïvete, and the nostalgia of old age are all apparent in his writing; but more than this, he shows the stronger qualities of winning personality, of ambition, determination, ruggedness, and perception that made him so effective as a teacher and so commanding as a pioneer in literary scholarship.

RICHARD C. MALONEY
LOUIS H. BELL
WILLIAM L. WERNER

The Pennsylvania State College
August 14, 1953

CHAPTER I

Five Hill Land Generations

B IOGRAPHIES OPEN USUALLY with genealogy—dull stuff for readers and generally skipped. I would skip mine, myself, did it not illustrate what happened in New England during the century that followed the Revolution. Luckily it is short, including only the family heads of five generations.

American history to date is a matter of some 10 generations, and it splits into halves on the year 1775. The colonial half may be illustrated by the five generations of the Mather family. My own line begins after the Revolution and parallels in its elements the Massachusetts family of the Adamses:

1. John Adams, 1753-1826	1. William "Patee," 1745-1810
2. John Q. Adams, 1767-1848	2. William Pattee, 1775-1820
3. Charles F. Adams, 1807-1886	3. Moses Pattee, 1806-1875
4. Henry Adams, 1838-1913	4. Lewis F. Pattee, 1834-1906
5.	5. Fred L. Pattee, 1863-

The Adams family represents the urban, the patrician, the academic, the professional New Englanders living on the areas won and settled before the Revolution, in the era when agriculture in New England was confined to the more accessible river valleys and the more easily-tilled land on the coastal plain. My family in its American beginnings was a landless group and after the Revolution was forced to turn to the Northern frontier mountain lands all but inaccessible and all but untillable. That Nature intended these hardscrabble lands for agriculture seems highly improbable, especially after one has seen her handiwork in the prairie lands of the West. Everywhere these earliest northern settlers found land, even the valleys made by mountain streams, littered with terminal moraine bowlders and cobble stones from the great ice age, and there was no escaping the stone-crop even if one took up land on the steep sides of the prevailing hills. But no hardship could stop these indomitable settlers. From the bowlders cleared from the stone-pocked lands they built stone fences, thousands of miles of them, and on hillside fields tilted on hazardous mountain slopes they grew crops that fed families of from 10 to 15 children. Only one element kept them from utter isolation: they must be within horse-and-wagon distance from the village church, the red school house, the town hall, and the blacksmith shop.

According to insistent family tradition, the American pioneer of our line was William who arrived in Boston from England during the Revolutionary era. According to my grandfather, who was born in 1806, the wife of this pioneer was Irish, *nee* Molly Hyde. Disembarking at Boston she saw on the dock for the first time in her life a negro and screamed in terror thinking he was the devil. Concerning this William I, little information has survived. By some genealogists he has been connected with other branches of the Pattee family, notably with the branches springing from the descendants of Peter Pattee of Haverhill, Massachusetts, but our family tradition is inflexibly against it. William's sea-chest, so called, is still to be seen. He seems to have drifted north to New Hampshire and his name, spelled "Patee," is to be found on an Alexandria, N. H. Revolutionary document preserved in the State Capitol. He seems to have had a part in the organization of the Alexandria township during the first decade of the American republic, and a deed is on file showing that he secured several holdings from the first division of lots, in the South Alexandria area, choosing level land that would be easily cultivated. His farm buildings he built near a lively trout stream on the main valley road just pushed through to Hebron on the North.

The eldest son, William II, broke away from this farm early, married Judith Worthen from a notable family in the next township, went up the steep hill from his father's holdings, and, securing more of the newly-plotted town lots, built a farm house after the prevailing New England pattern with huge fireplaces and arches with set kettles and brick ovens, dug a deep well, and attached to the house the usual woodsheds and barns. All this was extant while I was a boy and I have explored every part of it. So rocky were the cleared fields that the surrounding stone fences were veritable double walls six feet wide on top, the space between the two outside walls filled with cobbles.

This second generation William was a man of more than local importance, a justice of the peace, the only one in a wide area, and a rural judge and attorney. He died at 44, thrown from his horse, leaving a family of 10 children, six of them girls who early married young farmers of the neighborhood and helped them clear the inevitable hillside farms.

On the death of William II the estate was settled, as my father once expressed it, "on strictly mathematical lines." The widow, Judith Worthen, became heir to a third of the estate; William III became the family head, carrying on the farm until his death; and the other three boys became self-supporting at the earliest possible moment. Richard went to Holyoke, Massachusetts, learned a trade, invented the so-called Pattee hydrant, and flourished. The two other boys, James and Moses, left home together, found work on the Blackstone canal, became stonemasons, in time returned home, married local maidens, and after the pattern of their father went a quarter of a mile farther up the Pattee hill and hewed out two farms.

Again incredible toil, again stone walls made from cleared fields, again stump-pulling and burning and clearing. My own father has told me that he had often been awakened at night by the roar of a load of stones dumped upon a wall by his uncle James, who, after a hard day's work as a mason in the town two miles away, would work till near midnight by lantern light clearing land.

This Moses of the third generation, my grandfather, married Jane Gordon whose grandfather had been a member of the Gordon highlanders, or Black Watch Regiment. The farmhouse which he built is still standing. In it was born a family of 10 children. The first son, William IV, died early, as did Jesse Gordon, the second male heir, leaving my father the oldest surviving son. To rear this family of 10 children on such unpromising land required not only interminable labor, but careful planning and rigid economy. All his farm work he did with a single yoke of oxen. They did all his ploughing, hauled all his loads, twitched out all stumps and bowlders, and made possible the great stone fences. Jane, my grandmother, wove with a handloom nearly all of the cloth used for the family garments, spun yarn from the wool of sheep raised on the farm, and knit it into stockings and mittens, attended to the dairy products from three or four cows, made many cheeses, attended to all the work required at the fall butcherings, and in addition to all this cooked the meals for a farm family of voracious children.

Often have I heard the last survivor of these 10 children— he died in 1927, aged 84—tell of the good things that used to come out of the great brick oven. On Sunday all the family went to church, father and mother and the small children in the farm wagon drawn by the old work horse, and the older boys and girls, with Sunday shoes in their hands to be put on at the last moment, galloping on ahead. In the early morning grandmother had had a fire of "lightwood" built in the brick oven and when the heat had reached the proper intensity had put in her great roast thoroughly flavored with summer savory, sage and other fragrant herbs grown in her own garden, had added a huge pot of beans, and pans of vegetables properly guarded with water, and then dressing in the clothes worn only on the Sabbath day, was ready to observe, as it should be observed, the holy Sabbath.

Always, there were two services with an hour at noon between, an hour spent by the men in the horse-sheds talking crops and the weather and stock, and by the women in the vestry talking as over-worked, isolated farm women would talk of babies, and diseases, and accidents and hopes. Then home in the afternoon to find the great dinner in the brick oven done to a turn. After half a century my old uncle's mouth would fairly water as he described these Gargantuan Sunday dinners.

Many conveniences now the merest commonplaces were unknown, even in the early life of my father who was born in 1834. Friction matches were still in the future. Fires had to be carefully covered at night so that live coals could be raked out in the morning with which to kindle the new fire for the day. Failure at this point meant the borrowing of live coals from neighbors. Churches were unheated even in below-zero weather. Many worshippers, however, kept their feet warm with hot bricks or with foot stoves filled at home with live coals. For all her cooking my grandmother used maple sugar made on the farm. Kerosene lamps did not arrive until my father was in middle life. For lights during the long winter evenings nothing was in use save home-made tallow candles.

The fourth generation, my father's generation, filled the New England hill-farm land to overflowing. It cleared lands that nature never intended for agriculture, surrounded them with the stone walls which became their most lasting monuments, and built the great farm buildings, the barn connected with the house by a long wood-shed, many of them still in use in the mountain lands.

But this generation, born in the 1830s and 1840s, was also a migrant generation. It scattered its forces into every part of America. The fourth generation, children of William Pattee III, left the farm early as if it were a plague spot. The eldest, Joseph, a mere boy, struck out on foot for the West getting small jobs on the way. Arrived at length at a port of the Great Lakes, he found a job on one of the boats, reached Minnesota, found work on a new railroad and during the last years of his life was master mechanic of all the lines of the Great Northern Railroad. His brother Warren, reached high rank in the express department of the same road, and his brother Dick acquired a comfortable clerkship. Samuel, however, achieved success nearer home.

My father, Lewis Franklin, born 1834, also went west in the 1850s. For a time he settled in Milwaukee. Later he took part in the Kansas-Nebraska settlement to the extent of driving single-handed a herd of young cattle for settlers in the newly-opened territory. His return to New Hampshire may be explained by the fact that shortly after his arrival back in his home State, he was married to Mary P. Ingalls in 1861, and settled on a small farm near the South Alexandria border. After a year in this isolated spot, they removed to Bristol where I was born March 22, 1863. On August 1, 1868, father bought the Uncle James Pattee farm just above grandfather's home place where he had spent his boyhood, and took possession in November. Here I spent my childhood.

I have elaborated somewhat this family history since it illustrates with the exactness of a parable what happened to New England during the first century of the republic, especially to the vital hinterland among the mountains from which was to come so much of the bone and sinew and character that later settled the West, fought the Civil War, and made possible the industrial era that followed.

2

To say that mere chance directed the *Mayflower* to the New England area is to court argument. The Pilgrims themselves were confident that God held the tiller and directed the landfall. It must be admitted, however, that the Pilgrims themselves, were unaware that they were to settle in the New England area. So far as we can gather from their scanty records they simply sailed for America—a wide mark. Then driven in zig-zags by contrary winds and fierce gales, swept out of reckoning for days on end, headed now west, now south, by sudden squalls and tempests, at the mercy of a sailing master eager to land his cargo at the earliest possible moment so as to escape for home, why of all points should they have made New England their landfall? Why not Newfoundland? Why not Florida? Any one of a thousand chances would have veered them from the New England coast.

But whether it was chance or Providence, one thing is sure: that settlement never would have been made had the Pilgrims been able to view the whole Atlantic coast and choose deliberately the place for their permanent location. "A stern and rockbound coast" describes accurately their landfall. Solely from the standpoint of topography and climate and agricultural possibilities the land they settled should have been called not New England, but New Scotland or New Switzerland. Where else can one find terminal moraines heaped with glacial drift cultivated seriously as farms; steep hillsides jagged with rocks turned into corn fields, quaking mountain swamps bottomed with polypod roots, tough as wires, made into meadows; sky-line ridges bastioned with granite and snarled with hardhack turned into pastures, wrenched from Nature with incredible toil, fenced with walls of rolled-up bowlders by the labor of Titans; Arctic cold, with snow often for half the year; roads eternally up and down and branching with sharp angles, buried under great drifts in winter and washed into ragged gulches by the fierce cloudbursts of summer—where else will one find a seriously-cultivated farming region like that?

Of the generations of the Colonial period, who cleared the rich southern river valleys, built the harbor towns, and settled the arable lowland areas along the coastal plains, I shall say nothing. The second five generations concern me. Following the Revolution they were forced farther and farther back into the hill lands and the mountains.

The first generation of this second colonial period was a race of sturdy souls. It was this hardy brood that had fought through the Seven Years' War and the Revolution; a restless, free-born race, full-lunged and mighty-limbed, that at the close of the war crashed into the northern woods far up into Maine and New Hampshire and Vermont, founded towns by every water-power, surveyed the land into townships and the townships into lots, and carved out the first farms along the flats and river courses. Of this generation was the founder of our family, William I, as we call him.

For 40 years the northern wilderness rang with the axes of this generation, the crash of their old-growth pines, their shouts to their toiling oxen. Clearings became farms; trails were plowed into roads; wild mountain torrents were turned upon saws and mill-stones. That was the first generation of our national era, the generation that adopted the Constitution and added to it the sacred Bill of Rights. It was the first generation to be forced into the hill lands, and it was a generation of demigods who each did the work of five. And the women no less than the men. They it was who under sternest conditions and amid elemental surroundings bore and reared those families of 12 and 15 children, fed them, clothed them with cloth made on the kitchen loom, rested never a moment and died at last worn to the bone, their work all undone lying in heaps for the next wife to straighten out.

These children born on the frontier were the second generation of the national era. Swarms of them had been compelled early like spring robins to leave the home nest and forage for themselves. They too broke into wild lands and cleared fields and built farm buildings. They it was who organized fully the hill towns, built the steepled churches on the town commons, and completed roads far up into the hill lands where they had hewn out farms. It was this generation that built the most of the great farmhouses with their colossal chimneys and with their low-posted rooms sheathed with wainscoting of clear pine boards sometimes four feet in width. They completed the early highways, running them without thought of compromise straight over the steepest hills, oblivious of the fact, not discovered until a century later, that, as expressed by one old farmer, "the kettle bail is no longer when it lies down than when it stands erect." They multiplied the settled land by 10 and made the northern hills a neighborhood with growing villages and groupings of hard-won farms. To this generation belonged William Pattee II.

The third generation coming upon the scene in the early years of the new century, completed the expansion. When they had done their work, every acre of land that could by human effort be wrung from nature for farming purposes had been taken. The steep hillsides were dotted now with farmhouses. Everywhere now were little neighborhoods, often far in the mountain fastnesses. I am thinking of the farms I have seen myself under cultivation under the very shadow of Mount Cardigan, reached only by climbing mile after mile of steepest mountain roads. One might come upon isolated farms in mountain ravines where the winter sun scarcely ever shone after mid-afternoon, or clustered like Swiss hamlets about the bases of bare peaks sometimes 10 or 15 miles from post office and store. Not 40 years ago I climbed up an abandoned road to Tenney Hill which looms high over Newfound Lake in New Hampshire, and found old fields still used for pasturing cattle. For years no one had lived on the hill; the houses and barns had disappeared, and even the old cellars were not easily found. My father as a boy about 1845 had, with his Uncle Richard, climbed the hill on a hunting trip and had seen 10 or 15 farms there with broad fields, great barns and buildings, and droves of cattle in wide pastures. During a winter term in the red school house of that hill neighborhood there would be 60 or 70 vigorous youngsters, so vigorous indeed that it was the local tradition that only a man teacher could rule the Tenney Hill school. Today that hill is utter wilderness, a wilderness still traversed by stone walls, miles and miles of them. Walls that had once surrounded every field and pasture, and in every fence corner great stoneheaps like outworks of a fortress, imperishable monuments to a race forever gone.

And in all these vanished mountain farmhouses had been children, 10 and 12 and even 15 in each family. My father was one of 10 children as indeed was my mother. Born in the 1830s and 1840s, this fourth generation saw New England at the peak of its development. During their childhood the hills swarmed with life and work and promise. Nowhere was a section so remote that one might not find there a neighborhood of small farms. Sprung from generations of hill-born men, toilers in the open air, feeders on the wholesome fruits of the soil, lovers of the woods and the hills over which they scurried like the red foxes they delighted to hunt, reared in the great farmhouses where sleeping rooms were unheated and abundantly ventilated, this generation was as sturdy a race as the earth ever produced. They were as free as the hill winds they breathed; they looked one straight in the eye; they depended solely upon their own brains and muscles and wills; they were self-confident and undismayed by difficulties; they could adapt themselves to circumstances and improvise new methods; and their parents so trained them that they could work and indeed love to work.

That was the period when townships containing today scarce 200 souls numbered sometimes as high as 1200 or 1500 inhabitants. My home town of Alexandria, still vast in acreage, in the last census contained not much over 400 people; yet in the

1850s it came near having 2000, enough indeed to entitle it to two seats in the General Court of the State. Then it was that the town meeting day, held yearly on the second Tuesday in March, was the major event of the year. The whole population of the township assembled then at the town hall: hoary old grandsires of the second generation, bent and feeble, were there in full force, chattering like grasshoppers, and dwelling always on the strength of their youth and the vast changes they had seen since the town was a wilderness. Women and children came. A colossal dinner they prepared in the church: baked beans, brown bread, cold ham, apple pie, all for a quarter of a dollar.

The third generation men, now in their prime, ruled the day, heard the report of the town treasurer, the selectmen, the town clerk, passed or rejected by *viva voce* vote, one by one, the articles in the town "warrant," bid off the town poor, and then supervised the balloting for the "town fathers" who were to rule the new year. And outside of the hall flocked the young men under 21, a surging mass boiling with life, massive of shoulders, mighty of limb, clad in coarse and strong garments, and wearing heavy cow-hide boots that reached almost to their knees. What a magazine of stored-up energy! They were not still a moment; crowding and pushing each other, boasting, boxing, wrestling, laughing boisterously at rough jokes, jumping, lifting each other "stiff heels" with main strength, and finally massing together and crashing down the main partition of the town hall. What outlet was there to be for this pent-up mill-dam of power?

It was time for New England to send out swarms, as bees swarm from their home hives in the spring time. The old hive was full to bursting. Had there been no vent beyond the home domain it is hard to imagine what might have been. Had they followed the example of the three generations before them and sought to take up new land for farming, where could they have found it? Land already was being worked against the very protest of nature, and this virile new brood would have had to turn the very pastures and ledges into farms, and expend their lives in making gardens and fields out of what could hardly have been turned into goat runs.

The first overflow consisted of the older girls who found work as loom-tenders in the cotton mills of Lowell and Fall River. My mother and all her sisters were mill-hands in the Merrimack mills during the 1850s. The older boys found employment in the machine shops and the stores of Boston and the cities along the seaboard. But this was a mere nothing. The pressure in the northern farming lands was increasing. Something must happen.

And suddenly that something came.

The great West opened all in a moment as if the curtain had risen for the first act. Gold had been found on the far Pacific coast, fabulous masses of gold to be had for the mere gathering —in California, a region that seemed as vague and as far away as the Valley of Diamonds that Sinbad discovered. How it thrilled the northern farms! Then had come the Kansas-Nebraska call that sounded over New England like a trumpet blast! Squatter sovereignty—land for nothing—60 acres of fat land and a yoke of oxen free. "Iowa," "Minnesota," "Wisconsin," "Illinois"—the names were on every lip. Men talked of nothing else. Whole families started westward; young boys stole from their homes in dead of night and worked their way west to kill Indians and buffaloes and see the Great Plains.

Then suddenly like a fire alarm at night rang out the call to war. Seventy thousand, five hundred thousand, two million of men must come from the North, and there must be a thousand leaders raised at once, for this was to be a war such as the world never before had seen. Never had there been such a call for MEN, men for the armies of the North, men to break the vast West, men to develop the iron and the oil and the coal and to make the machines for its use, men to bridge rivers innumerable, to tunnel mountains, dig canals, make railroads and build cities.

There was no time to school and train this army of fighters and workers, no drill-masters to fit it for its new work. It must be picked from material already at hand for work to be done at once. And to the glory of the New World the material was ready. In 1838 Emerson had written: "This country has not fulfilled what seemed the reasonable expectation of mankind. Men looked, when all feudal straps and bandages were snapped asunder, that Nature, too long the mother of dwarfs, should reimburse itself by a brood of Titans who should laugh and leap in the continent, and run up the mountains of the West with the errand of genius and love." And even as he wrote, the brood which he described was in its cradles. When it had done its work Emerson could say, "We shall not again disparage America, now we have seen what men it will bear."

A generation of Titans it was indeed that carried through the Civil War, that conquered what even in my earliest school geography was denominated "the great American desert" and made it the granary of the world, and that in a single generation. They spanned the continent with railroads, penetrated the Rockies and the Sierra Nevadas, swept aside the Plains Indians, exterminated the uncounted millions of the buffalo herds, opened navigation on the great rivers, built Chicago and the cities of the Plains, organized iron works in Pittsburgh, uncovered the coal and the oil and sent them broadcast over the earth, and in their old age left what had been "the wild West" of their boyhood a dream-land as wild and romantic and far away to their grandchildren as the lands of the Arabian Nights.

But alas for New England! One day in 1861 there had been pitched on the town common of Alexandria, two miles from the Pattee hill of my ancestors, the tents of a recruiting squad seeking volunteers for the war in the South, and in a single day more than 100 young farm lads had signed the rolls. More came later. The Twelfth N. H. Regiment was recruited from an area nowhere more than 20 miles distant from this Alexandria Common. The fourth generation of the New England hill lands came in droves to the colors, and what they did all can read. The war over, they came back as veterans but they did not stay. They had seen the plantation farms of the South and for the first time they saw their native fields in their true light. And now everywhere was echoed the cry of Horace Greeley in his *Tribune* (which they pronounced Try-bune): "Go West, Young Man, and grow up with the Country." Congress appropriated wild lands to the young veterans who would go and settle on them. And the young veterans went and with them newly wedded wives. And the exodus drained the Hill townships until they became first the area of abandoned farms and before the fifth generation had passed wilderness again as in the days following the Revolution.

And here I come in, a representative of that fifth generation that saw the break-up period in its beginning, its middle and its end. In every way my generation has stood for swift change, for revolution indeed. Within my lifetime, New England, as my grandfather and my father knew it, has almost ceased to be. Indeed the world as I knew it in my boyhood has in all its phases and all its ideals completely vanished.

CHAPTER II

Civil War Baby

I AM QUITE SURE THAT, could I have been asked ere the "sleep and forgetting" called my birthdate, where I would choose to begin my next adventure in living, my answer would have been, "Drop me in the New Hampshire mountain land not too far from Dartmouth." Had I been permitted, however, to time my advent, I doubtless would have chosen an earlier date. During all of my early life I was haunted by the feeling that I had been born too late—too late to have been an actor in the colossal drama of the Civil War. That, in my early years. Later, I have been glad and more than glad that I came when I did. Like all generations after a great war, mine was able to view the great struggle not as did those who fought it, in blindness and suffering, but with perspective. Moreover, to my generation it came not as stark realism, but as romance to which time was to add more and more the gleam that is poetry. Had I been of the battle generation, I should not have been able to witness to its end and record the fifth act of the New England tragedy.

I was a war baby, born 100 days before Gettysburg, March 22, 1863. Five of my uncles were in the Union Army, all of my mother's brothers and one of my father's. Uncle John Ingalls died from disabilities received at Fredericksburg. Before me lies a letter from a Union camp near New Orleans, 1863. It was from mother's brother, Horace, and in it occurs the first written reference ever made to my existence: "Is it a boy or a girl?"

Thus I was nursed in my very cradle on war as a vanished glory—romance. All about me in my early years moved those who had been actors in the vanished drama, fathers, mothers, "old soldiers" still in their 20s, bubbling always with strange adventure. I was sung to sleep with Yankee war songs, many of which had been sent to my mother by her brothers at the front.

All of these songs were tremulous with sentiment and even sentimentalism. Before I could walk without waddling, I was singing with astonishing volume, *Just Before the Battle, Mother,* and *Tramp, Tramp, Tramp, the Boys Are Marching,* my version of the opening line being: "In the prison Sally set . . ."

The earliest lyric I ever learned entire was a recruiting song mother often sang to us. I quote from memory:

> We are sailing on the ocean
>> Where the stormy winds do blow;
> We are coasting down along the Rebel shore.
>> We have left our wives and sweethearts
> In our dear New England home
>> There to wait for us till the war is o'er.

Chorus:

>> Oh ye Yankees come away,
>> Come enlist without delay,
>> Come and help rout out these rebels as of yore;
>> For we never will give over till we plant the starry flag
>> On every fort along the Southern shore.

> Johnny Bull is getting angry;
>> We have heard the lion roar;
> He would gladly set his paw upon our shore;
>> But we think he'd better tarry
> And let Freedom's bird alone
>> For we've played him Yankee Doodle once before.

The sentimental songs of the '50s and the war years I knew by heart. My mother's family, the 10 children of Gilman and Sarah Ingalls, all of whom lived to maturity, all of whom were born and reared on the rocky little "Hemp Hill" farm overlooking Newfound Lake, a farm three miles from Pattee Hill, were as distinctive a group of singers and instrumentalists as were the famous Hutchinson Family, of Civil War fame. With organization they too could have given concerts, vocal and instrumental, but forced to leave the farm as soon as they were able to earn wages, an Ingalls Family entertainment group was impossible. Grandfather Ingalls for years was leader of the choir in the Free Will Baptist Church at Alexandria Village; his wife, Sarah Roberts, was leading soprano; and every one of the older children worshipped on Sundays in the "singing seats."

Two of the boys became professional musicians, cornetists of distinction and bandleaders. During the war Gustavus, the oldest of the family, became bandmaster of all the regiments stationed at Hilton Head, South Carolina, for winter quarters. His brother George was leader of the Twelfth N. H. Regiment Band. Once in an inter-regimental contest including all the bands in the encampment, Uncle George's band captured the first prize with a version he had made of the then new song *The Mocking Bird*. He had arranged it as a band piece and the chorus "Listen to the Mocking Bird" he had punctuated with bird notes to be played on the piccolo by a Meredith, New Hampshire, fifer, a new variation soon to become commonplace. In later years Gustavus became the inventor and manufacturer of the Ingalls reed which made possible the parlor organ, and established in Worcester, Mass., a plant that manufactured the Mason & Hamlin variety of this instrument, soon to become popular in small homes. Uncle George H. Ingalls became a band-leader, his "Cork-Leg" Band at one time being widely known.

My whole childhood echoed with sentimental song. Mother had one of the most moving voices I have ever known. She had not a wide compass of tone but she sang with rare expression, as if the feeling of the song was her own and as if it came out spontaneously. Her singing made of me an incurable romanticist. Listening to her set me into wild dreamings and imaginative adventurings. I remember she sang feelingly the old song *Gaily the Troubador*. This is my memory of it:

> Gaily the troubadour touched his guitar,
> As he was faring home, home from the war.
> Home from Palestine, no more to roam,
> Lady love, lady love, welcome me home.
>
> She for the troubadour often had wept,
> Often had prayed for him while others slept,
> Saying, "O Troubadour, why do you roam?
> Troubadour, troubadour, turn you back home."

To mother this was not a mere ballad of ancient days; it was a cry from the great war in the South that had taken her favorite brother's life and had filled with anguish so many homes she had known during four tragic years. "Home from Palestine" meant for me only one thing: the Civil War soldier, like my uncles, returning from the South, the mythical land where they had gone as crusaders.

Not all of my favorite songs of childhood were war ballads, however. Such songs as *In the Evening by the Moonlight*, and all of Stephen Foster's melodies chorded with everything that was within me. The prayer meeting songs mother had learned as a mill girl became a part of my education. Her favorite was *Shall We Gather at the River*. Feelingly she told us how mill-girls at Lowell, where she worked, caught in the ruins of the fallen Pemberton Mill sang until the flames smothered them: "Yes, we shall gather at the river, the beautiful, the beautiful river."

Mother boiled eggs to music: so many verses to each minute the egg was to be cooked. I remember one evening father as he started out to do his chores, including the milking of three cows, arranged that both were to sing the old hymn, *My Father's House is Bright and Fair*. Agreeing on the time-beat of the hymn, father went out singing, leaving mother singing over her dish-washing. Half an hour later, when father came in singing they were hardly a beat apart in time, and they finished the hymn together.

The Civil War atmosphere colored for me my childhood and my later boyhood. To me even now the old war in the South has over it the halo that must have stirred the imaginations of the generations following the Crusades. The stories told by my uncles and by the veterans who every year had regimental reunions in nearby towns were all touched with the dramatic and the heroic and the sentimental. The sons of many local families had never returned. Three of the Nelson boys had been killed at Gettysburg, many young veterans had come home minus a leg or an arm, the rest of their lives to live at the expense of the government. The pathos of the war was always dwelt upon and the anguish of fathers and mothers when battles were known to have been fought and no news came. In Bristol, two miles from

Pattee Hill, an eager mob of all the citizens was massed before the post office at the arrival of every mail, and just after Gettysburg private letters from the front were seized and opened and read to the crowd.

During all of my early years Decoration Day was observed like no other holiday. The war veterans marched in squad formation with a drum corps at the head and on every soldier's grave they placed a small flag and a wreath, closing the ceremony with taps blown by a bugler who had a brilliant war record. Always at the head of the column rode the most distinguished soldier of the town, Captain Bill Beckford, who once in battle had rescued at great personal risk the regimental flag which had fallen with its mortally wounded custodian.

Then there was the memorable day of June when the Twelfth New Hampshire Regiment held its reunion at Bristol, with regimental band, officers on horseback, and men on crutches marching with the line and cheered as they passed. No hall in town was large enough to hold the regiment and the visiting crowd, and the Grand Assembly was held on the town common, the speakers and the uniformed officers massed on the grandstand. I was greatly impressed by the glory of the regimentals worn by the speakers, but I was too young to get much from their speeches. Frank Beckford, brother of the captain, read a requiem to the unknown dead. All I now recall of the speaking was a very small officer who, the toast-master said, lived during the whole war up in the air, in observation towers, "He was so small the Rebs couldn't see him up there." I remember another veteran was brought to the front as an exhibit: he was "Ramrod Pittman," tallest man in the regiment. "When the Johnnys took him prisoner they didn't send him to Libby, they used him as a ramrod for cleaning out their guns." That evening during the story-telling rendezvous of the regiment, the British cannon which since the War of 1812 had been mounted on Sugar Hill just over the town spoke again and again, until finally, overloaded, it burst, throwing fragments down into the town square, though injuring no one. All through my youthful years I felt that somehow fate had cheated me: I had been born two decades too late and my life that might have been poetry had turned out to be mere prose.

I got small sympathy for my romanticism from father. The Pattees were workers, peasant-minded so far as adherence to the land was concerned, practical in the extreme, never a moment idle. Their outlook upon the domains of art and beauty and literature was Puritanic. Romance and fiction and all that pertained to the theater they reckoned among the major sins furnished by the devil. As a boy I was warned against dime novels, love stories, and all other fiction. "You admit that what's told in that novel never *really* happened?" my father would say. "Yes," I would reply, "but . . ." "Then it's a *lie*. Why read lies when you can read history and biography? Love stories! Pshaw." Never in his life did he read a novel. Mother, in 1861, however, persuaded him to listen to her reading of *Uncle Tom's Cabin*, assuring him that it was actual life as it was lived in the South. He was tremendously impressed, and after she had read to him the death scene of Uncle Tom, without a word he got his hat, went to town and enlisted as a three years' volunteer. The medical examination, however, disqualified him. He had a bad knee.

Mother was totally different. As a mill girl at Lowell she shared the excitement when *Jane Eyre* appeared, a title she always gave the mill-girl pronunciation, "Jane Erie." Through all her life it remained her favorite novel, equalled only by *The Lamplighter*, *Beulah*, and *The Wide, Wide World*. Her mill-girl sister Frances, who visited us often during my childhood, always brought copies of Bonner's *New York Ledger*, a periodical excoriated by father but read eagerly by mother. Mother furnished most of the literature that fed my boyhood, a scanty stock which she had acquired during her mill days: *Lives of Eminent Christians* bound in scarlet and gold with "Mary P. Ingalls" embossed on the cover; *Noble Deeds of Women;* a flamboyant gift book, *The Golden Gift* of the 1853 vintage given her by an early admirer; and a family Bible, pulpit size, illustrated, and beautifully bound with gold bordered covers. *Notes on Acts*, a small Biblical geography, and a school-sized *Webster's Dictionary* completed her library.

Mother had been a part of a notable movement, one that was made much of by Dickens during his first American tour. In the mid-years of the century the great cotton mills along the Merrimack made the first draft upon the growing over-population of the New England hinterland towns, a call for girls to tend looms and do other light factory work. And the farm girls were glad of an opportunity to go out into the great world and find congenial environments. Mother went to Lowell with her sister Mahala in 1850 when she was 16. Later she worked for several years in the Manchester, New Hampshire, mills, then in the cotton mills of Hooksett. As a loom operative she became exceedingly proficient, at one time being allowed to run six looms, the usual limit being five. I was told that she could join broken threads amid the flying shuttles with the dexterity of a magician, darting her hand here and there and joining threads so swiftly that an observer would not realize what she was doing.

The mill-girls, her room-mates and companions, seem to have been a remarkably religious, almost an evangelical, group of females. I have letters written to her in later years by these early friends, later happily married, and all of them are pietistically sentimental to the limit. In 1852, about the time of mother's first employment in the mills, there appeared in *The Boston Courier*, a poem entitled *Song of the Manchester Factory Girl*, written by John H. Warland. I quote it not for any poetic merit it may have, but for its revelations of a social movement forgotten now for a century. From the nine stanzas I select three:

> O sing me a song of the Factory Girl,
>   Who hath breathed our mountain air,
> She toils for her home, and the joys to come
>   To the loved ones gathered there.
> She tends the loom, she watches the spindle,
>   And fancies her mother near,—
> How glows her heart, as her bright eyes kindle,
>   And she thinks of her sisters dear!

O sing a song of the Factory girl,
    Whose fabric clothes the world;
From the king and his peers to the jolly tars,
    With our flag on all seas unfurled.
From China's gold Seas to the tainted breeze
    That sweeps the smokened room,
Where "God save the Queen" to cry are seen
    The slaves of the British loom.

God bless our Yankee Factory Girl!
    The rose of our mountain wild,—
Like a merry bird shall her song be heard
    Where'er sweet labor hath smiled.
From our forests green, where the axe hath been
    And the waters dance in the sun,
Through the southern clime to the thunder chime
    Of the surging Oregon.

Mother was 10 years in the mills, leaving them in 1860 to be married in January 1861.

3

Religion was seldom talked about in our home, but it was a felt, almost a ruling atmosphere. Religion awoke on Sunday and dominated the day. No weather, winter or summer, could keep father's or grandfather's family from the two services of the local church. Even the old family dog knew when the Sabbath day arrived. He was allowed to go with the wagon to town on week days, but not on Sunday when he might scandalize the family by slipping into the church. The result was that early every Sunday morning old Trip disappeared. But sometimes when grandfather and grandmother with the small children in the farm wagon had reached the foot of Pattee Hill, half a mile from home, the old dog would be found trotting on behind. Then he would be captured by the boys and led back, but more often than not he was discovered only after the family had reached the church. He seemed to learn by experience that it was not safe to be found until it was too late to return him home.

The Pattees were Methodists. The religion of the period was emotional. Much was said of "the Heavenly Home." Grandfather Pattee at prayer-meeting, called on to lead in prayer, would begin in a low tone, so low indeed as scarcely to be heard. Then gradually he would get "warmed up," would increase in volume until the very windows of Heaven would seem to shake. Most of the old "saints" of the time were highly emotional even when they were giving their "testimony" in the meeting, but in prayer they poured out their souls as if the Lord was hard of hearing, or else so far away up in the skies that only by shouting could they command His attention. None spoke or prayed without frequent allusions to the dear ones "over on the other side."

It was no formal thing, the religion that ruled the home of my Grandfather Moses. That the Bible came to men straight from the hand of God was never for one moment doubted. The family lived its daily life absolutely certain that after death they would be reunited in "the Better Land." Grandfather's favorite hymn was *There is Rest for the Weary:*

> On the other side of Jordan
> In the sweet fields of Eden
> Where the Tree of Life is blooming
> There is rest for me.

Undoubtedly the religion of his pioneer generation was the religion of tired toiling men and lonely women, who were here only for a night and then passed over to the Better Land. Two of my father's brothers, Jesse and William, died in their mid-20s. I have in my possession the Bibles given by grandmother to each of them when they left home. Both died in utter confidence that the separation was but for a moment. Jesse in his last hours asked that his funeral sermon be preached from the text Job 19: 26. "And though, after my skin, worms destroy this body, yet in my flesh shall I see God." His wish was obeyed.

All through my boyhood and far beyond it I was taught to divide humanity into two distinct parts: the "saved" and the "unsaved." Until one had been "converted" and had "professed religion," he was to be ranked as a sinner and numbered with the "unsaved." When I applied for the principalship of the academy in the small town of Northwood, New Hampshire, the first question asked me by Deacon Foss, one of the school trustees, was,

"Are you a professor?" meaning of course a "professor of religion."

Father, during my early boyhood, was not a "professor." His years in what was then the frontier West had modified to a degree his early training, and when angry he could swear profusely. Then in the early '70s the evangelist Henry Durant, the founder of Wellesley College and the school for deaf mutes, one of whose pupils had been my Uncle Wilbur, came to Bristol for a series of revival meetings. His influence on the town was tremendous. Nearly every "unsaved" man in town went to the altar, among them my father. I remember being awakened one night and hearing father come in from a meeting and saying to mother, "Kneel down with me. I want to pray." That was the beginning of a Christian life as genuine and as consistent to the end of his life as any I have ever known. Family prayers were established. On Sunday morning there was a Bible reading and a prayer, a special petition always being added for "the absent member of the family," if any were absent.

In both the Pattee and the Ingalls families it was an unbroken custom to give to the son or daughter who was leaving home, a Bible with an inscription on a fly leaf written by the mother's hand. There have fallen to me the small Bibles taken from home by several of my uncles. When I went to college I too received a Bible with the inscribed admonition written by mother to read it often if I were to avoid the way of sin. Mother herself certainly read the Bible. She intended to read it straight through once every year, having worked out a schedule that divided the Book into 365 reading sections. Seldom did she neglect this daily task, and if by any accident she was forced to miss a reading she always made it up the next time.

Until I went to college I never had a doubt that in the Bible was to be found all that God in His wisdom thought mankind needed to know. To criticize in any way the workings of Nature which God had made, the weather, the insect pests, the failure of crops, or any of the catastrophies of life, the seeming hard luck that came at times to all men, was to criticise the One who had made it all. Everything that came into our lives was a part

of His great plan that sometime would be made clear to us, but whatever it might be it would be for our good.

Attendance upon "divine worship" was about all the social life the community afforded. At times a singing school would be held in the school house and all the boys and girls needed no urging to attend it and pay the small tuition fee. The parents considered knowing how to sing the sacred songs a necessary part of one's education, but the youngsters were not so eager to learn as they were to see the girls or the boys. Christmas was celebrated with a community tree in the school house, and in my later boyhood there was organized a farmer's lyceum where farm problems were discussed and readings and amusing programs were often rendered. Everybody could sing, and music meant for most of the people only hymns—in later days the Moody and Sankey gospel songs.

As I look back now on my early New England life I see that the church was central in its thinking. Everywhere, no matter how small the town, one found in the center of it the commanding church spire or spires. Never were these houses of worship called churches: always in the New England argot they were "meeting-houses"—a highly significant term. They were primarily religious institutions, but they were far more than mere places for worship. They were social centres for isolated farm populations. On Sundays one saw one's neighbors and had a visit with them. Then too on Sunday the farmer wore his "Sunday clothes." The man with the hoe in his cornfield might look like the scarecrow he had planted, but on Sunday morning he could pass as a "city man" dressed in a neat suit with collar and necktie. Always there must be a Sunday hat. The weekday hat of the average New Hampshire farmer of my boyhood days would be refused even by a metropolitan tramp.

On Sunday the whole community became a social unit, no matter how scattered that community might be. In the South Alexandria of my early boyhood there was a large meeting house and near it the red school house where I began my education. There were no dwellings near these two central landmarks, only branching roads leading to a tangled maze of irregular farms,

now as I write all reverted to the primal wilderness. But in the days of my father and grandfather this isolated church on Sundays became a veritable *meeting* house. Every boy within five miles came and brought with him his family to the last member, all dressed in the best clothes they possessed. During the services farm wagons, all of them one-horse vehicles, stood with horses hitched to fences or else stalled in the horse-shed which was the property of the owner. Every church was flanked by a long row of these horse-sheds. Two services there always were, with an hour's intermission.

By no means were all of these church attendants "professors," and never, so far as my own experience goes, was the talk in the horse-sheds during the noon intermission of a religious nature. Often it was the very opposite. Many shiftless characters, "horse-jockeys and hard drinkers" and still harder swearers, never dreamed of going to church, yet even these could not be called irreligious. The community possessed no atheists and no real unbelievers. In all the years of my young life I never saw a farmer at work in his field on Sunday save when in haying time a sudden shower threatened to ruin the hay ready for the barn. That, even the minister agreed, could be done by the "saints," and he had Biblical texts to defend his position.

The recent critics of puritanism are ignorant of many fundamental facts. They generalize from exceptions. They are blind to the fact that multitudes of the Puritan descendants have been honest in their convictions and have tried so far as human weakness will allow to live up to their convictions. The Puritans in all generations have been law-abiding; they have been dependable citizens and good neighbors; they have paid their bills and have added stability to community and nation. Wherever they have settled they have brought law and order and honest living.

In every New England township white churches: who paid for them? Why, when money was earned with such expenditure of labor on stone-bound fields, was money paid so freely for church buildings and church expenses? There was no central church organization to bring pressure financial or otherwise. Hard-headed common sense ruled these Yankee communities

and to them religion was a necessary thing even though it brought sacrifices that bit deep. They had convictions that were deep and abiding. They had faith in the unseen that to them was as substantial as anything in the seen and the material.

The Puritan was a monarchist at heart. His God was an absolute ruler awful in His wrath. Removed to America and isolated by frontier conditions, he became a narrow individualist. He saw life only from his own farm and his own town. He was religious chiefly for his own sake and his family's sake. The very unfriendliness of the Northern hill lands, the rock-strewn soil that exacted from the tiller the totality of his powers, bestowing upon him no unearned increment; the fierce unending winters that blocked all roads with snow, and froze even banked-up cellars; the week-long northeasters; the New England disease, consumption, that took every year its ghastly toll, always the fairest, and youngest, and dearest,—all this called for escape. And there was no escape save in the religion that pointed to a better land where toil and sorrow are unknown. So "Amid the storm they sang," and patiently they endured until the end, for was not Heaven with its ivory towers and its ceasing from toil to be the reward?

The song book used in the prayer meetings held on Sunday afternoons in the South Alexandria school house of my boyhood was *The Pilgrim's Harp*, a small song collection published in 1869. Before I could read I knew many of the songs by heart and sang them lustily, often doing mayhem and worse to the text, for I had little comprehension of the meaning of what I sang. I remember that one of the hymns was vocalized by me as,

> "There are lights along the shore
> That never grow'd in;
> That never, that never grow'd in."

Recently I made a study of this collection of prayer-meeting hymns, so popular in the hill-town prayermeetings. Out of a total of 140 hymns in the book, 57 dealt with the Christian's heavenly home. From these 57 was drawn nearly all of the religious music that I heard during my boyhood. Every one attending prayer-meeting had a favorite hymn and called for it often.

My grandfather's hymns were *I Would not Live Alway* and
There is Rest for the Weary. Mother's favorites were all in minor strain, hymns that she had sung with her room-mates and
dear friends in her mill-girl days.

New England life was saturated with the Bible. All over
the mountainland were towns with Bible names. Near us were
the towns of Hebron and Canaan. Everywhere people with Old
Testament names. Among my near relatives, alive during my
boyhood, were Bartimus, Moses, Amos, Isaac, Hannah, Judith,
Joseph, Jesse, James, John, and a generation back of them there
had been many more. The New England Puritan found the land
he was inhabiting another Palestine. The two regions had many
characteristics in common, and as a result the dweller who lived
in sight of the White Mountains or the Green Mountains of Vermont was at home in his Old Testament which is full of arid
mountain land. The Old Testament God, the God of Law, completely satisfied him. Life in the hills exalted the individual soul
and family life and unity, and as a result he practised a religion
that an old Hebrew would not have severely criticised.

CHAPTER III

Life Under the Great Stone Face

𝔐ost writers on new england history and literature have defined New England in terms of Boston and Cambridge and Concord and the coast-line cities. To Barrett Wendell literature in America was a Harvard product. Van Wyck Brooks in his contemporary surveys of New England culture goes not far north and west of the Atlantic fringe. Reviewing the *Indian Summer* volume, Howard Mumford Jones found that "New England, for the purposes of this study is severely limited to southern New England and the Maine coast, or rather to that enchanted ground which belongs to the spiritual diocese of the Brahmins, their friends and foes."

Even the touring southern editor Jonathan Daniels, who in 1941 swept over the surface of New England in a swift glide lingering nowhere long, searching for materials for another "discovery" volume, felt that north of Boston one crosses a veritable line separating New England into two parts. Allow me to quote him. For this discovery alone his book, if for no other, deserves wide circulation:

> You cross more than the Massachusetts line on the road north into Vermont. There are two New Englands, and from Newburyport to Williamstown the northern boundary of the Bay State cuts them apart in a division almost as distinct as that of town and country. (More distinct than town and country in New England where the country may be in the middle of the town.) Below the line is the crowded industrial south, above it the comparatively empty rural north. Mason and Dixon did not draw the Massachusetts line but the region falls apart along it in a difference at least as clear as the nation separates along the line they did draw.

Of the barbarians of the northern hill areas, of the tillers of small mountain farms, of the rural villages with their white churches and their town halls—the great New England nine-tenths whose education went not at all beyond the winter ses-

sions of the red schoolhouses—little has been written. And yet this was the *real* New England, the autochthonic New England that put the Vermontness into Vermont, the Down-Eastness into "the State of Maine," the granite of New Hampshire into the sons of Dartmouth College, and that in due time created in its own image another New England in the Mid-Land Northwest.

"Yankee uniqueness" was bred not in Boston, the New England capital, but in the isolated "north of Boston" areas where Boston was only a geographical name. In the rural township where I spent my youth there was not more than one person who had ever heard the term "transcendentalism," and even today in many a northern village the term "flowering of New England" brings only suggestions of apple-blossom time, lilac time, mayflowers and golden-rod. I know whereof I speak, for I was 19 years old before I had ever even heard of Ralph Waldo Emerson, and I was by no means unschooled. When he died in 1882 and his name was everywhere in the papers, I thought at first it was L. O. Emerson whose name I had seen on church music.

To understand this unheralded New England one must begin with its geography. Somewhere I have read this, "In order to understand the ancient Greeks one must understand the extraordinary land that begot them." New England is pre-eminently a mountain land. It has been called "the Switzerland of America." Much of it is terminal moraine. The great glacial ice stream ploughed it from end to end. It polished the granite dome of Mount Cardigan, 3000 feet high, until it is smooth as glass. It left a landscape full of limpid lakes, gorges scooped deep, and soil thick with bowlders and cobbles. Mountain ranges traverse it, the White Hills, the Franconias, the Sandwich range, the Green Mountains, the Katahdin wilderness sentinels, and, in the south, the Berkshires.

It is a joke to contemplate much of this mountain land in terms of agriculture. I, who was reared on a rock-heap, heard early the rural estimate of the land that bore me: "It was created just to hold the world together." There were pastures, I was assured, where they had to file the sheep's noses sharp so they could graze between the rocks. And then would come the old

New England story of the weeping rabbit, in form somewhat like this:

The new minister was driving up Hardscrabble to call on Deacon Avery on Skyhigh Farm, and as he was picking his way through a "popple slash" he saw a rabbit sitting on a brush fence crying as if his heart would break. Pulling up his old mare, the preacher, a kindly soul, called to the rabbit:

"What seems to be a troubling you, Brother? Couldn't a fellow help you any?"

"No-o-o. Nobody can't help me none now," blubbered the rabbit.

"But why not, Brother? You know there ain't no sorrow Heaven can't heal. Tell me what's a-sorrowing ye."

"This morning father died."

"Why! You hadn't ought to cry about that. He must have been very old and was prepared to go to his Heavenly home, I haven't a doubt. Be thankful, Brother, that his pilgrimage at last is over."

"I ain't crying about father. It's worse than that, a million times worse'n that." He wiped his eyes with his cotton tail, then burst out blubbering again. "Ten hundred million times worse."

"What *can* be bad's that?"

"He went and willed me 500 acres of this land. Oh, bo-o-o-o ho-o-o!"

"Moses Washington!" The elder leaped into his buggy. "If it's that bad I can't help ye nor nobody else can. Git ap, there, old mare!"

"Switzerland of America" meant little to the tillers of these hill farms. The mountains they took for granted, and they did not sentimentalize them. They had to make a living out of them and they did it. The eternal up and down of the roads they had to travel was merely a part of life like the weather and the seasons. My father living for 70 years not 50 miles from the White Mountains never saw Mount Washington or the Great Stone Face or the Willey House in the Notch. He had always heard of them, a certain aura of the romantic invested them, but he never felt he could spare the time to see them. He did climb Mount

Cardigan which was nine miles from our farm. Climbing that in the Pattee family of my childhood was the ultimate of adventure. It is indeed a majestic peak as one sees it from the Alexandria meadows, an Alpine horn cut sharp against the western sky. "Old Baldface," the natives called it. Bald indeed it is for a thousand feet in air above the tree-line, and from it on the east stretches the bare range of Firescrew. First and last, I climbed this peak 10 times, once on snowshoes on the tenth of March. The first article I ever had printed was an account of a Cardigan ascent published in the *Bristol Enterprise*, while I was printer's devil.

The mountains, as in Greece, undoubtedly molded the people who inhabited them. "Mountaineers are always free." Life on isolated farms overshadowed by peaks made for independence, self-help, individuality, physical stamina. It used to be said by all New Hampshire orators that God placed the great profile on Cannon Mountain in the Franconias to serve as a model for the product He expected the hill-lands to produce—men. And the mountain lands made good. To-day one cannot drive long in any of these New England areas without finding roadside monuments to famous sons. Take Vermont alone; on one of its Green Mountain farms was born Joseph Smith of Mormon fame, from neighboring farms came Stephen A. Douglas, Thaddeus Stephens, Orestes A. Bronson and dozens of others. From New Hampshire farms came such men as Daniel Webster and Horace Greeley who rose to fame in other states.

The farming population of the New England hinterlands read few books. Life appealed to them in physical terms, in the concrete realities of every day, not as seen through the transfiguring haze of the theatre or the romance. Their music they got from the prayer-meeting hymns, their religious philosophy from Sunday sermons, and their political bearings from the weekly newspaper. By some unwritten law, the wickedest men of the community were supposed to be the somewhat vague clan of "horse-jockeys," those happy-go-lucky ne'er-do-wells who made a doubtful living by swapping worn-out old plugs with each other, or with worldly-minded deacons. To know what hill-town life really was, one should have spent, as I have done, winter evenings around the red-hot, pot-bellied stove in a country store, or in the village blacksmith shop of a rainy summer day while oxen were being shod and big stories were being told, or in a group of hired men hoeing corn in June or making hay in July. One, too, should have attended rural funerals, apple-bees, huskings, singing schools, and auctions.

To do so, even at this late day, is to learn what mountains do to men who live their lives in the seclusion they make possible. Not a neighborhood in the mountain township where I spent my early years but had its emphasized individual, its unusual "character," its "odd fish." Often one of these "cracker-box" dictators broke out of the environment that had produced him and made a stir elsewhere in the world. For instance, there was Ruel Durkee, small-farmer of Cornish, New Hampshire, a red-schoolhouse graduate, who as "Jethro Bass" dominates Winston Churchill's novel *Coniston*. By no means did the author overdraw him. The actual Ruel Durkee *did* become the state dictator and he *did* say that he carried the State of New Hampshire in his vest pocket, and there was truth in what he said. And even now his crudities and his rural philosophy are remembered and quoted. And think of the boy Thaddeus Stephens, reared on an impossible polypod-bound Vermont farm, sent by his marvellous mother through Dartmouth, who went on into the United States Congress which he dominated during the Civil War!

I have known personally but one man who could be called a "political boss," John Henry Brown, born on a tiny farm near my own birthplace. For years he was a dominating force at Concord. I spent an evening with him once in his later years and learned that to be a state boss requires an artistry that has to be born in a man. A story he told me illustrated his method: It seems that a mill precinct in Manchester had elected a stirring French-Canadian to the legislature and this man, inflated by the honor given him, began to visualize substantial perquisites. For one thing he must have free passes on the railroad for his wife, his five sons, and several of his relatives who were to go daily to Concord to see him in his glory. He was told he must see "General". Brown who handled such matters. Without difficulty he gained an audience and this audience the Canuck solon reported thus: "The Cheneral was glad to see me, awful glad. It was an honor, he said, to shake the hand of the representative of the great City of Manchester. From representative the next step is Congressman, and then Senator. When I told him what I came for, he said: 'Sure! I understand perfectly. You have five sons, you say? Marvellous! I congratulate you—five noble sons. And he asked all about them and their school grades, and when his secretary come in and said, 'Your time is up,' he followed me clear to the head of the stairs, smiling at me and telling funny stories, and I went out feeling jest like Teddy Roosevelt, jest grand. Then I felt in my vest pocket and by gar! he hadn't given me a damned thing."

I told Brown he ought to write his autobiography: it was a shame to let perish all he know about the State. Such a book would become a best-seller. "I can do better than that," he said. "If I let it get out I was writing such a book, a dozen men would club together and give me a million dollars not to write it."

Physical prowess counted for much in primitive days. During all of my boyhood I was told stories of the feats of strength that were common in my grandfather's early days. Rum ran freely at "raisings" and at "musters," and always in haying time when the gang was more than two men. Every working gang had its leader who held his place by sheer strength and skill. The leader on Squire Bartlett's great farm was Stephen Gordon. He always headed the 10 men who with scythes laid low the clover in the great fields and he allowed no man to "cut his corners" or endanger his heels.

On the hill farms a paid-for job meant extreme toil, sometimes during a 10-hour day, or even 12. I never was a strong man; a dozen of my boyhood companions could "throw" me at school, but I knew how to work. My college junior summer I was hired man on Calvin Martin's farm. I arose at five and milked five cows. After breakfast I turned the grindstone while scythes were being ground. Then I started for the field and mowed or else spread out hay-cocks till noon. One afternoon I pitched on seven one-ton loads of hay in the field and after sup-per milked three cows. All farmers, I was told, observe the eight-hour day: eight in the forenoon and eight in the afternoon.

Among the "characters" whom I knew in my young days at Bristol, Zeke Follansbee was much quoted; his malapropisms were long remembered throughout the region. Squire Zeke had moved from the lake region down to the town, but as he ex-pressed it: "If I live and have my health I want to be buried up on the old place."

And every small community had its mechanical genius. In my novel *Mary Garvin*, now forgotten, I had a character, Joel Green, a composite picture drawn from several actual personali-ties. One of them I saw much of during my boyhood. He taught me how to set traps, catch fish, and hunt squirrels and par-tridges. By trade he was an ox-shoer, but he considered himself no mere workman, and even his practical-minded neighbors agreed with him. All characterized him as "a mighty ingenious critter who might have been somebody, but he never had no show." With jack-knife and glue-pot he was a genius. He made long wooden chains from a single stick, rigged ships in bottles, and made balls within balls. Hardly an invention could be men-tioned without his saying, "I thought that whole thing out once, myself, and made a model of it, but I didn't have no money to get a patent. No money's what's ruined me." Once when I visited his little shop he showed me his double-acting, swing-door cat-hole model which worked perfectly. "There's money in it," he said. "The thing is waited-for all over the country. But it would have to be advertised and that would take a fortune, a hun-n-ndred dollars, I'll bet, and not a cent less. If I only had that, I'd jest flood the country with cat-holes." Then came his two favorite jokes, one about the farmer who had a dog-hole in the barn for his dog, and beside it a cat-hole for the cat; the other about the farmer who ordered his hired man to cut a cat-hole in the cornbarn, and when later he inspected the hole and found that it was covered when the cornbarn door was open, had roared out, "How in hell is a cat going to get into that cornbarn when the door is open?"

Once the old genius entrusted me with a profound secret. He was at work on a perpetual motion machine, and he had it perfect but for one thing. It would go "jest like goose-grease for a spell," then, in spite of everything he could do, it would go to work and stop. But he knew what the trouble was and he was working on it. "It won't be long now and then the world will wake up, I tell yeou-u."

Even up in the New Hampshire highlands one runs into stories of Henry Ford. Not far from the Alexandria line, lies a dreary range called the Danbury Mountains, peculiarly rich in sought-for minerals, notably mica and feldspar. The discovery of a rich vein of feldspar, noted in the papers, came to the attention of Ford who was in need of the stuff to be used as an abrasive. He immediately set out with an expert to inspect the mine, making the trip in his own personal Lincoln car. Now the discovered mine was near the top of Hardscrabble mountain over an improvised road which the natives declared would balk even a quillpig. Asking for directions, Ford was told how he could reach a farmhouse where he would be told how to get onto the mine road. Reaching the farmhouse, he was greeted by the robust old farmer living there:

"Wal, to get to that mine keep on a quarter of a mile, then turn sharp right and follow that rabbit track up a mile."

"Can I get up there in my car?"

"God no, not in that damned thing you're in. Nothing in God's world can climb that hill, over that devil's make of road, but a Ford, and you'll have to go afoot."

"Know where I can get a Ford?"

"Sure! Got one myself. Model T. Goes fine."

"Could we hire it with you as driver to take us up?"

They could and the old farmer delivered the Lincoln owner, much shaken up, at the mine. The episode so pleased Ford that on his return to Detroit he sent the old farmer a new latest-model Ford.

This story I can vouch for, since it took place not 10 miles from where I was spending the summer, and it was known to everybody in the region.

2

I was born in time to see the old New England before the debacle of the '70s, the New England at flood-tide as described by Harriet Beecher Stowe, Rose Terry Cooke, and Sarah Orne Jewett. The old regime was fading, but I saw enough of it to realize to the full its meaning. Not wide has been the realization that the Civil War destroyed not only an ancient order in the South but one as well in the North. To realize what New England was before the War and the West had taken their toll, read Whittier. He knew the northern hill lands thoroughly, and he was laureate of the lands and their people. *Snowbound* interprets the New England of his boyhood as perfectly as *The Cotter's Saturday Night* interprets the Scotland of Burns's day.

During my boyhood I talked much with my grandfather who had seen the region before it had been stripped for farms. All through my boyhood I fought the Civil War in my imagination. Even farm hands, hired just for haying, had fought in the South in bloody battles I was thrilled to hear about. I saw the westward movement begin its drain upon our neighborhood. One by one it took schoolmates from the red schoolhouse where my education began. Later I was to see farms abandoned until whole school districts lapsed into wilderness. My first letter-writing, crude stuff in capital letters, went to boys who had gone west with their parents, Ed Ballon and the Swetland boys, and from them came letters postmarked Iowa or Minnesota telling of life on prairie lands where one could "hunt all day and not find a stone to throw at a prairie chicken." I, too, wanted to go West.

Bristol was a manufacturing town that had been settled because a large stream from a lake had taken a precipitous plunge into the Pemigewasset River, furnishing unlimited water-power. During my boyhood gristmills, tanneries, sawmills, pulp mills, paper mills, and other water-driven plants made the town prosperous. My father was then working in these mills, earning the amount needed to buy the farm on Pattee Hill which was to be sold by the heirs of his uncle James.

My school life began in Bristol when I was four years of

age. I attended the first session held in the new brick four-room school house in 1868. All alone, day by day, I trudged down the quarter of a mile, and at noon often went with the children in my class to the town common where building operations were in process. Here occurred the first tragic event I can remember. The children, one day near where a new building was being erected, picked up bits of building tar and chewed them as gum. When the school bell called us in, I put my chewed piece on the brand-new shining desk I occupied on the front row. It clung fast. To keep the teacher from seeing it, I put my primer over it and that too stuck fast. Then came the primer class and I was there without my book. Never had I been so scared: I had spoiled the new seat and spoiled my book and I wanted to die. The kindly teacher, Sarah Day, however, made life for me again livable, and all culminated happily.

I must have been in that grade until I was six. I remember that one of our school songs celebrated the completion of the Pacific Railroad, and that was in 1868. I have never seen the text of this song and when I sang it lustily with the rest I had no idea what it meant. The chorus, as I recall it after 80 years, ran like this:

> See far away, see far away,
> The nation's proudest labor,
> The work is done, the triumph won,
> The East to West is neighbor.

It was not until I was six and a half years old that the farm became ours and I was given the thrill of my lifetime by being allowed to ride high on the load of family goods drawn by grandfather's oxen. The farmhouse, a rambling old structure after the prevailing fashion, had an unbelievably great brick chimney with arches and ovens and fireplaces. Standing in any of the rooms a grown person could touch the ceiling. Low-posted rooms conserved heat in the long cruel winters when fireplaces "roasted your shins and froze your back." So "run down" was the old building, and so comfortless, that father soon decided to demolish it and build a new residence. This he did largely with his own hands. Great hemlocks on the ridges above the farm were sluiced down to the field and then drawn by oxen to a South-Bristol mill to be sawed into boards and dimension lumber. His brothers helped frame the building and a neighboring farmer, who posed as a carpenter, put in the windows, hung the doors, and did the finish work. Bricklayers and plasterers came from the village and the house was ready for us in the autumn.

The house was planned with one thought in mind: comfort during the New England winter. The frame was boarded with hemlock boards an inch thick. Over this was spread heavy tarred paper, and over that the clapboards. The living room was on the south side to catch the warmth and cheer of the winter sun, and the large windows were reinforced by storm windows put on in November and removed in May. One of the autumn chores was to "bank up" the house, which meant thick windrows of leaves held down by green hemlock branches. Fallen leaves in the forest often were drifted in heaps by the November wind, and from these heaped-up corners load after load was secured and stored away for use as bedding in the cow "tie-up" during the winter.

In this new and comfortable home I spent my boyhood, not breaking from it until I had left college and was married in 1889. There were three of us children, Charley, a year younger than I, and Mary who was born in the new house.

The deed to the farm described it as "containing 70 acres more or less." Ten of these acres could be described as tillage "more or less." Twenty acres were rated as pasture land, certainly uncultivatable, since one could cross it from end to end stepping on nothing but protruding bowlders. It maintained, however, five or six head of grazing cattle, three of them milch cows. The rest of the farm was heavy forest. Some of it tipped at an angle of 45 degrees. The fences were all stone walls.

The road by which the house was reached was a long hill "steep as Jacob's Ladder," as one neighbor expressed it. From our yard we could look down into Bristol Village two miles away as if we were in a flying machine. The wooded ridge back of our farm shut off our western view, but on three-quarters of our horizon loomed foot-hills of the White Mountains. On the southwest horizon was etched the rounded peak of Kearsarge; on the south Periwig, on the east the Sandwich range, in the foreground the Bridgewater Mountains and Sugar Hill, and to the north the dim Franconias. Cardigan was hidden from us by the Devil's Den ridge, but as seen from this ridge it dominated the west like an Alpine peak. Overhanging us was Taylor's Ledge with a sheer drop to the west of 500 feet and at the top of this crag an old-growth pine rooted in cracks in the granite crag. I estimated that the tree was nearly 200 years old. A landmark it was for miles around.

The first poem I ever published had this pine as its subject. I sent it with the title *The Lone Pine* to the *Granite Monthly* and was thrilled beyond expression when it appeared in the April 1882 issue. In the poem I exulted in the fact that it had triumphed for centuries over seemingly impossible handicaps, had withstood all the attacks the elements had made upon it, defying the lightning and the storm. Unconsciously I was seeing in the tree a type of my own life as seen in my dreams. I too was facing the impossible and I too defied the forces against me. Now, half a century after my poem, the old pine lies in ruins. Lightning destroyed it. Ajax can defy the lightning, but the thrill of it dies with the moment. In the end the elements always win.

The Solitary Pine

Tossed by the North Wind's freezing flight,
    Rocked by the tempest's power malign,
Upon a tall crag's lonely height,
    There stands an ancient, time-worn pine.

Long has that old pine braved the blast,
    Long has its deep and sullen roar
Defied the storm-wind's furies cast
    Upon its withered branches hoar.

On thy grim form our fathers gazed,
    In boyhood's days to thee we came,
To thee our aged eyes are raised,
    But thou, old tree, art still the same.

Thine are the first dim rays of morn,
    The last faint tints of eve are thine;
Thine are the terrors of the storm:
    Dost thou not look in awe, old pine?

O stanch old pine! The years have flown,
    To earth thy brothers have been cast
Till now in age thou art alone,
    A weary spirit of the past.

Grim time at length will sweep thee down,
    And lay thy lofty crest serene,
Low in the dust, while all around
    The storm triumphant shall close the scene.

The details of this hill-farm boyhood concern my story only as they illustrate the life of a New England farming community in the years following the Civil War. Sometime I may write of it as Hamlin Garland wrote of his Middle Border boyhood or as John Burroughs described the farm that gave him his real education. I learned early the names of all the trees native to the region and I knew like a woodsman the habits of most of the wild creatures who were our nearest neighbors. Every farmer's boy is a trapper and a shot-gun expert early. The ruffed grouse was then abundant. In winter they fed on the buds of apple trees within gunshot of the barn. A walk in the woods on snowshoes would reveal their lodging places for the night. Headlong they would plunge into the snow sheltered by it from the cold, but they would never when disturbed burst out of the place where they went in. Foxes often pounced upon the place the bird had entered only to have it burst from the snow some six feet away. Even birds, we concluded, can think things out. Hen hawks preyed on our chickens; crows in the fall gathered in "windy congresses" on the ridge above us, marshalling their battalions for the long flight South.

Never were we out of work, save on rare spring days when father allowed us to go trout-fishing. The winter's work centered about firewood. First, trees on the hill were felled and then hauled through the deep snow to the back yard where they were piled in sled-length logs until the heaps were as high as the house. Then came the saw-buck job, and the splitting, and the piling of the stove-length sticks in neat tiers in the woodshed. After every winter storm came the road-breaking, a neighborhood jamboree enjoyed by all boys. All the oxen and steer teams in the district were out with sleds, snow-drags and plows.

Signs that winter was approaching its end were eagerly watched for. No one loved the winter save the farmers who spent it hauling cord-wood to the Bristol market where it sold for $4 a cord. Father and mother always celebrated March 1, for it was the first spring month. The dinner that day had a thanksgiving aspect, chicken of course, and as far as possible other dishes that had a summer reminiscence: parsnips dug from the frozen garden, and berries canned the previous August, and cucumbers which had been packed in salt, now desalted by being hung in a flowing brook and then plunged into vinegar.

Now, in early March, one listened every evening to hear if the frogs were peeping down in the thawing marsh. For some occult reason the date March 9 was given the frogs. As grand-father phrased it, "If the frogs don't peep by the ninth of March they lose their charter,"—"chatter" I think he meant. To many of his words he gave British pronunciations, and no wonder: his grandfather had passed his boyhood in England.

Another unwritten law governed a March day in New England: tomato seeds were to be planted on "March meeting day," the second Tuesday of the month. Mother never failed to observe this law. When father started for town meeting she would bring out her salt box filled with rich soil and plant the seeds she had saved the previous summer. When the plants were three inches high she would then transfer them, one by one, to birch-bark pots for transplanting when the garden was ready. In August we had bushels of tomatoes.

The first crop from the farm acres to appear on our table in the spring was dandelion greens, gathered while snow still lay in sheltered fence corners. And later another unwritten spring law was observed: when the first barn swallow sailed in the upper air, boys could lay aside their winter boots and go bare-footed the rest of the summer—save, doleful thought, when one must "fix up" for meeting on Sunday with the hated shoes.

In mid-March came the maple sugar season, hailed with shouts of joy by all country boys. Often after a big "run" we would boil sap all night. Several hundred pounds of sugar we made every season, selling some of it but storing the rest of it away in big crocks for home use. For years during my boyhood no "store sugar" was used in our house, save when the minister and his wife came to dinner. It was during the sugar season that we heard the first voices of the new spring, the bluebirds and the robins. What a thrill to hear the first bluebird note and then the voice of the first robin! The joy of Xenophon's army at sight of the sea with their "Thalatta, Thalatta!" had nothing on us as we hailed the new spring.

Following the sugar season came the "spring's work," and following this headlong blitzkrieg came "haying time," the major job of the entire year. This completed, for all the Pattee tribe there came a holiday, a tradition handed down through many years. Grandfather and his boys and, following his example, my father and his boys went on a fishing trip together, usually to Fowler's River where a boat was secured and during the day a tour was made of the "good holes" around the lake. What a day that always was!

The autumn season, however, most appealed to me. Then came squirrel shooting, coon hunting at night, trapping on the wild meadows. It was the time too of the apple harvest and Indian summer. The wild life of the woods tremendously interested me. As a boy of ten—1873, perhaps—I saw a flight of passenger pigeons, thousands of them, not in masses but in scattered flocks that filled the sky for hours. Flying west they were, high enough to be out of gunshot, and never, so far as reports later came to us, alighting anywhere. Not long after this flight the pigeon flocks disappeared, never to be accounted for.

Our winter evenings were short. As soon as supper was over and the evening chores done, my brother and I would take off our cow-hide boots—often no small job—then our woolen stockings, usually wet, and go with bare feet until bedtime with no thought of ever catching cold. Father's and mother's bedroom opened from the kitchen and so received the warmth of the cook-stove that furnished the sole heat of the house in winter. As small children we had slept in a trundle bed which at night was pulled out from under the parental four-poster. But soon we boys were relegated to the open attic which was the only room on the

second story. It was sweltering hot in summer and intensely cold in winter. Always on zero nights we undressed by the kitchen fire, and then, big boys that we were, would be put to bed in the attic by mother who warmed the cold sheets with a flat iron while we came charging up the stairs to plunge in before the sheets were cold. Tucked in warm we would chipper like small chickens under hovering wings. Cold it was in that unfinished attic. The January storm would make the window curtains wave and beckon like ghosts in the half light, and wavering shrieks long-drawn would rise and fall as the wind had its will. But we did not mind the howling storm and the cold at all. Snuggling down under the warm quilts, our heads covered, we were lulled to sleep by the storm. It did not take long.

Getting up in the morning, however, was quite another thing. Often the snow, sifting through cracks, would lie in small drifts on our bed. Descending in a headlong rush down stairs to dress before the newly-kindled fire, we would often find the water bucket frozen solid and the windows coated half an inch deep with frost.

As a farmer's boy with small outfit and no money for extras, I learned as all country boys do, how to use my hands and in emergencies my head. I was taught to handle an axe and a scythe, to drive the old square nails so as not to split the wood; to tap a sugar maple in the right place, to gather sap and carry it on a sap-yoke through heavy snow without spilling a drop of it; to boil sap, pour it off when it was at the right consistency, and to sugar off and pour into moulds for the market; to load a gun with loose powder and a newspaper wad, and hit what I aimed at, since powder and shot cost money; to build a "figure-four deadfall" for mink; to set snares; to drive a yoke of oxen; to grease wagon wheels, harness a horse, and make repairs on the road when anything broke; to drive a horse and at the same time hold plow handles—in short I was forced to learn something practical every hour I was awake.

Boyhood is the period of lusty eating; at least it was so during my years on the farm, for we had good food in abundance. In these days of tin cans, "boughten stuff" ready to eat, and

baker's bread all sliced, I recall the Gargantuan home-cooked and, to a large extent, home-raised Thanksgiving dinners of my youth. Family reunion times these were, when chicken pies of unbelievable girth were destroyed to the last drum-stick, and vegetables pulled that morning in the garden, Indian puddings, and mince and pumpkin pies were supposed to be completely consumed whether one was "full to the neck" or not. A small cousin one Thanksgiving watched the pie-making with hungry eyes, and announced that half a pie was to be his share. However, the chicken pie and all the fixings were greatly to his liking and when the pie course came he burst into tears, bellowing loudly, "Oh I'm afraid I can't eat any pie!"

We had very little fresh meat, save in winter when a quarter of beef could be frozen and packed in snow to be kept fresh for weeks. Often neighbors would club together to butcher a steer or a sheep and divide up the meat and the costs. In the winter frozen codfish from the Grand Banks could be bought in Bristol at reasonable prices and these were made into heavenly chowders, floating with cream. The art of chowder-making has seemingly died, at least in hotels and restaurants. Often father brought home a quart of oysters which mother made into surprisingly large stews rich with butter. Never was there any left.

On week-ends came a new menu. Let me quote from an old song:

> On Indian pudding, pumpkin pie,
> On week days let us dine;
> On Sunday bless the pot of beans,
> Nutritious, rich and fine.

"Bake" beans always were central at the church suppers prepared by the ladies for income toward the pastor's salary. No canned stuff these thoroughly cooked beans (10 hours in a bean-pot)—these home-prepared ambrosial lentils, abundant with completely cooked fat pork, the deliciousness of which could be celebrated only by the pen of a Charles Lamb who made a classic out of roast pig. Beans have now been popularized with the prefix "Boston," and they have now become one of the 57 products of Pittsburgh, but "bake beans," or "pork and beans" as the

church basement, the proceeds to go towards the minister's salary. The supper consisted of nothing but pies and one could eat as long as one wished at five cents a piece of pie. It was said there were 90 different varieties, but I am sure of only 20 since that was the limit of my pie-eating that evening.

3

After many years away from this land of my childhood, all incidents and scenes remembered are now veiled in a romantic haze of poetry. I remember with vividness days of the New England Indian summer, golden afternoons when a breathless hush held all the air as if the year were dead and lying in state; when the soft light which shimmered on the near horizon made all outlines vague and unreal; when all the maples were in scarlet and all the oaks in purple. Nowhere else in the world have I seen such royal glory in nature. The southing geese, high in air, making a great V against the sky, at the apex a guiding soul breaking the silence with hoarse voice, this always thrilled me with a longing I never could define. Escape was in it, freedom from the bonds that bound me to the earth. Fain would I follow that gallant leader into the unknown Southland where there was summer and freedom and the open air.

Always was I a dreamer, always a peerer beyond far horizons. Heat-lightning on summer nights, noiseless flashes betokening storms and tragedy in the unknown beyond the hills, filled me with unrest and longing. The long meadows that we saw from our hilltop held always for me on summer nights a something I could not define. Beyond them lay the river creeping through wildness and swamp and unknown bendings. In the summer the long stretch of cultivated land would be covered with hay-cocks like the tents of a sleeping army, in the autumn with shocks of corn like the wigwams of savages. In the spring floods would sweep over the lowlands leaving behind drift wood and mystery. Alive in the springtime were these meadows with bobolinks, and over them in the evening came the liquid notes of the hermit thrush. Later I was to throw all this into what I fondly thought of as poetry. Of the hermit thrush I wrote in my college days:

> Far far away in evening's hush
>   We caught a plaintive liquid lay,
> The lonely, love-lorn hermit thrush
>   Who sang the vesper hymn of day.
>
> A spell was on the meadows lush,
>   The day's dull murmur died away,
> And far away in evening's hush
>   We caught a plaintive liquid lay.

CHAPTER IV

Farming on the Rocks

*I*N ALL BUT NAME I AM AN INGALLS: in almost every way I resemble my mother's people. They were a buoyant clan, jovial and optimistic, and, though their schooling had all been gained in the red school house of their mountain district, they had artistic ambitions. A restless clan it was, ambitious, independent, venturesome, not one of the family of 10 content with the farm life of the parents. All of the four boys, as I have already recorded, enlisted in New Hampshire regiments at the opening of the Civil War and one of them, Horace, served enlistments in three different regiments, one of them for three years. The girls too left the home at the earliest opportunity, the most of them to serve as loom-tenders in the great cotton mills along the Merrimack River.

The Pattee clan with its Gordon strain in the fourth generation of the family was in many ways different. Grandfather may be taken as a type of those hill farmers who wrested from the wilderness enough arable land in the foothills of the Cardigan area to make possible the township of Alexandria.

First of all, he was a worker. Life to him meant toil, antlike industry, world without end. He was known as a "driver." Work as a thing to be planned and then rushed through without loss of time was his very life. He could keep a gang of men at work at top speed all day. For years he was the highway surveyor of his district, and on a spring day, "between planting and hoeing," he would order up all those who had their road tax to work out. Half a dozen yokes of oxen they would bring with them, with carts and plows. Each man and team was given a job and there was no loafing, no shovel-leaning, no stories told. Every man worked as if he were cultivating his own farm, and as a result grandfather's district always had good roads.

When he began a job everything else was put aside—"this

one thing I do." A sort of excitement seemed to take possession of him. At critical moments when judgment was called for and a cool head was needed, he was at his best. Almost fiercely he would chew at his tobacco, spitting in every direction, and issue orders in a voice that echoed from the hillsides. Once when a spring flood took out the largest bridge in his district, an old neighbor remarked, "Gosh! That will take for Uncle Mose two plugs of tobarker a day."

No kinder man, however, ever lived, or one more tender hearted. When pigs were killed in the fall he could not bear to be present, but would walk down into the woods until the tragedy was over. Then he would do his part. The most of his farm he had bought as uncleared land and he had himself felled the trees, "snaked out" the stumps by ox power, built the stone fences, and given the land its first "burn." The most prized of his fields was his so-called eight-acre lot, spoken of always by the family as the "ake-akers." With infinite toil he had made it as fine a field as one could find in the town. Literally he had spent the best part of his life in perfecting it. He had dug up bowlders and stumps, had filled and levelled slough holes and hollows, and had fenced it with double walls the entire extent—that is, he had built of the removed bowlders two parallel walls eight feet apart and had filled the space between with loose cobbles from the land. Even this had not exhausted the stone-crop. As late as my own boyhood I have seen him and my uncles on a newly ploughed piece load a drag with cobbles gathered on a radius of 40 feet. Grandfather used to say that stones grew just as gray birches grew on neglected land—something out of nothing. Undoubtedly they were pushed up yearly by the frost.

I saw this fine field in its prime, a part of it heavy with corn, a part in potatoes—"little rogues" grandfather called them when they were growing,—and other acres in clover or timothy or oats or white beans for the Saturday-night bean pot. Pumpkins by the cart-load grew in the corn. I am quite sure that grandfather would have agreed had some one told him that the creation of this perfect field would be his greatest contribution to his children, or to his town and state. His life-work was in it.

Beyond a doubt he built those double walls, smoothed and culti-vated those acres, and with infinite toil gathered those millions of cobblestones piled in all the fence corners and between the walls, with the thought that he was providing for his children. His sons, he dreamed, and his sons' sons would bless him in all the years to come for the foundations he had laid for them. But I, who saw the field in its prime with grandfather still turning its acres, have lived to see it lapse again into virgin wilderness covered densely with a growth of pines large enough now for lumber.

It has for years been a source of wonder to me how swiftly thousands of acres in Alexandria and hundreds of similar areas have lapsed into wilderness. Pasture land these once-fields now became, with young cattle turned in for the grazing season; then had followed cherry bushes and gray birches, then poplars, then pines or hard wood. The creeping forest takes no vacations, and leaves bare no areas save the granite ledges seamed with quartz veins.

It was always a part of the spring's work to go over the pastures and fence corners with a bush scythe cutting down all bushes and tree seedlings at their start. To save the tiny pines as a money crop never occurred to anybody.

I have in mind two farms in the region that were brought into high cultivation by two hardworking, clear-headed men, replicas of their fathers who had first cleared the land. Both were model farms. But the third generation inheritors of the two properties were as unlike as two men could be. One of them was "a chip from the old block" and he worked as his father and grandfather had worked, keeping the farm in perfect condition, sending men one day every spring to cut down the pine seedlings lest they grow and spoil the pastures. The other was called "a shiftless cuss." He loved to go fishing and in season hunting, and his work was always several weeks behind. The pastures were growing up to bushes, so he had to reduce his stock. He ne-glected his tillage and soon the farm was pointed out as an eye-sore of the township, while the other farm nearby with its per-fect pastures was pointed out with pride. Years went by. The good farmer had worked himself into helplessness. His sons all had city jobs. With hired help the farm barely paid expenses. Finally the farm, heavily mortgaged, was sold at auction. The other farmer, a hearty old dog, perfectly at home in a fishing boat, saying often, "What a hell of a fool John was," let his farm run down till it was no longer a farm but a forest. The other day, so I recently heard, the old man and his boys, who for a day had come up from the city, made a contract with a lumber company for the pine on the farm and the figure was $20,000. "Pine," said the old Yankee, "is a damn sight easier to raise than corn."

To win, as grandfather certainly won, with all but insuperable odds against him, required fundamentals of character not lightly to be passed over. His two oldest boys died in their young manhood after a lingering struggle with "the New England disease" now called tuberculosis. The family doctor, a practitioner of the blood-letting school, could be of little help, yet he made daily visits over long periods, and to collect his bill took at one time the yoke of oxen just as spring's work was opening and at another time all the hay that was in the barn a full month before pasturing time. Bills allowed to run perforce in the village grocery were collected by ruthless lawyers who bought them at a discount. For years, as grandfather once expressed it, he had "no more peace than a toad under a harrow"—"harrar" he pronounced it. For years, he said, he never saw anyone running toward him without his heart leaping into his throat: he thought they might be bringing bad news concerning the sick ones at home.

Cider was one of the standard farm products of the region, and never was it classed with the "hard liquors" which boys were taught to shun. Grandfather always made several casks of it and these 40-gallon, many hooped, once whiskey containers, sat on an elevated platform in the cellar under the kitchen, to be tapped on order when cider was needed. It was needed often in the winter time. When neighbors dropped in of an evening, the first thing done after the inevitable greetings and inquiries after health, was sending the boys down cellar to draw a pitcher of cider for the men. Few ever drank to excess, certainly not grand-father. Those were jovial winter evenings before the roaring fire-place.

Every New England family has its traditions of mystical happenings touching the unseen world, some of them bordering on the ghostly. No person dies in New England, but what some-body has had a premonition, the story of it gaining with each telling. Our family, too, had such a happening and often I have heard grandmother tell of it. One evening, according to the us-ual version of the story, grandfather, just home from his day's work, was washing his hands at the pump in the yard when, happening to look down the road, he saw his old Uncle Jonathan who lived many miles away, walking up the road. He was bowed and very lame, and grandfather recognizing him instantly, shouted to the house, "Put another tater into the pot, mother, and put on another plate, Uncle Johnty coming up the road." Everybody scurried about putting things in order, and then grandfather hastened out to welcome the coming guest. No one was in sight. He went down the road even to the old home place which was then in clear view from the farm. They had seen no one. The thing was an unexplained wonder for several days. Then came a letter saying the man had died the very hour grand-father had seen him on the road. No old New England family was without similar traditions.

One of my remembered glimpses of grandfather was caught of an evening when with his paper in one hand and a tallow candle in the other, he ran the flickering light along each line slowly, gaining the content of the article. For years he took the *Independent Statesman*, a weekly paper published in Con-cord, but he read little in it save the political matter. On the evening after this paper arrived he and his brother William would read and discuss it at length. Both were ardent Whigs and were thoroughly alive as to what Clay was doing, and the abolitionists and the Southerners.

The literary event of the year—at least so I considered it

in my childhood—was the arrival early in January of two or three patent medicine almanacs. The Joe Miller jokes, some of them illustrated, we learned by heart and often quoted. One of the few times I heard my grandfather really laugh was when one of these illustrated jokes was shown to him. A crude woodcut represented a pompous Southern colonel with goatee and broad-brimmed hat, standing before a grinning Negro who held under his arm a live skunk. Under the picture was this text: "Sambo had often been whipped for stealing his master's onions. One day he brought a live skunk to his master, exclaiming, 'I'se caught the rascal that stole de onions. Whew! smell him breath.'"

Rooted deep in New England life is a strain of humor that must have evolved from the climate and the soil itself. Such a soil necessitates rigid economy, an economy that extends, as we all realize, even to the vocabulary. "Any hills on this road?" I once asked a Vermonter. "Nothing but," he answered. Positive answers one seldom gets. At a fork of the road I asked a passing farmer which road to take and he said, "Take arry one of 'em and you'll wish like hell you'd taken t' other." A Yankee farmer will complain at times in the home circle about the roughness of his acres, but in public he'll render his hardships into exaggerations that will set the crowd into laughter. "Yes," he'll say, "my field *is* kinder tilted up, but it saves work. Dig out the 'taters and they'll roll all the way down to the house."

One summer walking with an experienced old native, he halted me before what once had been a cultivated field. Bowlders covered it thick and around them grew polypod with roots like wire. "That field ought to be fenced and a monument put in it," he said. "That's holy ground. Three different young men after working like hell one summer on that lot got a call to preach. They heard the voice of the Lord."

Grandfather never had family prayers; few farmers of the region did. There was no time for them. Prayers were for Sunday and church and prayer meetings. When the minister came on his annual call, he always ended his visit with a "let us all unite in prayer," and the whole family kneeled at their chairs and the minister would then one by one remember them before the Lord with appropriate preludes ending with a shower of besought blessings. When the minister was invited to dinner, that indeed was a thing to remember. The boys were sent to chase down the old rooster, which was then picked and boiled. Canned fruit was brought from the cellar, opened, and displayed in the dainty company dishes never seen at any other time, hot biscuits were prepared, "riz biscuits not saleratus," and sponge cake, and for dessert two pieces of pie, usually custard and apple, on a single plate. A day indeed it was for a boy to remember. I remember the observation made by an elderly dame, keeper of a boarding house: "Them that's pious eats awful."

Grandmother was a remarkable woman. During the earlier years of her married life she had woven on a hand loom all the cloth used by the family, had knit the stockings, and made the clothes. In addition she had done the cooking for her large family, taken care of the milk of three or four cows, and been the mother of 10 children. She was a positive soul with intense convictions. When statements were made that she could not believe or could not subscribe to, out would come her one expletive, "Fiddlesticks! Cat's foot!" Her kitchen garden was to me in my boyhood days, a replica of the Garden of Eden. It was bounded by a long row of ox-heart cherry trees always heavily loaded in summer, and there was an early pear tree, and many damsons. At one end was her herb garden, each herb of use for medicine or for dressings for meat or poultry. Summer savory and sage, spearmint and peppermint, marjoram and catnip, each one gathered in season and hung up on the rafters in the attic. She had her flower beds, all of them filled with old-fashioned blossoms like bouncing bet and bee balm. Vegetables there were of course in neat beds kept free from weeds by the children. In a bed across the road were clumps of cinnamon roses set out when she was a bride more than a century ago now, its ragged descendants still to be seen along the wall where they first grew.

3

The story of my grandparents I cannot leave without recording a family tragedy, and I record it not so much because of its value as a mere story as because it was a typical case, one that could be duplicated on hundreds of hill farms. A neighbor of my grandfather's was a Doctor Burton, so-called, whose wife Molly was indeed a "character." Many believed that she was a witch, though no one had ever seen her on a broom-stick flight. Externally she was pious. She always attended prayer-meeting in the South Alexandria church and always when the time came in the meeting for "testimonials," she was prompt in the delivery of hers. And not at all was her testimony conventional. Singling out a member of the congregation who had offended her, she would rehearse his whole history, dwelling only on his mistakes and his meanness, growing louder and louder in her condemnations until her voice fairly broke. There was no calling her to silence. The only way to stop her was to "sing her down." The more she would screamingly berate her victim, the louder would rise the volume of song until at length she would stop in sheer exhaustion.

One evening grandfather was the object of her maledictions. Just what her charges were I never knew: I think a broken fence and cows in her corn. The singing grew louder and louder but not loud enough to drown her final curse: "Mose Petty, I curse you in the devil's name. May you never have a daughter that won't be a curse to you nor any of your line forever and ever."

The curse was neighborhood talk and it was not forgotten when the oldest daughter was born a moron, and the second daughter died mysteriously in infancy. Seven of the children were boys, but the last of the 10 was a daughter, Rosa, and no man ever loved a child more than the father, given in his old age the girl child he had longed for. God at last had sent him a daughter. A beautiful girl she was, sprightly and joyous, and her father died happy in the knowledge that the curse that had haunted his life had been forgotten.

The widow, Rosa's mother, feeble now and helpless, needed this daughter, and there was her deaf and dumb son Wilbur to be cared for. That brought at once the complex which furnished Mary E. Wilkins with so many materials for her grim stories of the New England decline. Tied to the farm by bonds unbreakable, unable to find the social contacts she dreamed about, forced to do the unending drudgery that her mother no longer could carry, Rosa seemed doomed to dreary spinsterhood. The thought of it horrified her. In her provincial inexperience she pictured the life that she imagined was being lived in the social areas of nearby Bristol Village in terms of Mrs. Astor's New York. And it was impossible for her to enter it. All her beaux were country nobodies whom she had known in the red schoolhouse. She had dreams; she wouldn't look at such clods. I remember once as a small boy sitting in grandmother's kitchen and seeing Rosa leap to the door and pull down a four-leafed clover that she had hung above it, gasping: "Merciful heavens! I wouldn't have Sam Clark come in under that clover for a million dollars."

One young man of the neighborhood, fine looking and on Sunday well-dressed, saw Rosa one day at church and the next evening came to see her. Soon they were seeing much of each other. But he was not only penniless but in debt; he peddled fish in a slovenly old fishcart, and investigations proved that he was from a family that "was not much." Rosa's brothers, therefore, with families and farms, discouraged the match, and so effectively that the young man ceased to call. Whereupon the headstrong girl declared that she would marry the first man who asked her to marry him, and this she did. She married a veritable tramp, a man of the patent medicine barker type, with a flowing "gift of gab" and a romantic history that, as he told it, was indeed fascinating. Certainly he had seen the world—the worst of it, and he certainly had received its worst stains. She eloped with him, leaving her mother soon to die. The baby that came died, and Rosa followed not long thereafter. It was a Mary E. Wilkins story in real life.

4

There comes to me sometimes the conviction that some men, and perhaps all men, live more than one lifetime upon this earth. Our earliest American ancestor, who settled at the foot of Pattee Hill, lived for a century on the farms registered in his family name. My grandfather was a reincarnation of this ancestor and my father was my grandfather over again. He too was a worker, a driver, obsessed with the idea that work was the primal necessity for man. Like his father before him, he classed fiction with falsehood, and namby-pamby sentimentalism; of poetry he knew nothing save as he found it in hymns; and music, outside of its sacred areas, he thought created laziness, shiftlessness, and worldliness generally. During all of my youth I was warned against five cardinal sins: dancing, card-playing, swearing, fiction-reading—especially in its dime novel forms—and drinking.

Never did we talk religion in the home. Like sex it was never mentioned, yet it was always present. There was a sense of security in our lives that came not from government or from physical absence from danger or from economic independence. We knew our world and had no doubts. God, as He had been revealed to man through the Bible, was to us as much an actuality in our thinking as were our parents. It gave a standard from which to fix values; it made for us a rounded philosophy of life. We knew why we were living and what it meant for us to live. I am sure that my father and mother were as convinced that they were preparing for a life to come, where dear ones were to be found again and sin was to be unknown, as they were of the life they were actually experiencing.

5

Schooling came of course. The very fall of our removal to Pattee Hill I was taken to the South Alexandria red school house by my Aunt Rosa who was then an attendant. For four generations all the family had received their education within the walls of this old structure and the wooden benches were covered with their carved initials. None of them had had schooling elsewhere, all of them had walked the two miles from the Hill, and all had eaten their dinners at the noon intermission out of their tin dinner pails. I did so until I was 15. The curriculum was limited, the teacher, home educated, strong in nothing save discipline. Reading she taught best, always from readers in a graduated series from first reader to sixth, the reader used by the student serving as the only means for grading the pupils and forming classes. Never did we use McGuffey's Readers; I have never seen them in New England, but we had at various times Hilliard's series and Wilson's which were practically the same as the celebrated series that educated the West. From these readers came my first taste of classic literature. In every school I attended before entering college I was forced often once a week to commit to memory a piece of poetry or prose and recite it before the school. I have still in my memory poems learned for these knee-shaking occasions. It would seem that what most interested me in those callow years was the resonant and the martial. I declaimed "Marco Bozzaris," as did many of my schoolmates. "The Seminole's Reply" I spoke with all the defiance I could command:

Blaze with your serried columns,
I will not bend the knee.

and once I spoke "The Combat" canto from *The Lady of the Lake*, beginning:

The chief in silence strode before.

Scotch martial lyrics impressed me greatly, perhaps because of the Gordon strain in my ancestry. To the blinking, cud-chewing cows of an evening in our old barn, I droned weirdly "Lochiel's Warning," and then did my best to thrill them with the execution of Montrose:

Come hither, Evan Cameron! Come, stand beside my knee:
I hear the river roaring down towards the wintery sea;
There's shouting on the mountain side,
There's war within the blast—

and so on to the end. Great poetry I thought it, supremely great, but the cows went to sleep on it and the school, when I delivered it, simply giggled.

Some years later preparing for college at New Hampton Institution, from a literary standpoint I was debauched by my training in public speaking, a required subject. I was fed with the flowery and the melodramatic and it chorded with my aboriginal soul. I liked it; I made it a unit of measure for values. Much was made of prize speaking. There were no athletics and in place of them the students competed in oratorical contests. The literary value of a piece, I inferred, could be determined by counting the number of prizes it had won. Accordingly I compiled a list of all the prize-winning pieces during a period of years, and as I read that list to-day I find it packed with fine writing, melodrama, and sentimentalism. At the head of the list stood Kellogg's *Spartacus to the Gladiators*. I spoke it once myself in a prize contest and was much impressed by what seemed to me its poetic opening paragraph:

> The moon piercing the tissue of fleecy clouds, silvered the dew-drop on the corselet of the Roman sentinel, and filled the dark waters of Volturnus with a wavy, tremulous light. It was a night of holy calm when the zephyr sways the young spring leaves, and whispers among the hollow reeds its dreamy music. No sound was heard but the last sob of some weary wave, telling the story to the smooth pebbles of the beach and then all was still as the breast when the spirit has departed.

I thought it literature at its best and strove to write in the same key. Would that there had been on the faculty a critic who knew values. The principal of the academy had published a novel for boys *Through Struggle to Victory* after the Horatio Alger pattern, sermonic rather than literary.

In the South Alexandria red school house I was taught thoroughly the multiplication table, the usual elementary arithmetic, penmanship to the degree that my handwriting become almost legible, and geography in which I learned that beyond the Mississippi lay the great American desert and that bordering the African Sahara were the Mountains of the Moon. The teacher was always a woman chosen not so much for her ability to teach as for her ability as a disciplinarian. Her weapon was a ruler, and when a victim who had broken a rule was detected in *flagrante delicto*, the summons was always the same, "Come out on the floor. Hold out your hand!" and the ferrule would descend an appropriate number of times according to the gravity of the offense.

The school in our district was known as a hard one to manage and its teacher was always the best disciplinarian the committee could find. The result was that ferrulings became the leading entry in my juvenile diary, now burned. At one time the owners of the near-by cider mill ordered the teacher to keep her "scholars" out of the mill when cider was flowing, for the whole school, each pupil with a capacity of quarts, had been visiting the mill daily. The teacher thereupon issued an order: Go to the cider mill and you'll be severely punished. We knew what that meant, and we at once applied logic to the problem. If the *whole* school went in a mass, both girls and boys, she couldn't lick the entire bunch. To our amazement, however, she did. She lined up the whole school on the floor and beginning at one end of the line ended at the other pounding severely the palms of every pupil. It was an unwritten law among the younger ones to bellow lustily at the first blow, believing it might temper the teacher's wrath, and now by the time the whole line was licked the school room was a roaring bedlam. It was found, at least under that teacher, that it was painful to disobey and consequently we obeyed. "No larning without licking," the old parents would say. "If they get a licking in school they'll get another when they get home." My own father used to say when I brought home monthly school reports, "If your grades are low, you are not to blame for being born dull, but you are to blame if you get below 100 in deportment. When that happens, you'll have a session with me in the wood shed." School in the red school house always adjourned for the winter, and after I was 10 I was sent to the Bristol school two miles away, for the 10 weeks of winter term there.

6

One cannot dwell long upon any phase of New England life without encountering religion. Churches were everywhere, three or four in a single small town, and membership in these churches constituted a social caste: "Without are dogs, and sorcerers, and whoremongers" and all the other members of the "unsaved." To my parents the two castes meant two different worlds: those who go to church and those who go to dances. The church-member class was not at all a homogeneous unit; it was sharply divided into denominations. To many denominationalism was a fundamental part of their religion.

Sunday always descended upon a New England town like an Indian summer day after a week of storm. No transition could be more complete. Church bells, the Methodist in one key and the Congregationalist in another, sent out their mellow alternating notes to be heard far into the hill lands. A hush was over the streets as if a magician had waved over them his wand. Everywhere orderly processions of devout church-goers, all dressed in their Sunday best, little girls and boys gayly decked in perfect order, the same small "brats" that had whooped and yelled down the same street the day before when school was out.

Our family attended the Methodist church of the village, driving out in the farm wagon, and hitching the old horse in the horse-shed behind the church. Father taught a Sunday school class, and I was long a member of Deacon Butterick's class of boys, two of which later became Methodist ministers. The small Sunday school library had in it few books that interested me— not a single *Oliver Optic*. One of the class taught me how to pick out a good book to read: "If the pages are solid stuff without any short lines, the book is hard reading. You must pick a book where the page is all broken up into small pieces with lots of spaces." That was my first lesson in literary criticism.

Denominationalism then ruled the churches to a degree hard now to realize. One inherited one's denomination as one inherited one's political party and one never broke from it. With many a church member denominational doctrines were as inflexible as the laws of nature. To some, not to have been baptised by immersion was to be damned on the Day of Judgment.

7

A recent discoverer of New England was Jonathan Daniels whose volume *A Southerner Discovers New England* came out in 1941. A mushroom growth, to be classed with *Russia in Ten Days*. During his eccentric sweep through six states he found what he was looking for—materials with news values. He edits a paper in North Carolina. Everywhere he demolished Yankee traditions. The pie-belt held for him no pie; pie for breakfast was a myth; the land of Coolidge was actually voluble; and the leaders of New England in politics, industry, or literature were natives of the West or the South, among them Dorothy Canfield Fisher. That her father President Canfield was a Vermonter with a long Green Mountain ancestry and that his daughter came back to the primitive nest there to abide, he seemingly did not know. Most of those he designated as westerners were really, like Mrs. Fisher, returned New England stock. When Daniels in a later book dealt with his own people he could speak with authority. He was a "tar-heel" and he knew Tarheelia to its roots, but New England to him was foreign ground.

When I criticise his interpretation of New England I do it standing on my native sod and knowing it down to bed rock just as he knows North Carolina. I admit that Vermonters can be voluble, but it depends on who is listening to them. In home groups or gatherings about a grocery winter stove with neighbors to listen, they loosen up like a January thaw, but let a stranger appear and attempt to cross-examine them, or attempt conversation when a job is in progress, or a land trade, or a horse-swap, and there will be no volubility to speak of. In a class-room lecture at Dartmouth, Professor Richardson, lecturing on Lowell, gave us an adaptation of his story of two Vermonters who met on a country road and drew up to "pass the time of day." Richardson, I remember, improving on Lowell, told it something like this:

"Kinder good-looking hoss you got there, Deacon."

"Wa-al-l." (With a rising quaver. Pleased surprise.)

"Sorter aiming to sell?"

"Wa-a-ul?" (Nasally drawled. Tone indicates, "that depends.")

"Sot a price on him?"

"Wa-a-a-al!" (Drawn out. Tone indicates, "Hadn't thought of it, but—")

"Spose I offer seventy-five?"

"Wa-aa-l." (Incredulity at such a low offer. Disgust.)

"Dunno but I could add twenty-five."

"Wa-a-a-al." (Drawn out hesitatingly with nasal whine. Doubtful.)

"Make it one-twenty-five."

"Wal!" (Snapped out with finality. Hands him the halter.) The sale is made.

To get the full import of such a folk trade one must hear it. It is wholly true in its dialect, whatever one may say about the rest of the story.

Much of the dialect of my boyhood days depended for its meaning, as did the Deacon's "Wal," on intonation. I can understand easily how in the Japanese language the same word may have different meanings all depending on the intonation. For instance a Yankee farmer in haying-time may say:

"Thunder shower coming, don't you think?"

"I guess so." (Tone doubtful. Eyes exploring the sky for evidence.)

"I dread 'em. Been struck myself three times."

"I *guess* so!" (Second word stressed. Incredulous. Don't believe it.)

"Pretty serious being struck by lightning."

"I guess so." (Hearty approval. You are dead right.)

Had a question followed, asking why lightning sometimes kills a man struck by it and sometimes strikes and does no harm, the answer might bring out another New England characteristic:

"Dunno's I know,"—as far as any Yankee will confess ignorance.

New Englanders are by no means icy individuals, but certainly they are not demonstrative and they are not gushing and sentimental. In none of the Pattee families did I ever hear anyone addressed as "dear" or "darling," and there was no kissing. We boys were never praised for any work excellently done; nothing but good work was ever expected. Yet kinder people never lived than my grandfather and his family. When on a job they never talked. They worked with intensity, issuing short commands to helpers and turning deaf ears to those who lightened their toil with streams of talk. "Talk never gets work done," father would say. "Don't ever talk unless you have something on your mind, and when you're on a job, there'll be nothing on your mind but the job. Work, don't talk."

That New Englanders are Scotchmen when it comes to affairs of the pocket book need not be denied. Both peoples had to struggle with a soil that gave no unearned increment. To raise a family on a New Hampshire hillside one must count every penny. I know this thoroughly from personal experience. I was never given an allowance during my boyhood and I spent no money. A few pennies I earned by selling brook-trout to a man in the village too ill to catch them for himself, and these pennies we saved for celebrating the Fourth of July. One farmer boy whose father was a synonym for "tightness" asked for 10 cents for firecrackers and was harshly refused. All his playmates in the village had money for firecrackers, and he went again to his father begging with tears for just 10 cents. His father was touched, and pulling out five cents said to the weeping boy: "Well, here's five cents, but don't you go and make a damn fool of yourself spending it." Tillers forced to support a family on a hill farm were frugal from necessity, but even the poorest of them had a contempt for miserliness. Tight-fistedness furnished humor for many a grocery-store gathering on a winter evening. There were men in the region undoubtedly, like Uncle Aaron Sleeper, who, so the phrase went, would "clutch a dollar till the eagle on it screamed." According to one miserly old Yankee I knew, the way to get rich is to "Make a dollar a day and save a dollar a day."

Daniels mentions the lack of aesthetic taste in the early New Englanders as evidenced by the location of their view-hiding barns. Scenery as mere scenery affected the farmer not at all. It was merely a part of the world. Asked by a summer tourist if he didn't think the mountain near his farm beautiful, he might reply: "Yes, but think of the cussed Jacob's ladders it makes of the roads."

I have in mind the Gale farm high up on Hemp Hill just above the farm where my mother spent her childhood. To the north, seemingly just below it, lies New Found Lake ringed about with the peaks of the lower White Mountains, on the west Mount Cardigan cut like a cameo against the sky. No more beautiful landscape in all the hill lands, but when the pioneer Gale cleared away the woods for a farm on the hill-top and built his farm buildings, he placed the great barn between the landscape and the house. In later years when a Chicago family bought the farm for a summer home, the first thing they did was to move the barn, an expensive job, but inevitable as they saw it. "Fools!" cried the old farmers of the region. "They have spoiled the farm. That barn was placed in the one position where it could be driven into with loads of hay, and driven under when manure was to be hauled out. Now look at it. You can't drive even a wheelbarrow into it or under it."

"But it killed the view," the new owner objected.

"Killed nothing! You can't make a living up in this neck of the woods jest looking at views. You have got to farm and farm like hell and keep your eyes down on the ground every devilish minute or you'll land in the poor house." So spoke the last owner who had farmed the place.

To the incoming tide of summer folk, however, the view is the greatest wealth a New England farm can bring. But for the view, the Gale farm would now be a bush-lot like my mother's birthplace just below it. The view sold the place. The old woodshed was found to be the focal point commanding the whole north and west, and it was glassed in and refinished and refur-

nished and called the library. Here over a book, one can see the cloud shadows chasing over the mirror of the lake and watch the changes creep over the old peak as the afternoon fades into evening.

Winter in The Hills

Steel-blue and cold as primal adamant
 The cloudless sky. The air is tempered steel,
 And rings and trembles with metallic peal
With every sound. The sunbeams shoot aslant;
 The frost wreaths glitter like a magic band
 And like a marble frieze the hemlocks stand.

The slowly-moving sleds now creak in every seam,
The toiling oxen blow out clouds of steam.

CHAPTER V

Printer's Devil

*W*HEN I WAS SIXTEEN I secured a job in Bristol for the season—May to October—as farm hand on the Bartlett estate, the largest farm in the region. The proprietor of the estate, "Squire" Frederick Bartlett, son of Levi Bartlett who for many years had been a dominating force in the town, was a graduate of Dartmouth College, a lawyer, and after the death of his father, inheritor of the Bartlett holdings. The so-called "Bartlett's Plains," an extensive farming area, free from stones and perfectly level, had been brought to a high state of cultivation. But since the death of old Levi it had steadily deteriorated. The "Squire" had failed as a lawyer and now was making a greater failure as a farmer. When I came as a farm hand, things were certainly at sixes and sevens, at least they were so when compared with what they had once been.

There was plenty of work to do, however. With a hoe or a scythe I found myself able to keep my heels from being rapped even when the best men in the gang were behind me. I enjoyed the work. It threw me into a new environment. Indeed the six months I spent on the Bartlett estate I reckon as the beginning of my education. The old Dartmouth graduate had what to me seemed a very large library. Naturally most of it consisted of law books, but scattered through it were volumes that I took pleasure in reading in the few hours that were at my command. Rare treasures he had inherited, among them an autographed bill sent by George Washington to one of the early Bartletts.

The old mansion I found was full of relics and it was surrounded by buildings that were relics. Beyond the vegetable garden was the original Bartlett store which dated from the days when the town was first settled. Originally it had stood at the edge of the town common, and through it had passed hundreds of hogsheads of rum and West India molasses, countless bales

influence in mid-December, 1879, I found employment in the office as "printer's devil." It was the only printing establishment in a wide area, and in addition to the usual run of job work it published a newspaper, *The Bristol Weekly Enterprise*. The proprietor, Captain Richard W. Musgrove, a veteran of the Civil War and later a soldier in the regular army stationed in the Indian country of the Northwest, was a man of sterling religious character, a strong influence in all movements for community betterment. From the first his vigorous personality made a great impression upon me.

I soon found I had entered a new world, one of which I had had no conception. I had to learn a new language, the argot of a peculiar tribe: "quoin," "chase," "galley," "quads," "leads," "live copy," "dirty proof," "pie," "long primer," "brevier," "pica" and the rest. An exclamation point, I found, was "screamer," type were "stuck," and the job press was "kicked." Type was measured by the "stick," though in city offices it was by the "em." The "type-sticker" often got "out of sorts"—certain letters in the case all used, requiring renewal. My work hours were given to sweeping, tending the fire, cleaning ink-fouled rollers, running errands, distributing "pie," picking over the "hell-box" for usable "sorts," and "type sticking," an art which in time I mastered, though it was long before my spacing and justification were good enough for anything but the "Guts-ache," which was the office name for the weekly (often spelled weakly) newspaper which we issued. In time the paper was enlarged to four pages, an improvement caused by the new "wrinkle" in rural newspaper work, "the patent insides," plate matter that could be procured in any quantity desired.

As I gained in type-setting skill, I began to find the boss's copy on my "live copy hook," and it was not long before I began to dream of the day when I too could sit in the front office and like him dictate the policy of a newspaper, and through it of a town. It impressed me, too, that he was gathering materials for a history of Bristol, a work that he later completed in two large volumes. His vivid stories of Chancellorsville where the Twelfth Regiment was decimated, and of Gettysburg where it was all but annihilated, always thrilled me. He had been at the apex, he said, of Pickett's charge, and had not seen any of it. His regiment at the very front of the Union lines, lay flat on the ground, firing as they could without aim, the air above them seemingly solid with missiles from the Rebel batteries that roared so that a soldier's ears would be stopped up for weeks afterward. And during it all, the regiment was thinking of only one thing, as he expressed it, "wishing with all their might that they were flap-jack thin and could make themselves thinner. I wouldn't have raised my head to see that charge," he said, "if I knew that by doing so I could have seen the Day of Judgment or the devil sitting on his throne."

My job as devil was no "soft snap." I got 50 cents a day, and boarded at home, two miles from the village if one cut across the woods. In the dead of the New Hampshire winter it was my job to arise at five, have breakfast, plunge out into whatever storm might be raging, wallow through the woods, build the office fires and have the rooms warm enough so that at seven when the gang arrived, ink would run smoothly on the presses. My job it was to "tote up" the firewood and keep the fire in order during the day. Hazing came as a matter of course. I was sent out in the usual way to borrow left-handed monkey wrenches and four-foot yard-sticks, and was shown "type-lice," which meant having a wet column of type suddenly closed, squirting inky water into the victim's eyes.

The big day of the week was Thursday when the paper went to press. The foreman made up the forms from galleys of type brought to the composing stone by the type-setters and by 10 o'clock had them on the platen of the old Washington Hoe press. Then the devil took the big roller and the pressman became furiously active. Fred Ackerman, who followed me as devil, declares that our record run was 400 an hour and he is positive that he once "kicked" 9000 circulars in one day on the Gordon press. The fraternity of Washington Press Pullers can have no recruits. It is all but extinct. I am one of the last leaves on its tree.

My three years as an apprentice I look upon now as a preliminary school course that grounded me in fundamentals useful to me during the rest of my life. Without it, I should have taken another road and have arrived I know not where. Over my type cases I awoke to the fact that education is a practical thing, a tool for one's life-work. I found that I had dawdled with life and had mastered nothing. Perforce I learned to spell. Fellow workmen educated each other. Constantly we were asking over our type-cases how to spell this and that word. Moreover, one must be able to read whatever penmanship one might find on one's copy-hook—type-writing we saw little of. Accuracy too was demanded, and rapidity and ability to "justify" and space the lines so that the paragraphs would look not ragged and haphazard but uniform and beautiful. Furthermore, it was forced upon me that reading matter existed first as manuscript and that manuscript had to be composed and put into form—no small art. As a result, I began myself to write. I wrote a criticism of the village morals and Franklin-like slipped the thing under the boss's door. Later in the day when I burned the contents of his waste basket, I found it therein and burned it. Then I wrote the story of a trip I had taken to Mount Cardigan, left it on the boss's desk and was thrilled to find the manuscript on my copy-hook. "A good piece," he said as he passed me, and the thrill came as it should have done.

During my second year my pay was raised to 75 cents a day and a new devil was engaged to do the work that for a year had devolved on me. More and more I was doing job work. It had been discovered that I had a sense of form that could express itself in the type varieties and display work of auction bills and "dodgers." I still boarded at home, but my dinners I took at the Bristol House at 15 cents per meal—believe it or not.

A by-product of my apprentice work I found highly enjoyable and in some degree educative: the run of free tickets to local shows and lectures given out by advance agents for newspaper publicity. I used all that came my way. It was H. Price Webber of the Boston Comedy Company who gave me my first glimpse of the world of the theater. In his time he was an outstanding figure in the barn-storming line, travelling through

New England small towns and presenting what then were called "clean shows." He came every winter to Bristol to give a series of plays of the type represented by *The Hidden Hand*, *The Octoroon*, and *East Lynne*. The melodramatic Webber was to me a veritable Garrick or Forrest or Booth.

Lecturers came, among them an old phrenologist who tried to convince me that he was presenting an exact science coordinate with mathematics and physics and medicine. In his evenings in the town hall he would examine the heads of well-known citizens, summing up their characters and characteristics often with ludicrous results. From the first I was doubtful, but to reassure myself I consented to have a chart made of my own head and a year later I had him make another. Comparing the two I no longer doubted. Phrenology was a fake, and I began to wonder if some other sciences were not also fakes.

No longer was I deprived of books and magazines. I had access to the exchange list of papers and magazines which came flooding into the office, and my fellow workmen, I soon found, were all readers, their tastes varying widely. One of them was well read in *Oliver Optic* and kept me supplied with volumes, one of them had an amazing stock of dime novels, *Denver Dick* central, and these I freely sampled, but I was most influenced by a fellow type-setter, Will Randolph, who could argue fluently about the tactics of the Franco-Prussian war, then only 10 years in the past. Soon I discovered the source of his fluency, a sub-scription-book history of the war, and I soon made this my own, swapping, as I now remember it, a new jack-knife for the volume. Quickly I knew it by heart and was able to counter with warmth the fellow-workman's military science. But this was not my first book. Volume number one in my library was a Quacken-boss *Rhetoric*, a book bought at full price when dollars looked to me like balloons in size. The copious selections from the English classics I learned by heart. They furnished what really was my first extensive adequate reading matter. The printing office had awakened me to the need of education in English if I was to be a newspaper man, which was now my ruling ambition. The books in the Sunday school library no longer appealed to me.

Advised by a bookish lady whom I met, I read *The Scottish Chiefs* and finished it to the interminable end, but I much preferred the Maine woods stories of C. A. Stephens in the *Youth's Companion*. He made the Maine lakelands alive for me and for one period my ambition was to be a guide in the wilds about Parmachenee Lake and the upper Magalloway.

My Sunday school attendance at Bristol, which for years was unbroken, did much to civilize and culture me. One of my class was preparing to be a doctor, and several others had the ministry in mind as their life-work. I remember that one of them, who in time became a presiding elder and a churchman of note, had read the *History of Methodism* through twice. In time a little group of us considered ourselves sufficiently literary to form a club, the "D. F. L.," letters which (I am safe now to tell the secret) stood for what was supposed by us to be the Latin for "Disciples and Sons of Literature." We held frequent meetings with varied programs and in the spirit of the times soon determined, lyceum fashion, to engage a lecturer. After much discussion the choice of the club was Josh Billings, and after exciting preliminaries Josh Billings, a much-bowed, white-haired old man was with us. The town hall was crowded, for he was then known to everybody as a leading humorist. Sitting on the stage and delivering monotonously scrap after scrap of his wisdom, he was greeted with little laughter and little appreciation. The audience was disappointed and the editorial comment of the local paper was anything but flattering. I remember but a single fragment of the miscellaneous jumble he gave us. Holding up two fingers to represent gun barrels, he said, "I've known a man to load a double-barreled gun clean to the muzzle just to shoot a bird and then not hit the bird."

3

What I now realize as a major turning point in my life came in the third year of my apprenticeship. My lifework I now felt sure was to center about the trade that I was learning, but more and more there was growing in me an ambition to live in

the front end of the office rather than in the rear. I talked now of
"journalism" as my profession, and my workmates did not
laugh. They too dreamed of themselves as journalists, though
not one of them in later years became a newspaper man. One of
them, Will Randolph, became the Register of Deeds for the
county and another, Fred Ackerman, Postmaster and leading
citizen of the Town of Bristol.

My educational deficiencies confronted me at every turn.
The boss was using me as copy-reader, my job being to read
aloud the copy while he followed on the proof. In this way we
read the catalogue of the New Hampton college-preparatory
school. Frequently he corrected my crude pronunciations. I remember I pronounced the *Anabasis* "Anna-bay-sis." Then and
there I resolved to take courses at New Hampton, and in due
time I broke away from my apprenticeship and enrolled myself
as a student. A bold step it was. All unknowingly I was climbing out of the rut worn by my tribe and entering an area from
which I never could return. No one of the Pattees and no one of
the Ingallses had ever had educational ambitions beyond the red
school house three Rs.

The New Hampton Institution, a school under the auspices
of the Free Will Baptist Church, a school of ancient lineage, lay
five miles from my native Bristol. It was then highly prosperous,
for at the head was a masterful personality and real educator,
Atwood B. Meservey, a man who had much the same influence
over his students as did Dr. Arnold of Rugby.

There were two separate departments, the academic and
the commercial, the latter concentrating upon book-keeping, penmanship, business law and methods, and the rudiments of bank-
ing. In the academic department were taught the conventional
subjects required for entrance to college: Latin and Greek
Grammar and Reader, Caesar, Cicero, Virgil, Xenophon's *Anabasis* and Homer. Sweating over these old classics, I had no sus-
picion that they were great literature, works of supreme art and
beauty. From first to last, even into college days, they were simply conglomerations of ablative absolutes, vocatives, gerunds
and gerundives, caesural pauses, conjugations and inflections,

maddening irregular verbs, and Latin prose composition to anguish over. Thus were we taught the classics.

In later years, at Penn State, the professor of Latin was called out of town to attend a funeral and I was drafted to teach his class. The first assigned lesson was one of the Odes of Horace and I resolved to teach the ode as I wished it had been taught to me when I was in college. First, I read to them the incomparable Latin, dwelling on the music of the rhythm and the felicity of the phrasing. Then I read to them six versions of the ode made by master poets, beginning with Milton. In every way I could I tried to bring to them the exquisite beauty of the poetry, and the peculiarly Horatian qualities that it contained. And I failed completely. A day or two later, one of the class was overheard to say, "Old Pat had better stick to English; he don't know no Latin. Instead of teaching us, he brought in a horse and read it to us."

The students at New Hampton were for the most part from New Hampshire farms, many of them from adjoining townships, crude lads like myself, compelled to cut down school expenses by studied economy. Canvassing for subscription books occupied many during the summer vacations. A publisher's agent would appear in town in the early spring, gather a group of students and, using the students who already had had experience "on the road" as examples, would set forth the fabulous success many agents had had with the books. Older students who had handled the book would recount their successes. Then would follow a free course in the science of book-peddling, with a dozen different approaches, and carefully rehearsed rebuttals for all the possible objections that might be made by canvassed victims. The popular subscription book one year was *Our Deportment, Detailing the Manners, Customs and Dress of the Most Refined Society*. Some did well with the book. It did only one thing for me: it convinced me that I was no salesman. To argue a person into buying what he did not want to buy, and really could not afford to buy was no job for me. I made several trips, once with a dollar home dictionary and another time with Dodge's volume, *Our Wild Indians*, but I lost money on both ventures.

Like most of the older students I boarded myself, with the aid of a weekly box sent over from the home kitchen. Two or three terms I had to miss in order to earn means for continuing my course. Once I served as clerk in a Bristol store, once or twice when work was pressing in the printing office I took a hand there, and always in summer, work could be found in hay-fields. But all this broke into my courses and kept my school grades low.

Public speaking was made much of in the school, as was dramatics, several plays being presented each term. Soon I was called on to take parts in dramas, and greatly did I enjoy the experience. Never such delicious thrills as came when the rented costumes arrived from Boston and were donned for the final re-hearsal. That indeed was treading on the very heels of romance. I never got far, however, in the fascinating art. I played Ralph Stackpole, I remember, in the play, *Nick of the Woods*, and I was applauded for my Negro part in another play, though never in my life had I seen a Negro or heard one talk.

From every graduating class a limited number went to college. The greater number, however, considered themselves educated and began their life-work. Especially was this the case with those entering the ministry. The school, though small, had a remarkable alumni roll. Several governors of Massachusetts were on it, several New Hampshire governors, and one author of national import, Orison Swett Marden. I think I have the dis-tinction of introducing his first successful composition to the world. While I was an editor of the school paper, he sent, at my urgent request, a manuscript which I issued in the *Hamptonia* and which later he reissued as a chapter in the volume, *Getting on in the World*. Handwritten, this manuscript would have puz-zled even a Horace Greeley handwriting expert. For days we puzzled over it.

I had had no intention of attending the New Hampton school for more than two or three terms, and I had planned to study nothing in these terms save English and grammar and other kindred subjects useful for journalists. But soon I became conscious of my classmates, and was persuaded to take Latin as

I was two summers at Block Island and my memories of it are all poetic.

4

The first reading matter to influence me toward self-expression by the written word I found in *The Youth's Companion*, stray copies of which I was able to find here and there. Father had no $1.75 to spend for a story paper, but one year by selling muskrat skins we secured the amount necessary for a subscription. From the first, the Maine Woods stories of C. A. Stephens fascinated me,—I can find no other word to describe their effect. At length I began to copy their style and attempt similar stories of my own. The first book of fiction I ever bought was Stephens's *The Young Moose Hunters*, the money coming from my printing office wages. I wrote to Stephens and his letter thrilled me. I was then in college.

> Your kind letter of the 3d instant gave me quite a good deal of pleasure. I was but a boy myself when I wrote *Camping Out*, etc., (in which I condensed the results of numerous jaunts and trips with various objects, into the Maine woods, Canada, and other localities). This town Norway Lake in Oxford County is my native place; and, situated somewhat like yourself I should think, I struggled through all sorts of tight places while trying to get an education and make a start in the world. When I wrote *Camping Out*, I was badly in debt for tuition, etc., and not a little discouraged at times. It chanced to sell pretty well and that set me on my feet. I graduated at Bowdoin College, and, two years ago, took a degree in medicine at the Boston University. I am not a practising physician, however, but have embarked in a line of biographical research which I am trying to do some honest work in. I still write for *The Youth's Companion* and am sometimes quoted as being on the editorial staff, but in truth am little more than a contributor there.

Among my letters from Stephens I find this one, dated March 20, 1893, when I was principal of Coe's Academy:

> I have received and read your letter of last Monday with unusual pleasure. Why, you have done remarkably well to get ahead so far! I know what it is to "begin and be born" on a rocky New England farm, with every conceivable obstacle in the way of an education or progress of any sort. I know what it means to climb that hill! No play about that! I worked my way, off and on, through a preparatory course at Kent's Hill and Lewiston, Maine,

and afterwards through Bowdoin. For nine years I hardly had decent clothes and sometimes not even proper food. I worked by the day, cut cord-wood, canvassed for books, sewing machines, insurance companies, and at length kept school. (I cut 78 cords of wood at one time when I was about 17.) I know whereof I speak when I say that *you have done well*. In that particular, at least, my judgment ought to be sound.

Ah, but were there not *blue days* in those years! And yet I would not willingly have missed those days—of toil even—for always there was a sustaining faith that held me to the task and often a secret sense of exultation over victories won. Yet I would not like to see a child of my own go through a similar ordeal. Still, it may be the better thing for a boy, after all, for it is that sort of man that oftener than any other reaches the top of the ladder.

I hope you will get that professorship. Thank you for the suggestion to put some of those Maine woods sketches into a book. I doubt whether they would be worth it. When your poems are published please send me the address of your publisher. By same mail I am sending my photograph and should be glad to get yours, if quite convenient.

C. A. STEPHENS

This letter describes my own life almost in detail. I think it could be used as a type letter describing the lives of thousands of boys of more than one generation in the New England hill lands.

I still think Charles Asbury Stephens deserves from the literary world more credit than ever he received. He became a contributing editor of *The Youth's Companion* in 1870 and held the position for 60 years during which time he is said to have written some 3000 short stories, 100 serials, to say nothing of short sketches. He was not at all a stylist or a consciously literary creator, but he had the rare power of presenting a region and an atmosphere that became to the reader a veritable reality. One of his last books, *My Folks in Maine*, is the story of his family in the hill lands, "a reminiscence of incidents as we youngsters of the fourth generation used to hear them at the old farm." Like my father, he was of the fourth generation. He was much older than I. The book is a priceless document in the history of the settlement of the New England hinterlands.

Schoolhouse in South Alexandria, N. H., attended by F. L. Pattee for 15 years. Four generations of Pattees were educated here.

F. L. Pattee
as a schoolboy.

(Left) Typical
stone wall on the
old Pattee farm
near Alexandria,
N. H.

Haying on the Pattee farm. F. L. Pattee on the hayrack.

Dartmouth Hall as Pattee saw it (1884-1888)

These Dartmouth men climbed Mt. Cardigan in 1888. From left: Christian P. Anderson '89; Benjamin S. Simonds '88; Walter S. Sullivan '89; and F. L. Pattee '88

CHAPTER VI

Dartmouth College

IN MID-SEPTEMBER, 1884, with father driving the old horse and with my small trunk in the back of the farm wagon, I started for the Danbury railroad station, nine miles from home, to take the train for Dartmouth College. For both of us it was a serious journey. As I think of it now, there comes to me the story once told me by H. O. Houghton, head of the Boston publishing firm, of the old Massachusetts Puritan whose boy was starting for Harvard in the family buggy driven by the hired man. The father could not take time for the trip, yet he followed behind the wagon steadily giving the boy advice for six miles. My father gave me no advice as to morals and manners, but he filled the whole three hours of the trip with a discussion of ways and means. I was embarking on a desperate venture, he thought, and it worried him, it gave him at times "the blues." He was positive I could not do it; only two in Bristol had ever tried it and they were the sons of rich men. He, however, would not stand in my way.

I was positive that I could make it. I had been for two summers in the atmosphere created by Orison Swett Marden, hotel manager, the most starry-eyed optimist of his generation. I had once spent a half day with him in Boston, and he had assured me that a student worth his salt could even make going-through-college a money-making job. This he told me about himself:

He had been orphaned at the age of three years and had been "bound out," after the old New England custom, to a farmer who lived 24 miles from the railroad, and had been obliged to work from dark to dark with no educational advantages. When he was 21 and free, his guardian's wife made a remark that angered him: "You'll never amount to anything," she had said, and to spite her he had retorted, "I'll show *you!*" He found a job in a sawmill and later, to earn funds to attend The New Hampton Institution, turned bobbins on a lathe, was shoemaker, barber, hotel waiter, woodsawyer. Fitted for college at New Hampton, he had entered Boston University. Though never strong physically, he had found work enough in Boston to enable him to win the B.A. degree in four years. He had then done graduate work in the university, and in time had won degrees in law and in medicine. After a graduate course in medicine at Harvard, he travelled in Europe, and later became a successful manager of hotels. His career as magazine editor and author is known to all now.

After listening to him I was sure I could make the grade, sickness and death not interfering. Esquire George Emerson of Bristol loaned me $25 and father from time to time took my note for small amounts, safeguarded by my life insurance which was made out to him. I was sure, so I told father as he drove "Fanny," the old mare, to Danbury, that nothing could stop me save moral slumpage and that was unknown to our breed.

Arrived at the college, I at once reported to President Bartlett who was running Dartmouth single-handed, passing on student credentials, and admitting freshmen without secretary, typewriter, or college dean, the latter office not even a dream at Dartmouth at that time. He was not only president, he was the whole administration. He wrote all letters by hand, attended personally to all matters of excuse from duty and all cases of discipline. Already I had secured from him a scholarship that required the holder to sign a pledge reading, "I hereby deliberately declare and affirm that during the present academic year of Dartmouth College I will on no occasion make use of tobacco or of intoxicating drinks," and at the close of the year again to declare or affirm that I had not so used these articles. I had also through him been given the job of pumping the college organ in the Dartmouth Hall chapel and in the White Church, and through a New Hampton student at the college had secured a position as table waiter for my board.

Applying for entrance, I was asked by President Bartlett for my certificate from New Hampton. I told him it had been sent by mail at the end of June. He could not find it, even after turning over the whole heap of papers littering his desk. I told him I was one of four candidates from the school, and that he had already accepted the other three. "Well," he said, "it will probably turn up," and he put my name on the freshman list. It was not for more than a year afterward that I learned, what I not even had dreamed of, that no certificate had been sent. My Greek teacher had considered my Greek preparation below college requirements, but had allowed me to graduate from the school. I had missed one whole term, the critical one when the class was beginning Homer, and, work as I would, I had never been able to overcome the effects of this handicap. I passed my freshman Greek, however at the college, though not with a high grade. Years later, by irony or fate, I was asked by this same New Hampton instructor to use my influence to secure him a professorship in Greek he was working for in some college. This I did. He was a thorough teacher and deserved my testimonial. President Bartlett never again thought of that lost certificate. With today's organization I could never have entered Dartmouth.

2

The Dartmouth that I found in that September of the mid-1880s was vastly different from the Dartmouth of today. The freshman class of which I was to be a member numbered 98 men, two-thirds of them from New Hampshire and Vermont. I was soon to discover that of the 318 students in the four college classes, one-half were from New Hampshire alone. Only 48 of the entire student body came from outside of New England, and these were mostly sons of alumni who had been born New Englanders. In the words of the Dartmouth laureate, Richard Hovey, Dartmouth for a century had been the college of "the lone and silent North," the college built on the mountain granite, a *vox clamantis in deserto*, in every sense of the word. Compared with the early Harvard and Yale, Dartmouth was what Edinburgh was to London in the eighteenth century: an outpost of culture on the northern border. Behind the little college which Wheelock had moved into the cultural aridity of upper New England, lay a vast, Scotland-like area, ragged with mountains, the stern nurses of free men. To the breakers of this granite land, "Vikings of the North" Hovey called them, and to their sturdy sons, the Websters, the Thad Stevenses, the Salmon Chases, Dartmouth was a God-sent opportunity. To the glory of the old college, it can be said that the greater part of those sterling, mountain-born individualists, the early alumni, would never have found college training at all but for this outpost of culture on the Northern border.

As I see it today, I was indeed a crude specimen, but as I got acquainted with my classmates, I found that many of them were as crude as I. Like myself they had come from small towns, many of them from small farms. For all of us it was indeed a new world. Latin saluted us even in the slang vocabulary of the town. We were hailed as "paenes," meaning *almosters*. The local boys who knew the town were our first instructors: of college customs and traditions they knew more than even the seniors. Many of them had been born in Hanover and had seen much college history as it had been made. As in a criminal gang, we at once acquired picturesque names by which we were always saluted. Sawyer became "Tom"; Whitcomb was "Josh"; Chandler, "Zack." Slightly bald even as a freshman, I became "Father Pat." We were told in language that had to be interpreted to us that we would have to take "Quibe" under "Tute" which meant Professor Quimby's algebra taught by Professor Worthen, and also "Nixon," Latin, taught by tutor Owen Hamilton Gates, and Homer's "Eyelids," taught by "Roots"—Professor R. B. Richardson. It seemed to us a heavy load. Surely it meant hard study, and the sophomores did little to lighten our burden. Even now I seem to hear their harpy chorus as they sat on the college fence, forbidden to freshmen, and sang:

> Green, green, green, as the grass is on the lea,
> Green, green, green, as the waves are on the sea,
> And oh that my tongue could utter
> The deeps of their verdancy.

All of the Dartmouth traditions I found were rich in native humor. One of them was grounded in the New England habit of making fun of the agricultural deficiencies of the region. As a freshman I was sent by a senior to see "Prexie's garden," an ungodly stretch of granite ledges at the south of the town. On my humiliated return I embalmed the legend in the amber of my youthful verse:

When I was very, very young
   In Dartmouth College ways
And had so many things to learn
   It took me several days,
A lordly senior said to me,
   "Now I'm your friend indeed:
To visit Prexie's garden plot
   Is just the thing you need."

Now it was very plain to me,
   A man of such renown
Would have the finest garden plot
   Of any man in town;
So on a Sunday afternoon,
   For I was there to learn,
I went to Prexie's garden plot,
   And saw the whole concern.

Now you who never yet have felt
   Old Dartmouth's shaping touch,
And think you know a thing or two
   Of gardening and such,
Just let me whisper in your ear,
   For I'm your friend indeed:
A visit to this garden plot
   Is just the thing you need.

An earnest group this freshman class, vigorous of body, ambitious, individualistic. Hardly a man in the class had riches behind him. We educated each other. I got more from my associations with fraternity mates and from fraternity programs than from any class-room. Everywhere I was given the impression that college years were the time for the reading of classics, and I read in all the hours I could steal from my studies. In the library I discovered the early books of John Burroughs, *Birds and Bees*, *Wake Robin* and others. These I pored over until I had determined to be myself a Burroughs and write of Nature as I should discover it in the woods. I took long walks every Sunday making notes of my observations. Once I cut classes for a whole day—an Indian summer day when the trees were ablaze with color, and all the world dim with its haze was as silent as a dream. In my journal, I remember, I jotted this, "Devil take the cissoids and the Greeks, I'm off for the woods to spend the whole day. Why squander riches like this Indian summer vision of beauty? I'm off alone, though one has said, 'He who wanders in the wilds alone is either a devil or a god.' Devil or god, I'm off alone for the day."

The marvellous beauty of Hanover Plain with its mountain setting thrilled me more and more every year of my stay there. On the South, etched like a cameo against the sky, was the sharp peak of Ascutney, once in a sonnet written in senior year hailed by me as the Soracte of the college setting:

> "Behold Soracte white with winter snow"—
> Ah, sunny poet of the Sabine Farm,
> I never read thy memory-haunting psalm
> But what Ascutney, lying blue and low
> Upon the South, and clad in mellow glow
> Comes back to me.

The campus with its ancient elms and its bordering maples a blaze of scarlet and yellow in autumn, made an ideal setting for the old Dartmouth Row, strictly academic like the architecture of the buildings. Behind it all arose sharply the observatory ridge crowned with the commanding old pine, during our day vigorous and seemingly, like the very college, a landmark forever. But lightning was to destroy it. Now in its place stands the round tower, first suggested by President Bartlett. Our class built the second section. Below it was the picturesque glen known as the Bema woods, with many trees dedicated to college classes in a ceremony following the "sing out" when the Juniors furnished the lemonade for a "wet down."

No college had more facilities for walks and outings. One might explore the "Vale of Tempe," follow "Stump Lane" through a matchless stand of white pine to the Connecticut River, "frog it" around the five-mile square, or one might climb

Balch Hill and view the town from the upper air. And endless were the possibilities of the great river, the Connecticut, often in the spring filled with logs that sometimes jammed against the Ledyard Bridge even threatening the old structure. Near enough to the college for a week-end trip were the Franconias, with Mooselauke, and farther away Mount Washington and the Presidential range. Few of us, however, dreamed of actually visiting them.

Intense loyalty to Dartmouth came early to all of us. When the president addressed the student body as "Men of Dartmouth," it always brought to me a strange thrill. The spirit of the fighting old college that had been planted in the forest of the frontier by a man who had had a vision was instilled into our very souls. We would be *Men* of Dartmouth ourselves and worthy of the name. For most of us Dartmouth had been our one chance for a college education. During our four years we were living in a golden dream realized.

3

In every way the college adapted itself to the young Vikings it had in charge. As compared with college expenses today those of the 1880s seem of "believe it or not" texture. Board was $3 a week and room rent $10 a term. I left college with what seemed to me a tremendous debt—$550. All my other expenses I had paid from money earned at college or during vacations. Using the experience I had gained in the printing office, I made for the college the blank books used in the college examinations, and I peddled through the dormitory rooms blocks of paper and various kinds of stationery. One summer I waited table at Revere Beach, another summer at Nantasket Beach out of Boston. In my junior summer I worked as a hayfield hand at $1.50 a day and, haying over, I got a job running a boring machine with a gang that was building a pulp-mill in Bristol. During two winter vacations I taught school, once in Candia, N. H., and once in Maine. It had long been a college tradition to allow students to teach 10-week terms in rural schools during the mid-year vacations. One of the jokes of my era had it that Cape Cod had been educated by Dartmouth winter pedagogues, and as a result many of the fair Cape Cod sirens wore Dartmouth fraternity pins, later to be exchanged for wedding rings. Be this as it may, dozens of Dartmouth students turned schoolmasters, were found all over New England during the winter months. I have no doubt that "the master of the district school," who, according to Whittier in *Snow Bound*,

> "Sang songs, and told us what befalls
> In classic Dartmouth's college halls, "

was one of these embryo pedagogues let loose for a winter term to lighten the darkness of a rural school.

To make this teaching plan possible, the Christmas vacation had been lengthened to four weeks, and by incurring an absence of six weeks, the student would have time to complete a 10-weeks school term, the absence to be made up on his return in early March. Such absences, however, raised havoc with one's grades. My own standing, because of my two winter absences, was affected to the degree that I did not make Phi Beta Kappa (honorary membership was awarded me by the chapter in later years) and in a graduating class of 65 I was able to be only number 17. During my senior year, which was unbroken, I was number six.

The school in Maine which occupied my junior winter was secured for me by a teacher's agency run by two seniors who had bought the business from the preceding senior class and who in turn, for a consideration, would pass it on at the end of the year. Of the inner workings of this agency I was soon to learn. I had registered with them early in the fall, signing an agreement to pay to the agency a percentage of my salary in any school they provided for me. Accordingly early in December I was told that a school had been found for me at Bowdoinham, Maine, and that I was to open it the day after Christmas. In high spirits, therefore, I started for Maine little dreaming what was ahead of me. Bowdoinham I found was a town on the Sagadahoc, a branch of the Kennebec. It was a tide-water town with a unique fertilizer mill run by a tide wheel so adjusted that it could be used for power both on the incoming and the outgoing tides. A shipyard was there too, but unused during the winter.

I soon found that I was not expected in Bowdoinham. It seems that the student at the head of the agency, an experienced teacher with a wealth of recommendations, had engaged the school for himself, and just before my arrival had telegraphed the committee that he had broken his leg and had sent me as a substitute. All at once I found myself in an embarrassing position. The committee was divided. After a meeting discussing the situation, Dr. Cheeny, a physician of the old school much loved by the community, called me in and looked me keenly in the eye. "What is the truth? Tell me squarely," he said. I told him all I knew and after a searching interview he said he would let me open the school. There seemed to be nothing else to do. The school was to open on Monday and I was the only teacher in sight.

Then came another attack on my nerves. The school was a "teacher-killer," so I was told by every one I met. The boys one winter had thrown the master from a window and he had landed head down in a snowdrift. Walking up to view the school house Saturday afternoon, I was stopped four or five times, welcomed to Bowdoinham, and then showered with advice: "They are a tough lot and the only way is to begin licking 'em the very first day. Thrash 'em or they'll thrash you." I did not sleep well the Sunday night before the opening.

As I viewed the 70 boys and girls, all of them of high school age, I realized that I had tackled a job that needed experience, and I was a mere college junior who had taught only one term in a small school. In one corner sat eight or ten strapping young men who worked during the summer in the shipyards, raw-boned Yankee lads boiling over with life and mischief. My first problem was discipline, and unconsciously I did the one thing needed to rule the turbulent youngsters. I took no pains to conceal the fact that I was a member of the Dartmouth track team with a record for the two-mile run, and that I played football in the fall. I weighed then 185 pounds and had no more fat on me than a fox hound. I talked athletics with the boys, told them how to organize teams, and how football squads are dieted and handled. They were impressed, but action was needed to convince them. A half dozen of the students were better men than I was physically and they knew it. The test was not delayed. One morning I found the key-hole plugged and the door unopenable save by a carpenter, with the school lined up to see what I would do. From the academic standpoint I did the wrong thing. I was melodramatic in those days, full of adventure stories, and I felt that difficulties must be met not with argument but with action. Accordingly I made a flying-tackle rush at the door, the strength of which I knew, and smashed it down. Then in true Oliver Optic fashion I stripped off my coat and shouted, "If you are men, come on one at a time. If you are yellow rats, come in a bunch." I laugh when I think of it now, but it worked. For a moment no one stirred, then the leader, a giant of a shipyard worker, came to me and said, "We's only jokin'. We didn't mean nothing. Don't go to work and get mad." Thereupon I laughed and said, "Oh, I didn't mean nothing either. I was only just joking too. Hurry up; the bell's going to ring." I had no more trouble. A glorious fellow I found the leader after that. His name was Jake Rideout—I still remember it. The 10 weeks over, he came to me and half bashfully said: "Kinder wish you wan't goin'. We sort er like ye." The local paper gave me a three-inch write-up, praising my work, but the paragraph was evidently put into type by the printer's devil. The editor had written, "The Prof. was well liked by his pupils," but as it appeared in type it read—"well licked."

One of the pleasantest episodes of the winter was a weekend visit to Bowdoin College where a New Hampton schoolmate, Clarence B. Burleigh, later well known in Maine journalism and authorship, was a senior. The Dekes gave me a reception and I saw much of the college. The Hawthorne-Longfellow room in the library with its wealth of editions and souvenirs greatly impressed me. On another Sunday with W. B. Kendall, superintendent of the local phosphate works, I walked down to

northern New Hampshire. It was at one time a saying that if you wished to see Dr. Gile, all you had to do was to sit by the side of any road within 50 miles of Hanover and wait a day or so. He would be sure to drive by, his son John at the wheel of the car.

With him as close companion, I passed one of the pleasantest summers of my life. In our off hours we explored the region thoroughly for miles. Three of us, Gile and H. C. Gross and I were expert swimmers and we took, as I now realize, great risks. The hotel was built on the low tide mark and was protected from the ocean by a high and heavy bulkhead, and at high tide the surf broke violently against this barrier, shaking the entire building. When tides were especially high we three would give exhibitions for the guests on the upper decks. We would dive under the breakers and dare them to dash us to death against the logs. Once on an outgoing tide we swam easily out nearly two miles where the house fisherman was catching mackerel. On our return against the tide we got so exhausted that for a time it seemed that we never could reach the beach. I consider it the narrowest escape from death I have ever experienced. We all lay for an hour on the sand completely exhausted.

4

The 14 men of the academic faculty during the four years I was in the college deserve more comment than I have space to give them. After 50 years spent in college class-rooms and faculty gatherings I give it as my conviction that no college anywhere could have given us better training for the life that was to be ours. Never have I seen a faculty better fitted for its work. There were no young instructors to use us as practice material. First and last we sat in the class-rooms of major professors, the most of them heads of their departments or else the whole department staff in a single chair. We were taught only by scholarly masters, several of them of national renown.

There was the president who had led an expedition to determine the route taken by the Children of Israel during its 40 years in the Wilderness; there was John K. Lord, noted editor of Lord's *Livy;* there was R. B. Richardson, Professor of Greek and later head of the American Classical School in Athens, Greece; there was Arthur Sherburne Hardy, mathematician, novelist, and later ambassador; there was Charles F. Richardson, Winkley Professor of English; and there were others who were as distinctive.

Perhaps of them all C. F. Richardson made upon me the deepest impression. At a glance one noted that he was a personality. He lectured in staccato volleys, making even commonplaces seem startling. He abounded in what the college man of today would denominate "wise cracks." He had arrived at Dartmouth two years before our class entered, from New York where he had edited the magazine *Good Literature*, and already there had been issued by one of his classes a tiny brochure entitled "Smart Sayings of Clothespin Dick." I have never seen it. It was my privilege to hear as lectures volume two of his *History of American Literature*, read from the proof sheets. Volume 1 had appeared in 1886, a pioneer work of which much was made at the time. Delivered as lectures with dramatic intensity, the book seemed more valuable than it really was. One felt like taking notes just for preserving the numerous *bon mots* dashed at us. His presentation of the old sea poet Philip Freneau so attracted me that in later years I made a complete study of the man and his works, and Princeton University published it in three volumes. After my graduation, Richardson made it a practice the rest of his life to write me one letter every year.

Professor Hardy's *But Yet a Woman* was on the bookstands, and was so distinctive that a Boston critic ruled that henceforth the name Hardy would infallibly bring forth the question "Which Hardy?" In my senior year was to come his *The Wind of Destiny*. All this appealed to me tremendously. Never before had I seen a real novelist in the flesh. About him was the atmosphere of a larger world of which I had had no experience. Son of Alpheus Hardy of Boston, he had breathed from infancy an atmosphere of books and culture. So greatly did he appeal to my imagination that just to be with him I elected his course in higher mathematics, a course I was wholly unprepared for, and as a result had to study with intensity just to keep my head above water. As I remember it now, my grade was low, though Hardy's memory in later years recorded no such grade. "You are altogether too modest," he once wrote me, "about your math, having doubtless forgotten what you once knew." In later years I saw much of Hardy. He lectured for me at Coe's Academy, and I visited him in Berne when he was minister to Switzerland. As a writer he always delighted me. There was a French quality in his prose style, a clearness of expression, an epigrammatic crackle, and often a poetic gleam over a page that adjectives are powerless to describe.

In the faculty too was Professor Parker, known to seven lustrums of Dartmouth history as "Picker." He had taught Latin for years, until the soul of the great classics had so possessed him that he forgot the accusatives of specification and the gerundives and gave to his class the thrill of great literature. It was "Picker" who awoke me over my Horace to the realization that there was poetry even in the 60 Latin lines to be translated daily. Since that day in the old Dartmouth Hall classroom, Horace has been for me one of the great poets who have touched my life. Again and again have I read him. A genuine soul, old "Picker." Even the "naughty sophomores" loved him. A man of character he was, rather than a professor with glamorous scholarship. It was a tradition of the college that once on a leave of absence on account of ill health, he spent a winter in a Florida hotel and while there so impressed a certain rich man from the North with his genuineness that the man later left a rich legacy to the college, though before knowing "Picker" he was totally ignorant of Dartmouth.

5

Greatly different from today was this college of the 1880s that catered to the sturdy individualists who had been reared on the granite by the fathers of the fourth generation of New England after the Revolution. There was something still Puritan about the college. Every week-day morning, prayers in the chapel: the scriptures read by the Hebrew-loving old president, a hymn sung by the students, a prayer, and then dismissal by classes, the seniors in the lead. On Sunday a required service in the white church with sermon by "Pa" Leeds, a Puritan surviving from the old order. Once years later when I was at a class reunion, I heard him offer prayer at the commencement service, and then heard Colonel Pearson's appraisal of the effort. "It was shaped," he said, "largely as information given the Lord concerning the character of President Tucker." I countered him with the story of a prayer once made before our student body at Penn State containing the sentence, "As thou doubtless hast read, O Lord, in the morning papers, there is a terrible famine in China and millions are dying."

Vastly different too was the old town of Hanover, seat of the college. It was without a water system, and so was without sewers and water-served toilets; there were no concrete or brick sidewalks and no hard surfaced streets. Electricity did not come until 1893. In the summer, dust everywhere, and in the spring sidewalks and roads were mud. At one time I considered this condition worthy of rhyme and produced this with the title, "Hanover Seasons," published in the *Aegis* of which I was D. K. E. Editor.

> From the time the Fresh are here
> Till the Seniors disappear
> All the seasons teem with miseries by the
>   Band, band, band.
> For the autumn streets are dust,
> And it loads each passing gust
> Till we wade through worlds of choking, blinding
>   Sand, sand, sand.
>
> And the winter brings the snow
> In one swift, heart-sinking flow
> Till the streets resemble Greenland's dreary
>   Land, land, land.
> And the mercury freezes fast,
> And forever howls the blast.
> Oh the happiness when spring is near at
>   Hand, hand, hand.

But when comes the prayed-for spring,
When we thought the world would sing,
Then the streets are ankle deep with oozy
    Jam, jam, jam.
And the grave professors tear
And the wicked students swear,
And from morn till night the air is full of
    Damn! Damn! Damn!

Traditions, not easily broken, ruled the college, when I arrived. There were "football rushes"—the freshmen to bring out the ball and the other classes to kick it around the campus until a sophomore or a freshman captured it and ran it off after a furious fight to some place of safety. There was too the cane rush, a ferocious affair usually won by numbers and weight. And finally in the spring the hat rush. An athletic freshman would wear a silk hat out of the chapel service and Bedlam would take place. One morning I was told to cut chapel and with three other athletes hold the sophomore door closed while the freshmen went out of their door with the hat. I was holding furiously when a hand was put on my shoulder and a voice spoke: "Young man! Young Man!" Turning I saw it was President Bartlett. That meant being "called in on the carpet" by the faculty, which I was that very night. I am still scared as I think of it. The president was determined to stop the various rushes, and to an extent he succeeded.

Traditions of quite another variety also ruled. For many years the senior class had assembled at the first period on Monday morning to read the New Testament in Greek under the direction of the president. Dr. Bartlett, a foremost authority on Old Testament History, had dared to change the tradition. The Monday morning hour he now devoted to Old Testament criticism, a course the students dubbed "Godology." I got much from the course. For the first time I was in the presence of a constructive critic, and his methods fascinated me. The higher criticism of the Scriptures, then so fiercely denounced by the churches, I soon found was nothing other than the methods of research used by all literary critics. It was a vital discovery for me. I still have the notes I made and often refer to them.

There were four Greek letter societies when I arrived at the college, Alpha Delta Phi, Delta Kappa Epsilon, Psi U, and Theta Delta Chi. I pledged D. K. E. and from my four years in the fraternity I got as much as from any department in the college. At the weekly meetings there was always a literary program: an oration, so-called; a humorous paper with personalities; a book review; a reading from current literature; and a report from an appointed senior critic who overlooked no defects. Sometimes the program was a Shakespeare play to be read by assigned readers; sometimes it was a hotly-contested debate; sometimes a prize-speaking, the prize always a humorous thing of small intrinsic value.

During my four years there was a great deal of literary activity in the college. The coming of C. F. Richardson and A. S. Hardy as professors of the college was no doubt a contributing cause, but there were in the student body several genuine poets, the leader, Richard Hovey who was a senior during my freshman year. In my class were William Byron Forbush who issued a volume of lyrics while yet an undergraduate, and Warren F. Gregory who later became owner and manager of the Boston publishing house of Lee and Sheppard. In other classes during the four years were several who arose to distinction in the field of journalism: Morrill Goddard, later a force in newspaper New York; Robert Lincoln O'Brien, later editor of the Boston *Herald;* Wilder Dwight Quint, later editor of the Boston *Traveller;* others as distinctive. Richard Hovey had started his literary career at Dartmouth with a published history of his freshman year entitled *Hanover by Gaslight*, a collector's item now rarely found. Later he contributed frequently to the *Dartmouth Literary Monthly*, which was inaugurated during my junior year and of which I was an editor during my senior year.

For the first time in my life I now had access to an adequate library and I made fullest use of my new riches, exploring the snug alcoves of the old Reed Hall labyrinth where the books were housed. The new library (Wilson Hall) was then under construction. My reading, totally unguided, certainly covered a wide area. I read haphazard from *Clarissa Harlowe* and *Tom*

Jones down to *The Rise of Silas Lapham* and the Tennessee Mountain tales of Craddock. A surprisingly large number of the students, it seems to me now, were reading, as I was, the books that a well-read student was supposed to know. Frequently one would be asked, "How much Shakespeare have you read?" or "How much Hawthorne, or Scott, or Dickens, or Tennyson?" Much was made by certain magazine writers of the time, O. S. Marden especially, of the amounts of classical reading one could cover if one devoted certain hours each day to the mastering of a certain number of pages or chapters. By reading a designated number of pages every night just before going to bed, one could finish Gibbon and Boswell and Prescott in a few weeks. That many students had begun on such a course and had not completed it, I proved once by finding volume one of most of the standard sets greatly worn while the other volumes of the set were untarnished by use. I attempted no such system, but I did use all my spare time. I have found a library card listing the books I drew from the library during two months of my senior year:

> *Mosses from an Old Manse.* Hawthorne.
> Shakespeare, vol. IV.
> Shakespeare, vol. III.
> *Astoria.* Irving.
> *Winter Sunshine.* Burroughs.
> *Algonquin Legends of New England.*
> *In the Wilderness.* Warner.
> *Poems.* Sarah H. Whitman.
> *Yamoyden.* Eastburn and Sands.
> *Vanity Fair.* Thackeray.
> *Fifteen Decisive Battles of the World.*

At graduation I took "Final Honors in English" and in preparation I had had to submit a thesis on "The Nightmare School of Fiction Writers of the Eighteenth Century," a work which necessitated the reading of Horace Walpole, Beckford, Anne Radcliffe, "Monk" Lewis, and Mrs. Shelley.

In my senior year I wrote my first regular piece of literary criticism, a review of the poetry of Sidney Lanier, which appeared in the *Dartmouth Literary Monthly* while I was an editor. The greater part of my contributions to the college papers, however, were poems. The college seemed to look upon me as a poet, and I wrote surprising quantities of verse, much of it buried now in the columns of weekly papers. I was poet at most of our class banquets, beginning with the freshman year, and twice at least I was poet at the D. K. E. initiation banquet, my poem afterward issued by the fraternity in pamphlet form. I was class poet also when we were graduated.

To be able to write publishable verses seemed in the 1880s a mark of genius, and I seemed to be able to produce poems that the college papers were glad to publish. Professor Richardson pronounced my final class-day ode the best ever delivered at Dartmouth, but he had helped me very little in the way of guidance. And I sorely needed the touch which Brander Matthews, for example, had given the young Stewart Edward White. As a writer, I was forced to educate myself and I did a poor job. A new literary period was in its opening days both in America and in Europe, and a judicious critic could have changed the direction of my work. The college helped me not at all at this critical moment. Its whole vision was directed toward the past. I was told to form myself on Addison and Macaulay and the purists of the eighteenth century. In the field of poetry I was wholly unguided. I read with eagerness the exquisite chirpings of Aldrich and Bunner and the makers of French Forms, Gosse, Dobson and other masters of *vers de societe*. Masters in his "Petit the Poet" lyric in *The Spoon River Anthology* might have made the title "Pattee the Poet":

> Triolets, villanelles, rondels, rondeaus,
> Seeds in a dry pod, tick, tick, tick,
> Tick, tick, tick, what little iambics,
> While Homer and Whitman roared in the pines!

I was greatly influenced by Bayard Taylor's early lyrics, his "Daughter of Egypt, veil thine eyes," his "Moan ye wild winds around the pane," a monody on the death of his first love, and the volume of oriental echoes, *Poems of the Orient*. Living in such a poetic atmosphere did me no good as a developing writer.

6

The story of Whitman at Dartmouth has been told, but not widely. There had long been at the college a tradition that the commencement orator one year and the poet the next were to be chosen by the graduating class. In 1848 the graduating class had chosen the then much criticized Ralph Waldo Emerson after five or six notables they had invited had refused the honor. The class of 1872, replete with headstrong personalities, had, in order to shock the faculty and the town, voted to call as their poet, "the smutty old bard who had been dismissed from a government job because of immoral writings." The faculty was powerless, and in due time Whitman appeared. The first surprise came from the dress and the bearing of the poet. This was no "New York rough," as Lowell had termed him, no "flannel-shirted rowdy." He was faultlessly dressed in a neat blue suit. According to custom, the visiting orator or poet at commencement was the guest of the college pastor, but "Pa" Leeds was abroad. His wife, however, undertook the duty and found him delightful. At the commencement exercise, the faculty holding its breath, the students expecting momentarily to burst into laughter, and the college church members expecting the shock of their lives, Whitman read them the magnificent poem opening in his unexpanded version:

Like a strong bird on pinions free.

Years later at a Dartmouth "potlatch" held in Boston, with many of New England alumni present, I told the college that it had the honor of being the only educational institution in America to call Whitman to its platform and recognize his genius, and that a marker should be placed somewhere on the college campus. Furthermore I told them that in the poem he had read in the old White Church was a definition of what education in a *modern* American college should be, and that this definition should be on the marker commemorating the poet's visit:

Brain of the New World, what a task is thine,
To formulate the Modern—out of the peerless grandeur of the
    modern,—
Out of thyself, comprising science, to recast poems, churches,
    art
(Recast, may-be discard them, end them—may-be their work is
    done, who knows?)
By vision, hand, conception, on the background of the mighty
    past, the dead,
To limn with absolute faith the mighty living present.

The college did not heed me.

The most notable visitor during my period was Matthew Arnold, then on his American lecture tour. Hanover, isolated, a full day's journey from the great centres of art and literature, determined at least for once to rise above its handicap and bring Mohammed to its mountain. A lecture by the great Englishman meant $500, in those rural days a considerable sum, but even this mountain was not insuperable. One hundred professors, students, and townspeople pledged each $5 and the great lecture was assured. He came on a dismal spring day of rain and fog and mud. Alighting from the train at Norwich, he glimpsed the fog and rain and mud and remarked, "How beautiful! Just like dear old England." The lecture according to one student's report was a "flop." Pulling a small pamphlet from his pocket, a reply he had once made to Huxley I think it was, he read in monotonous drone to the dreary end. And few heard him.

I was more interested in a far less famous writer, also a winter lecturer, Julian Hawthorne. He had published 10 novels, none of them best-sellers, save perhaps *Fortune's Fool*, 1883, but he was fiercely in the limelight because of his *Nathaniel Hawthorne and His Wife*, 1885. Ought he to have published all of his father's love letters? Would not the old novelist turn in his grave at this deed of his son? The romantic two-thirds defended the deed. "He has enriched a world where all are lovers," they cried. But the other third was shocked. "Happy the man," said they, "who has had famous parents, for he can enrich himself by publishing the family love letters." It was whispered around the campus that the man resembled his father, and after the lecture everyone was asking, "Did you see the likeness?"

Viewed in profile the face certainly suggested the elder Hawthorne, and many were unkind enough to remark that the lecturer, who evidently was aware of the resemblance, lectured for
the most of the time so that his audience had a side view of his
face. "A lecture delivered in profile," said one of my classmates.
His topic was "The Novel," but I remember only a single sentence of the lecture. "Wilkie Collins," he said, "so terrified himself with his *The Lady in White*, that his pen was paralyzed,
and nothing he attempted since has mattered." After the lecture
a few of us spent several hours with Julian in his room, and,
college boys though we were, we were shocked by his stories.

7

For the most part, what help I got at Dartmouth toward
literary training came indirectly. Latin and Greek laid foundations of utmost value, but no classroom during my four years
suggested even remotely that literature is a present-day matter.
English literature meant Anglo-Saxon taught as Greek and Latin
were taught, Shakespeare, and major English writers taught as
something remote and esoteric like Homer or Vergil.

Dartmouth had been fortunate to have for nearly half a
century, 1835-1882, on its teaching staff the scholarly Edwin
D. Sanborn. After a professorship of some 20 years in the Greek
and Latin department, he was made in 1863 Evans Professor of
Oratory and Belles Lettres, then in 1880 Winkley Professor of
Anglo-Saxon and the English Language and Literature. His
radiant personality, his vast knowledge of literature in many
tongues, his eloquence as a public speaker, and his marvellous
memory that enabled him to quote entire classics are now one of
the rich traditions of the college. His influence came largely
from his personality. English literature he taught as he taught
Latin and Greek as precious art material rescued from the dead
past. Seldom did he come nearer the present than the romantic
age that produced Scott.

Charles Francis Richardson, Dartmouth, 1871, inherited
in 1882 the professorship bestowed on his illustrious predeces-

sor two years before, Winkley Professor of Anglo-Saxon and the English Language and Literature. But "Clothespin Dick," as the students at once named him, had been for 10 years in the vigorous currents of modern American literature. In New York City he had been editor of the up-to-date magazine *The Critic of Good Literature*, later under the editorship of the Gilders to become the widely known review *The Critic*. He had in 1878 issued a pioneer text-book in American literature entitled *A Primer of American Literature*. He came to Dartmouth, therefore, with a peculiarly modern outlook on literature. He was soon given a privilege, rare indeed in the colleges of the 1880s, of giving a course in American literature to the senior class. Four years after his arrival he issued Volume I of his *History of American Literature*, truly a pioneer volume.

Very soon the new professor found that he had inherited, as Oliver Wendell Holmes once said, not a chair but a settee. He was the whole English department in a college with 400 students. Anglo-Saxon, a course execrated by most of the students compelled to take it, was a part of the name of his professorship. He had inherited, too, a course in Shakespeare, a requirement for all liberal arts students. Only one thing do I remember about this course: each student in the class was assigned one play to read carefully and to embody his findings in a theme. I was assigned *Henry VI*, and duly wrote my theme, working hard upon it. In time I got the theme back unmarked and un-remarked upon. Some weeks later, however, I happened to meet "Clothespin" on the street and he stopped me to remark, "As to your Shakespeare theme, it contained too many misspelled words. Improve your spelling." This was the only written work required during my four years in college—a thing worthy of note when one thinks of the daily theme contagion that soon spread from Harvard through all the colleges. English composition was simply not taught in my college days. Richardson gave courses in English literature, using as a text-book for the first the *English Prose Masters* by "Granny" Hunt of Princeton. No drier book was ever written. Not even Clothespin could find any life in its mummy case. But the senior year course in literature with

Taine's epoch-making volume as text-book was a vastly different matter. The translation by Van Laun had in it a French tang that fascinated me, and the philosophy of the critic, totally new to me, swept me along and colored all my thinking. I am sure if ever I have achieved a prose style of any effectiveness or if I have maintained in my criticism any consistent point of view, the seeds were planted during this course in Taine's *History of English Literature*.

Then in senior year had come the course in American literature which greatly impressed even the unliterary elements of the class, since the professor was using for his lectures the proof-sheets of Volume II of his *History of American Literature*. Here indeed was literature in the making, literature up to date and American. Naturally we did not realize the uniqueness of what we were getting. To have Bret Harte, Cable, Mark Twain, Sarah Orne Jewett, Joel Chandler Harris, and Charles Egbert Craddock, all of them among the best sellers of the period, presented as a course in a classical American college was something explosively new. Until very recently, the class-rooms of ancient Princeton University have never been polluted by this unscholarly modernness. As late as the 1920s a leading member of the English department there wrote me, "I fear you will think Princeton very backward and old-fashioned when I tell you that we do not regularly conduct any courses at all in which American literature is treated by itself." Even English literature as it is presented today in all American colleges is a comparatively recent arrival in the academic curriculum. Professor William Cranston Lawton, Harvard, 1873, wrote me in 1923:

> In *my* time, '69-'73, 'Stubby' Child was professor of 'Rhetoric and Oratory' (both of which he despised,) and gave the only English instruction. I took his courses throughout. I think Dryden's political verse was the most modern 'literature' we touched. I gave at Hobart, 1914-18, a course in 19th century poetry, which was really Wordsworth to Tennyson, Bryant to Holmes' death.

American literature did not enter much into college courses until the mid-1890s. Professor Lane Cooper, Rutgers, 1896, once wrote me from his chair of English at Cornell:

I have done my best to keep courses in American literature from flourishing too widely . . . In general, courses in American literature, given for any reason other than the welfare of the student, have done harm by diverting his attention from better literatures. I suppose there are advocates for the teaching of Australian literature in Australia, Bolivian literature in Bolivia, and so on . . . There was no teaching of American literature as such in my day at Rutgers.

Moses Coit Tyler at Cornell undoubtedly antedated Richardson as a historian of American literature, but Tyler was a professor of history and wrote his two classic volumes primarily as a study of American history as revealed by its writers of books.

A study of literature in the colleges I presented before the Modern Language Association in 1923. This I published in the *Educational Review*, May 1924, with the title "American Literature in the College Curriculum." Later it appeared in my volume *Tradition and Jazz*, 1925.

8

Commencement, always a climax period for seniors ending their four years of calm before the plunge into the world where they must make their way alone, had for me as its most moving moment "the sing-out," when at the last chapel exercise the senior class marches out while the three lower classes reverently standing sing the hymn that has been sung at this service for a century:

> Come, let us anew our journey pursue,
> Roll round with the year and never stand still . . .
>
> * * *
>
> Our life is a dream, our days as a stream
> Pass quickly away
> The fugitive moment refuses to stay
> The arrow is sped, the moment is gone,
> The Millennial year rushes on to our view
> And Eternity's here.
> Oh that each in the day
> Of His Coming may say
> "I have fought my way through
> I have finished the work that thou gavest me to do."

I had indeed, I thought, fought my way through, and now was ready, it so seemed then, to fight my way through the larger battles that life, I was sure, would offer me.

I had been elected poet of the class, and my poem read at classday was the usual adolescent war-cry. Every new genera- tion sees visions of a new world of their own creating, visions (as mine have now done) that at last become only dreams. This was the opening stanza of my poem:

> "About to die, we hail thee!" one has sung,
>> When on the hoary verge of four-score years,
> Full freighted with the garlands Fame had hung,
>> With life all tried—its conquests and its tears,—
> He sought again the haunts where first had rung
>> His magic flute, when life and hope were young.
>
> We come not with the ripened fruit to-day;
>> We come not to salute, "About to die!"
> Agirt for battle stand we for the fray;
>> About to live, we hail thee! is our cry.

The old century was drawing gloomily to its close. Like an atmosphere lay the feeling that the era following the Civil War had been a shameful one, a "gilded age." The dreams that had gendered the great war had vanished in a fog. The 1890s that were upon us seemed yellow. In literature *The Yellow Book* and the *Philistine*. Everywhere one saw the word "decadence." But there was still hope. A new century was coming. A new era was opening. Glorious! I caught a vision of it in my poem and turned prophet:

> The coming age will be a golden age;
>> The lyres to sound its epic are unstrung;
> Of all its thousand volumes not a page;
>> Its heroes and its prophets, who has rung
>> Their welcome in? Its battles are unsung.

That in 1888, and the golden age is still in the future. No epics yet. But I still stand by my youthful prophecy. I have, however, hazarded no guess as to dates.

9

Shortly after my graduation at Dartmouth, I wrote an article entitled "Working One's Way through College" and in 1891 it was published in *Golden Days*, a magazine edited by James Elverson. The article is really autobiographical, and parts of it I am reproducing:

120

> We will confine ourselves to the class of colleges represented by Dartmouth, Williams, Bowdoin, and Amherst. In every college of this grade can be found at least 25 per cent of the students who are working their own way. They are the backbone of the college; the faithful workers who give individuality to their classes and the ones who are heard from in after life.
>
> I have questioned scores of these young men, and have found that their expenses seldom exceed $200 a year. In all colleges of this grade, scholarships can be obtained, thus cutting down tuition to a low figure. Room-rent, where two share the room, is very reasonable. Books, if one wishes to sell, as soon as one has finished their content, cost practically nothing. One term's books will almost pay for the next term's. Board, in clubs run on the co-operative plan, has been brought as low as $2 a week, and even lower.
>
> A careful investigation of the subject warrants me in giving the following as the cost of an average year in college, when the student is willing to economize:

Tuition	$ 25
Board, 30 weeks at $3	90
Books	12
Room rent	10
Laundry, oil, fuel	25
Incidentals	10
Total	$172

> This is my estimate, with the understanding that eight weeks were passed teaching school. But even this seems like a big sum to the average boy. However, one who is keen and active and in earnest can earn even this during a college year. I have known especially wide-awake fellows actually to earn money while in college.
>
> First, there is always a call for teachers of rural winter schools. In January you can find undergraduate college students in every country town from Canada to Cape Cod. The pay ranges from $40 to $60 a month. Most colleges will allow a leave of absence for such teaching.

Thereupon I took as an example a man of my own class who established what he called the "Codfish Club" at the college:

One morning we were startled to see in his window the notice:

"Gentlemen's Restaurant.
Regular Board for 17 cents a day."

Oat-meal, crackers, salt codfish, and baked beans were his staples. In a week he had 13 boarders. The club flourished for a time, but one by one the boarders returned to their flesh-pots, and after six weeks the proprietor was again alone.

There are always demands for student waiters at the seashore during the summer and one can earn from $50 to $60 there. Tutors are also in demand at summer resorts. Some students are reporters for newspapers. A considerable number of students can earn their board as waiters at the college commons. In a city one can always find a job that will pay for board.

The poor boy who really wants to attend a college has little excuse today if he is frightened out of it. All that is needed is perseverance and an ability to do hard work. College authorities are always in sympathy with those who are struggling along, and, once in college you are pretty certain to graduate.

My clothing bill during my whole course was small. I wore heavy woolen shirts and, though often in the winter the mercury crept to 30 below zero, I had no overcoat. I wore my shoes completely out and though the sidewalks often were veritable mudholes, I could not afford rubbers. Seldom did I end a day with dry feet. I had a suit for Sunday wear, but no evening clothes, since we never went to social gatherings save once a year to the reception given to the seniors.

I remember at one of the alumni dinners at commencement, Dr. John Ordronaux of the class of 1850 deplored in his response to a toast the extravagance he found all around him in the Dartmouth he was visiting. "When I was a student here," he said, "my washing cost me only ninepence a week and I was regarded as a cleanly boy." To which President Tucker, as toastmaster retorted: "If you were a student here now, in this day of the sweater, your washing would not cost you anything." It was about this time that the famous coat-of-arms emblem for Dartmouth was suggested: "A green sweater on a snowdrift."

One heard many rare stories of the old Dartmouth in those days when we believed everything we heard. It was told that shortly after the Civil War, Salmon P. Chase, Dartmouth, 1826, was the central figure at a commencement and the college outdid itself honoring its famous son. A great tent, circus size, was central on the campus during the week and in it was served the alumni dinner, the *piece de resistance* of the menu being salmon and peas. More alumni came than were expected, the food supply ran short, and as a result the banquet became a "salmon pea chase."

Some years later while I was at the Northwood Academy, I found Dr. Bartlett a fellow passenger on a train out of Concord. It was in 1891, just after he had retired from the presidency,—been forced out, would be nearer the truth. Professor John K. Lord was filling the presidential chair for the rest of the year. The old Prex seemed glad to meet me and cordially invited me to share his seat which I gladly did. I confess that I was flattered and somewhat thrilled to have him open at once and with characteristic impetuosity his own side of the case, as if I were a fellow executive and not a mere alumnus who had graduated during his administration. I was not surprised, however. I knew the case thoroughly from the side of the prosecution but had heard little of the defense.

From the beginning of his administration he had clashed with the more modern elements of his faculty, and with the more headlong personalities of the younger generation. Even the college students considered him antiquated in his ideals. As an undergraduate I had myself opposed him, though not actively. I had, however, been an editor of the college class annual, *The Aegis*, and had not objected to the publication of the historic cartoon depicting a suggested memorial window in the new Rollins Chapel, to "1817. Rev. . . . . . . D.D., L.L.D.," representing the funeral of Ananias, the accompanying text being, "The young men arose, wound him up, carried him out, and buried him." That the cartoon all but finished the careers of some of us editors, goes without saying, but that it made a stir goes also without saying. It was indeed prophetic. Soon the younger alumni were to do just what the cartoon suggested. And now I was hearing the victim present his defense.

For the first time I saw the tragedy in its true light. The man had been a victim of his own Puritan inheritance and he had tried to carry his ideals into the new generation beyond his own. He had brought with him into the closing century conceptions that should have died with the century. He had fought without quarter the new order that was setting in like a spring tide with the new generations that were to live their lives in the century soon to be born, and with true Puritan inflexibility he had refused to yield an inch or to modify one tittle his chosen course. Even his enemies must admit that he was honest in his ideals, that he worked incessantly for the good of Dartmouth, as he saw the good, and that, like the Puritan he was, he believed with his whole soul that he was standing on immovable foundations, and that opposition to these fundamentals was a thing from the Devil.

I parted with the old man with pity in my heart, even sadness. It is a moving thing to be in the presence of a strong man who was seeing the dream and aspirations of his life lie shattered at his feet. He was 75 years old, but he talked as if he might have gone on indefinitely to final success, had he not been brutally cut down. Though he said to me, "I'm glad I'm out of it! It was slavery,—slavery!" The impression was deep upon me that I was listening to a defeated man, one who had started with the highest aspirations, and that the defeat had come through no weakness of his own. I could not argue with him. One with such deep foundations of conviction cannot be changed at 75 years of age. I could have told him his failure came not from his ideals and not from his standing on the foundation he had chosen, but that it came from his refusal to consider at all the ideals of the new generation that so soon was to rule. He was a Moses who could bring law and vision to his own day and lead through the wilderness his own generation must pass through, but who was compelled to surrender his own leadership to the young wilderness-born Joshua, who alone was fitted to lead into the new and larger period. And soon all were to see the new Dartmouth grow into reality under the vigorous leadership of his successor, the young President Tucker, who like Joshua was in tune with the living present and not inflexibly bound to a dead past.

Prexy Bartlett, nevertheless, had strong elements for leadership. He did much for the college despite his inflexibility before new ideals. He did work now done by four or five. He was a strong soul, in many ways to be admired. Once, of late years, asked to address in Florida a gathering of alumni, I read them this, a poem as yet unpublished:

Prexy Bartlett

Strong leader in the brazen age
    Ere Tucker came and Tuck,
He taught one lesson to us all:
    He never passed the buck.

They piled on him a giant load,
    He did not growl or duck;
He did the work five men do now,
    And never passed the buck.

Fierce warrior in a fighting age,
    We honor now your pluck;
You added iron to our souls:
    You never passed the buck.

And where your men to-day are found,
    They lead and not by luck;
They learned from you to stand alone
    And never pass the buck.

10

As secretary of my class for some years, I found much that interested me. Out of the 100 who entered the class 65 were graduated, and of these 65 twenty were alive 56 years later. Five of the graduates entered the ministry, six became doctors, 10 lawyers, nine teachers, 18 business men, and two journalists. Only five returned to the farm. Many were highly successful in their professions. G. F. Hardy became the world's leading authority on paper mills; L. C. White became general superintendent of Federal Prisons; W. F. Gregory became president and manager of the publishing house of Lee & Sheppard, Boston; Lee F. English became general attorney for the Santa Fe Railroad Company; William Byron Forbush organized the

Knights of King Arthur, a far-reaching fraternity for boys, and published a long series of books on "the boy problem"; A. A. Fisher became general superintendent of the Railway Mail service; Fred A. Walker became president of the Association of the New York Newspaper Publishers. Others, less famous, were leaders in the communities where they lived. What Dartmouth did for all of us is evident if you but study what we looked like when we went *up* to the college and what we were when we came *down* to make our way in the world of men.

CHAPTER VII

Alexandria, N. H. in 1890

T HROUGH COLLEGE AND NO JOB. My ambition to be a "journalist," the urge that had caused me to leave the printing office and go to college, was still with me. Professor Richardson had advised me to apply to the Springfield *Republican*, calling it the best training school in the nation for young reporters. At my suggestion he wrote to the editor, an old friend of his, and advised me to follow his letter with a letter of my own. A reply came several weeks before I left Dartmouth:

> I want to take on a new man now, as soon as possible. We are accustomed to take beginners for one month's work without compensation. We then pay them at the rate of $6 a week, and advance gradually above that amount as their work improves and we are able to pay more. If you want to come on these terms, please inform me when you will be able to begin.
>
> SAM'L BOWLES

It seemed like the break I was looking for. No start, I felt, could be more promising. But I was $550 in debt, an amount that seemed to me national-debt-like in size. It was, indeed, nearly half as large an amount as father had paid for the farm on which I had been reared, money that had represented a lifetime of labor and careful saving. There was interest to be paid on this debt, and regularly-due life insurance fees to be met. Six dollars a week would not pay for board and lodging in a city like Springfield, Massachusetts. The chance, golden as it seemed to me, I had to turn down. Thinking of my old father who held the notes of my debt, I could not make the venture. Often in later years I have wondered what my career would have been had I been able to enter this profession for which I had been preparing myself. Poverty at times speaks in the imperative, and poverty ruled me now.

For "strapped" college graduates there is but one profession that will pay beginners a living wage from the start—

none of them giving any previous notice or making reservations in advance.

The automobile has changed completely the White Mountain region. No longer is it the rich man's reservation. It is now patronized by flying thousands of people of moderate means. One can hardly now go a crooked mile in the mountains and not come upon groups of tiny one-night cabins to be rented at low prices. Many of the big hotels nationally known are gone: The Flume House, the Profile House in the Franconia Notch, the Waumbek House, the Glenn House, all of these were burned. My verb in the passive is not accidental. Many of the large houses still remain but they are often "in the red" at the end of the season. But in the golden summer of 1889 all mountain resorts made money. They were crowded to the very doors with paying guests. All through August I reported veritable mass attacks upon the hotels I visited. I quote at random from my *Herald* letters:

> The season is wide open and at its gayest. There is not a dull moment in the whole day now. With every house in the hills crowded with merry-makers, with prancing four-in-hands on all the roads, and with merry alpine horn notes echoing from every hill, what wonder that August is a Mid Summer Night's dream?

Again, this from another resort in Jefferson, N. H.:

> The place is totally unprepared for the incoming hosts. There is not a vacant room in the town. The farm-houses even are full. One party last night, after searching the town, found accommodations for half of the family in one farmhouse and the rest in another two miles farther on.

The beauty of the summer mountains got me early and I find my reports to my paper often bordered with roses. When I wrote of Jefferson I found poetry slipping from my pen. One of my letters was republished in the Sunday *New York Times*, August 11:

> Its altitude, its bracing atmosphere, its coolness and quiet, and its matchless scenery make it nearly a perfect Summer resort. Here one is not hemmed in by near and overtopping mountains, which, grand though they are, soon have a suffocating effect. Nor is one so far from the mountains that

one is forced to use a glass to see them. From Jefferson the main range of the White Hills can be seen at its best. Its peaks loom on the sky line, scarred and furrowed, their bare summits glistening in the sun, so near that one can see with the unaided eye the railway and the houses on Mount Washington, and yet so far away are they that the majesty of the entire line impresses one more than would a single prominent peak. Towards the west stands the unbroken forest, sloping off from the foot of Mount Washington to the broad savannas of the Connecticut, and robing to the top the broken ranges between. In the south stands the blue mass of the Franconias, and on the North looms the overhanging peak of Starr King. There is something restful in the scene. Its moods and tints are as changeful as those of the sea. One never tires of it. Its charms increase with every summer one worships at its shrine.

2

My health still precarious when the season closed, I did not continue as a reporter. In the autumn I took charge of a high school in Mendon, Massachusetts. Here we began housekeeping for the first time, in a small apartment which we found ample for all our needs. The school was small and well graded and I found myself for the first time really enjoying my work as a teacher. I organized a class in American literature and was so successful with it that the students gave me a set of Hawthorne as a present. Soon I was dreaming of a school text book in American literature. So far as I could find, only one was in print. The year closed in May with a graduating class of 10, several members of which went to college the following fall.

Again, June 1890, we were at the home farm in Alexandria and soon my wife found employment in a neighboring school. I too got a job: I was appointed census enumerator for the town. The work interested me greatly. Here was a typical New England mountain town for me to study under ideal conditions. No part of it was nearer a railroad than five miles, and at the upper limits of the cultivated area under the bald peak and hedges of lilac. These could not be transported with the old house and without them, and without the setting of the forests and the hills, the soul of the ancient building was lost.

Not one of the ancient cellar holes I visited but had its story, often a tragedy. Some of the stories have been told. Sarah Orne Jewett was at home on the sea coast of Maine and New Hampshire, and she seldom put the hill lands into her tales. It is Mary E. Wilkins alone who has recorded the New England tragedy as found in the mountain lands. I could match almost every one of her pathetic old maids and forlorn deserted old fathers and left-alone mothers in the Alexandria area that I know. But only a few of these tragic tales of deserted hearth-stones will ever be told. There is no one left who knows them, or could tell them.

The township was divided in several ways. First, there were some 12 school districts, each with definite bounds, and each with a red school house in which one and sometimes two or three sessions a year were held, taught by local teachers, usually women meagerly educated. Then too, the town was divided into road districts, each with a local agent, usually a farmer whose duty it was to see that the roads were broken out after winter storms, and in the spring to make arrangements for a general gathering of the men of the district for working out their road taxes. Such road gangs usually plowed the gutters on the sides of the road and then shoveled the loosened soil up on-to the road bed. Always at such times came from the workers the ancient "wheeze" that the town had decided to mend its ways. The executive body of the township was composed of three se-lectmen elected one each year at the March meeting. To this town meeting every voter not "bed-fast" always went. Nowhere can one find democracy more complete and more effective. The town is run by its citizens, every one of them present and priv-ileged to speak and then to vote on every town measure.

Alexandria village, where during my boyhood and until I was 30 years old, I often attended these annual elections, is on a broad meadow bottom that in days prehistoric had been cov-ered by the near-by lake before it had been lowered by breaking through a barrier at the southern end, a break-through which had created the plunging Newfound River, parent of the manufacturing village of Bristol. A white church there was in this Alexandria village, flanked by a long row of horse-sheds. In front of the church was the town common, an acre of level ground bordered picturesquely by ancient elms and rock maples. On the side opposite the church were the village store and the town hall, and not far away the blacksmith shop, an institution greatly needed in horse-drawn days.

On the four roads leading from the Common there were half a dozen farmhouses with near-by barns joined to them by long woodsheds. Behind these lay the inevitable kitchen garden and the cultivated acres of the farm. One of the roads led to Bristol, another to the Newfound Lake areas, another to the South Alexandria section that once had had its own church and blacksmith shop, and another with many branches leading to the hillside farms even to the limits of Mount Cardigan. Like many of the cultivated lands in the Swiss Alps, many of these farms had been hewed out against the very protests of Nature.

I had a long talk with every farmer left in the town in 1890. Every one of them told me that attempts to realize a profit from live stock, whether in the dairy line or the beef market line, meant back-breaking work and small returns. To haul grain week after week from the distant mills at Bristol, to feed it out day by day with hay cut from the farm, and then to realize from the products sold scarcely enough to pay the grain bill, was to get little for your work save the society of the cows and the steers.

The farmer's year, as I gathered it, seemed to round up into some 12 major events. The March meeting began the new year; then came the annual visit of the selectmen who appraised the stock and other taxable property; then came the maple sugar season; early in May opened the pasturing season when the young stock was sent up into the mountain clearings for the summer; then had come planting, hoeing, road-mending followed by the major job of the year, haying; harvesting, wood-with "caterpillars," he branded then as "cockney rhymes." Cockney nothing! They were straight New England ruralisms. Whittier rhymed "faster" with "pasture" because he himself always pronounced the words "farster" and "parster," just as my grandfather and all his neighbors did.

Edmund C. Stedman, to whom I sent a copy, was less severe:

> This year I am compelled to cease letter-writing, as far as possible. But your own letter pleases me by its good sense and direction. Let me say, in a word, then, that there is no doubt you have a poet's ear and touch, and I like some of your verse—especially a few of the closing sonnets. There is some true descriptive poetry in the volume.
>
> But *jam satis* of description and merely contemplative verse. You ask me whether to go on. Not unless you have something new and strange and dramatic to say in your song. Frankly, you need some struggle, or experience, or great motive, or change of life—that is, you need it if you wish to reach the world as a poet.

Remarkably sound advice as I see it now, and surely I needed it. Thomas Wentworth Higginson also was helpful:

> Thank you for the book, which has, I think, freshness and vigor and promise, but nowhere so fortunately concentrated and brought to bear as to make a really great and complete poem. When I offered something, as a boy, for the last volume of *The Dial*, Mr. R. W. Emerson wrote to me: "These verses have truth and earnestness, and a happier hour may add that external perfection which can neither be commanded nor described." This is all I can say to you, but this simple and pregnant formula did me good for my whole life, and it may help you in the same way.
>
> Go on writing verse by all means, but do not expect to know for many years whether it is of real value or not. I am just 70, and have never quite ascertained that as to my own alleged poems.

Harriet Beecher Stowe was motherly rather than critical. She commended the book because there was in it "sweetness, gentleness, and sympathy for the weak," and because in it was a poem appreciative of the song of the hermit thrush, a bird loved by her brother Henry.

Boston critics disagreed about the book's value. *The Bea-*

con warned the poet that "he has much to learn in the way of technique and not often does he achieve the genuine lyric note." *The Traveller*, however, found the book commendable: "Mr. Pattee has written poetry and there is a distinction to be made between verse and poetry. He has the genuine insight of a poet as this volume abundantly testifies."

Long ago I realized that the little book was all that Stoddard said it was, and diligently have I sought copies of it for destruction. Many times I have counselled young literary aspirants not to issue their early immaturities at their own expense, but to wait until a publisher has found their writings of enough value to take a chance on. And yet, unless one publishes one will not find the criticism one early needs. Enemies help an author more than friends, and yet to most young writers the word "critic" is synonymous with the "the devil." It was with me.

Curiously enough this little volume of immature verse, made for the most part in undergraduate days, a book justly damned by judicious critics, was to become a turning point in my life. President Atherton of Penn State once told me that the little book which I had sent him with my application for a professorship in the college was the deciding factor, so far as he was concerned, and had got for me the professorship. The stern old administrator had a vein of poetry in him. He told me once that the only poetry to which he had access as a boy was a copy of Burns that his father had once bid off at an auction mishearing the title and thinking he was bidding on a law treatise.

Verse-makers in early America and even up to the time of my college days were looked upon by the great majority of readers as beings peculiarly gifted, geniuses rarely evolved. My native Bristol in its whole long history had produced but two writers who had had actually seen their verses published in reputable papers or magazine. Mrs. Frank Robinson, who wrote under the pseudonym "Marion Douglas" had contributed many verses to the Harper magazines during the decades after 1850 and later she was to have the distinction of having one of her poems reproduced in Stedman's *American Anthology*. During my late boyhood I found in Mother's scrap-book one of her lyrics

originally published in *Harper's Bazaar*, "Cinnamon Roses." I
am sure that this lyric strongly influenced me.

> It is but a break in the woodland
>   This wall of young poplar encloses;
> There is not the trace of a dwelling
>   Save only these cinnamon roses.
> A glow like the cloud of a morning,
>   Each bloom with its heart's hidden gold;
> The dear threshold flowers of New England
>   Our grandmothers cherished of old.
>
> All sweet with their fragrance, the south wind
>   Sways softly the boughs to and fro;
> "We planted those flowers," a low whisper
>   Floats down from the dim long ago.
> Who were they? We know not; the wild-wood
>   The place with its green wall encloses;
> A home that has vanished forever,
>   Still lives in its cinnamon roses.

More influential for me was the poetry of Josephine A.
Cass, also a resident of Bristol, a woman eight years my senior.
She was a graduate of Wellesley, class of 1880, a teacher in the
college and later in Urbana, Illinois, and then a student for a
year at Cambridge, England. It is an unrecorded tragedy in the
history of American literature that her poetry has been allowed
to perish. In her sophomore year at college she won a prize offered by Mr. Durant, founder of the institution, for the best
German boat song, and in the early '80s she won the most distinctive poetic prize of the decade with her lyric, "If Life were a
Banquet." Put into type by me for the *Enterprise* while I was a
workman in the office, it greatly moved me and influenced me:

> If Life were a banquet, and Beauty were wine,
>   And Being the cup to contain it,
> What duty had man but at ease to recline,
>   Drink deeply, and never disdain it?
> If Life were a banquet, and Beauty were wine,
>   And Being the cup to contain it.
>
> If Life were a banquet and Glory were wine,
>   And pain were the strong bowl that held it,
> Would any man pause ere he quaffed, or repine
>   At the cost; though his heart's blood had swelled it?
> If Life were a banquet, and Glory were wine,
>   And pain were the strong bowl that held it!

If Life were a banquet, and Love were the wine,
And pure lips alone touched the chalice,
What soul would refuse for a draught so divine
To purge himself wholly from malice?
But Life is a banquet and Love is the wine,
And pure lips alone touch the chalice.

She died of consumption the year I was graduated from Dartmouth, 1888. She was 33 years old when she died. No collection has ever been made of her poems.

5

During all of my four years at Northwood I wrote poetry and showered it upon the magazines, collecting in the process enough rejection slips to paper my room with. It brought me adventures, however, none of them stranger than a friendship continued for years with Hezekiah Butterworth of the *Youth's Companion*, Boston. Having read one of his *Zig-Zag Journeys* volumes, I sent him my poetry collection, and one of the lyrics seems to have bowled him over. Strangely enough, it was entitled "Song of the Vaquero." I had never seen a vaquero or even a Mexican, but I had read a thrilling book of life on the Mexican plains and had burst into song over it. I had not the slightest idea of how a fandango is danced and Spanish belles for me existed only in my imagination, but this was one of my stanzas:

Ah, there's life on the Mexic plain,
Where the fierce hot passions reign.
In the Mexic dance,
In the fandango,
One may catch a glance
From eyes that glow.
Oh, the witching eyes! Oh the eyes of Spain!
And the dainty hands one would die to gain . . .

As a result I received the following letter, and late in June I spent a weekend with him:

I thank you most cordially for the tasteful volume you have done me the honor to send me. Of course the literary art is correct and elegant, but it is in the incidents of your poetic inspiration and purpose that I am most greatly interested. I regard 'July' as the perfect gem of all, but am personally most interested in the Spanish and Mexic trend of your fancy.

Every one should have a hobby! My own follows Edwin Arnold's prophecy that "the greatest development of American life will be in the equatorial regions of South America,"—a climate akin to Egypt, Syria, the isles of Greece, the cradle lands of the world's first inspirations and achievements. I have been to the Valley of the City of Mexico—the loveliest spot on earth—to Caracas in the Andes, and am making a study of the progress of the South American Indian races, of which Gomez of Mexico is a noble historic representative. The N. A. Indian is dying; the S. A. Indian is advancing true to the prophecies of his great destiny in the temples of Yucatan and Peru.

I wish I might meet you. Northwood is not far away. Why will you not come down to Boston and pass a Sunday with me? We would talk of those things common to our imaginations—and you have this new South American world of the Sun and the Southern Cross in your person as well as I. Why not come down to Boston, say June 10th, and pass Sunday with me at my home 28 Worcester Street? I would be greatly pleased to meet you.

Cordially,

H. BUTTERWORTH

I found him a somewhat sentimental old bachelor living in a rented room. For years, so he told me, he had chosen all the poetry published in the *Youth's Companion*. He introduced me to a Boston boarding house table such as the Autocrat had ruled over. Fellow workers on the *Companion*, and a varied Boston miscellany, were his table companions. Over not alone the breakfast table, but the dinner and supper tables as well, Butterworth ruled like a veritable Dr. Holmes. Wit and wisdom flashed and scintillated. I remember that someone at the table announced that James Grant Wilson was advertised to lecture in Boston.

"Who's James Grant Wilson?" came a voice.

"Why! Surely you have heard of Wilson," answered Butterworth. "He's the man who murdered William Cullen Bryant."

"Murdered Bryant? What do you mean?"

"Killed him. Murdered him in hot blood—very hot blood."

"I never heard of it. Tell us about it. How did he murder him?"

"Big time in Central Park. Hot day in New York—nothing hotter on earth. A monument being dedicated. Bryant the last speaker. Orator of the day, James Grant Wilson. And he talked! and talked! Hour after hour he talked, till Bryant fell dead. Horrible death, don't you think?"

I smiled when on Sunday evening Butterworth invited in a group of Mexicans and South Americans to meet me as a fellow traveller. They brought instruments and played and sang Spanish and Mexican songs. When I left the next day he gave me the surprise of my life by affectionately kissing me goodby. It was the first time in my Puritan young life that I had known a man to kiss another man.

Butterworth's exploitation of newly-found young poets once created a situation much laughed at: A newly-located Tennessee mountain poet who wrote under the signature Will Allen Drogmoole contemplated a visit to Boston, and the genial Butterworth, as he had done with me, invited the young poet to share with him his room and not go to a hotel! Imagine his consternation when the poet appeared in petticoats!

CHAPTER VIII

To the Centre of the Keystone

AFTER FOUR YEARS at the academy I was restless. I was 30 years old, and where a teacher is at 30 he is likely to be at 40, the deadline for teachers. I wanted college work now, but before me loomed the six-barred gate of the Ph.D. degree required for entrance to the profession. I corresponded with the Graduate Department at Harvard, but found no hope. I was still in debt and the earning of a Ph.D. meant several expensive years without income.

Then came a letter from a Dartmouth College mate, Fred P. Emery, 1887, who now, after graduate work in France, was serving as the entire English Department of a college in central Pennsylvania. He was resigning, he said, to become an instructor at Dartmouth, and he advised me to apply for his present position. I lost no time. With my application I sent all my testimonials and with them my book of poems and my *Literature in the Public Schools*. Lean bait I now realize, but I got a bite that thrilled me like a tarpon strike. This was the letter:

> If you are willing to come here without considering yourself or us committed by that fact to any engagement, I shall be very glad indeed to see you, and think it may be of mutual advantage. I ought to mention two points:—
> 1. We are looking distinctively for a teacher of the English language rather than a teacher in Literature. The work is hard and exacting, involving a continuous and rigid drill in writing and speaking the language, with an incidental study of formal rhetoric, and, necessarily of course, to some extent, the use of the literature. I emphasize this because the point of view of the instructor in the two cases would be necessarily quite different, and might be decisive in one's judgment of whether he wished to enter upon the work or not.
> 2. We shall probably not be able to offer, for the first year, more than $1200 but with the promise of some slight regular increase, if the engagement should prove mutually satisfactory.
>
> Yours very truly,
>
> GEO. W. ATHERTON

Again I lost no time. Although the commencement at the academy was near and I was scheduled for the graduation address, I dropped everything and started for Pennsylvania. The trip was a memorable one—for me, at least. I had never been farther west than New York City, and the marvellous clover fields of Lancaster County and the Susquehanna Valley as I saw them in their June ripeness, thrilled me. Then had come more dramatic territory. The great bridge across the Susquehanna at Lewisburg had gone down in the spring flood and we crossed the river on a flat boat. Then had followed the unique ride west on the single track line that wormed its way through the welter of the Seven Mountains, dramatic with glimpses of wild valleys, rock-filled like the tailings of mines, varied by dashing trout streams, and all of it bowered in laurel and rhododendron in full bloom. To me it was a new world, arousing all that was romantic within me.

Finally came the little station Lemont, nestling under the low peak that later I was to learn was "Mount Nittany." Then a horse and buggy ride through "the vale of old Mount Nittany" to the borough of State College, elevation 2000 feet. I had arrived, and, eager with curiosity, I looked around me.

A small town, a mountain hamlet in fact, unprovided with sidewalks save for paths along the street sides, with here and there mud holes occupied in warm weather by hogs which without let or hindrance seemed to have the run of the town. A wag on the college faculty once had proposed that the State's name be changed to *Pig*sylvania since nowhere were there pens. The town was without sewers and the streets were unpaved. All vehicles were horse-drawn or mule-drawn, and in wet weather all the roads leading from the town were swimming in mud of a depth not predictable.

I found commencement at full tide at the college, all available rooms being taken by friends of the graduates. A room was provided for me in "the Lodge" and a student guide was assigned me, who at once took me up six flights of stairs to the Mount Nebo of the town, the tower of the great limestone building known to all Penn State students as "Old Main." From its tower could be seen a most remarkable landscape.

Dozens of times in the years that followed I was myself to act as guide to pilgrims visiting the college, and always I was to tell what my student guide now told me, Dr. Atherton's dictum that this tower is the real hub of the United States. For Pennsylvania is a parallelogram and the diagonals intersect at State College, making the town the exact center of the commonwealth. But Pennsylvania is the keystone of the famous arch. This Tower of Babel, therefore, at the centre of the Keystone, must be the Hub of the Union, out-centering even Boston.

President Atherton was positive in his belief that from this tower could be seen the most beautiful landscape in America. A view it was, indeed, not to be forgotten. In the foreground the vale of Mount Nittany with its scattered farms with cultivated fields like different-colored patches on a garment, with the two visible ranges of the Seven Mountains in the east, the two following each other as if drawn with a pantograph, with the smoke-hued Alleghenies dominating the whole west, and midway between the two, at the head of the valley, Mount Nittany like a sentinel peak.

Less dramatic was the foreground of the picture, the great college farm with its hundreds of acres, rich in orchards, grain fields, corn rows, and gardens. The near campus had been landscaped by a master of his art. Everywhere rare trees and shrubbery, laid in picturesque patterns, with walks and flower gardens and lawns. College buildings not many, the most notable after the great five-storied stone structure on which I stood, being the Engineering Building newly built from the first large appropriation to the college by the State legislature.

At 10 o'clock I was to meet the executive committee of the Trustees, General James A. Beaver, once governor of the State, presiding. It was more like a reception than like an interview with a candidate. I was introduced to the men one by one, talked sociably a moment with each, but no questions were asked as to my qualifications as a teacher. Then I marched with the faculty to the graduation exercises. At the annual dinner following this meeting the president presented his report for the year and in it was an announcement that electrified me: I had been elected. Later I learned that a dozen other candidates had been considered, but that I had been the only one applying in person. It furnished me with a text much used by me in later years: "Always apply for a job in person. A man in sight is worth a dozen on paper. Of all worthless trash the most inane is the letter of recommendation sent by mail. The best set of signed testimonials I ever saw was presented by a Harvard graduate who failed so completely in his first term that I had to drop him."

Back home in Northwood I received formal notice of my election:

> At a meeting of the Executive Committee of the Board of Trustees, held June 13, 1894, you were unanimously elected Professor of English and Rhetoric, to succeed Professor Emery, at a salary of $1200 for the first year, with an increase of $100 a year until the amount shall reach $1500, and with the promise of a house free of rent as soon as one can be provided by the College consistently with other obligations. As you have already stated to me that you will accept the appointment on these terms, I have only to add my expression of sincere gratification, and my desire to co-operate with you in every possible way to make the work of the Department everything that the best friends of the institution could desire.
>
> If our plans for the future succeed we shall witness within the next few years a rapid enlargement of this general work of the College in the direction of Literature, History, and Philosophy; and I have every expectation that we shall be able to offer you a field of work that will satisfy your highest ambition as an educator.
>
> Faithfully yours,
>
> GEORGE W. ATHERTON

Arrived at State College in September, I found myself in a new world. I was being transplanted, as I now see it, into a new soil. Professor Emery, a Dartmouth Yankee like myself, had refused to take root in it, had rebelled at his first contacts with it, and after a single year had escaped back into the world which he knew. It reminds one of the way, a little later, the newly organized Chicago University appeared to the college men of the cultured East. Despite sensationally heightened salaries, college

Looking toward Old Main and the Penn State campus from an elevation south of College Avenue about 1894 when Fred Lewis Pattee came to Penn State.

F. L. Pattee about the time he came to Penn State in 1894.

Campus home at Penn State where Pattee family lived for 17 years, now Benedict House.

View from Old Main tower (1894) characterized by President Atherton as "the most beautiful landscape in America."

Class in bibliography taught by Professor Fred Lewis Pattee in the Old Main library about 1894, shortly after he came to Penn State as Professor of English and Rhetoric.

professors for a long time refused to live in the cultural border lands.

Little did I realize it, but I was entering the trenches of a revolution. Later I was to find that I had been born within a year of the date when President Lincoln had signed the bill creating the Land Grant Colleges with their slogan: "the unity and democracy of education," a movement upsettingly new in education. For three decades the movement had been slowly gaining headway, with fighting centers at Cornell, at the University of Illinois, at The Pennsylvania State College which had elected Dr. Atherton president in 1882, and at other state colleges established under the Grant.

Utterly unaware of the meaning of it all, I had myself already seen one tiny phase of the evolution which was in process. The agricultural funds of the New Hampshire land grant appropriation were being expended at Dartmouth College. A farm had been acquired, buildings had been erected, a curriculum adopted, and instructors secured. It was in the catalogue as a department of Dartmouth, and daily we saw the agricultural students in the chapel with us. During my freshman year there were 39 of these students enrolled, "dungies" we called them in high-hat contempt for a college education not centered about Latin and Greek. I remember a doggerel outburst of mine in our Junior year annual, *The Aegis*. I quote it to illustrate the spirit of the period that produced it, and the prejudice that possessed me when I began my teaching career in the Land Grant College, Penn State:

The Dungies

Horny-handed sons of toil,
'Tis for us to till the soil
 And night and morn
 To milk the meek-eyed kine;
We delight our days to pass
'Mid the growing garden sass
 And to suckle calves,
 And feed the lusty swine.

For a time we go to school,
For we wish to farm by rule,
And to learn to kill
The "pesky tater bugs."
If there's hayseed in our hair,
What the Dickens do we care!
Were we dudes we'd shave,
We'd shave our ugly mugs.

President Atherton, I soon learned, a Yale graduate with a full complement of the Latin and Greek conventional in that college, had served as a captain in the Civil War, had been for a year a member of the faculty of the newly organized Illinois Industrial University, later the University of Illinois, which he had helped organize according to the demands of the Land Grant bill. Then for 12 years he had served as professor of economics in Rutgers College. Chosen as president of The Pennsylvania State College in 1882 when the entire collegiate student body numbered only 34, he had commenced at once to organize the institution according to the ideals of Senator Morrill's bill of 1862. The college had been granted the funds allowed by this bill and the state had accepted the grant, but it was as yet unsettled as to whether the State had thereby obligated itself to support the institution, to maintain in all the coming years the child it had fathered. The result was a battle, a series of skirmishes fought in legislature and courts, and just before I arrived on the scene the first battle had been won, with Dr. Atherton as a leader. Penn State not only had been given appropriations, but had even been granted from State funds an elaborate engineering building.

But the "new education" to be given, as outlined in the Morrill bill, what was that to be? Early in my conferences with Dr. Atherton I found that "two natures were struggling within him," to quote the title of the Barnard statue that soon was to grace one of the college halls. He had felt strongly the cultural force of the old Greek and Latin education that he had been given at Yale, and to throw this all overboard and to substitute for it the industrial training that could be furnished in mere trade schools troubled him.

But the Morrill bill had stood for "the unity and democracy

of education"; it had stood for "the liberal and practical education of the industrial classes in the several pursuits and professions of life," and it had ruled that courses in agriculture and the mechanic arts were as valuable in their training effects as courses in the more patrician Greek and Latin subjects.

Mr. P. Gray Meek of Bellefonte told me in 1908 that in 1883 when he was clerk of the House at Harrisburg, Dr. Atherton, just inaugurated President of the State College, came down to the legislature for the first time. He sought out Mr. Meek and asked him what the sentiment of the legislature was toward the college. Meek told him he would find out. Accordingly he interviewed many legislators and soon found that, aside from Senator Mylin, not one favored it. One senator referred to it as "that sink-hole." When Dr. Atherton came down the next week, he had said, "Doesn't look very bright, does it? Well, I shall be at Hotel Lochiel; have some of the leaders come around and introduce them." This Mr. Meek did. As the weeks went by he would hear now and then some one remark, "That's a pretty fine old professor they've got at State College." Dr. Atherton never went up the "hill" to the Capitol save once or twice when he appeared before a committee. All of his lobbying he did in his hotel room where legislators found him. When the bill finally came up it was passed by both House and Senate. Governor Pattison, however, vetoed it. Thereupon Dr. Atherton said, "Well, I got far more than I expected. We shall come out better next time." His first move was to get the Governor up to the college to make the Commencement address before the graduating class. The next bill was not vetoed. Mr. Meek told me that Dr. Atherton never made himself a nuisance with his lobbying as many who wanted appropriations did. He never buttonholed his man and never asked for his vote. He simply sat in the hotel lobby and talked to those who were there. He had a certain charm and a compelling personality redolent of sincerity that swung men to him. The only man in the House who voted against the 1883 appropriation was a member from Annville who thought the United Brethren College more worthy of an appropriation than was State College.

152 It was years before I realized what was happening to American education, years before I could think of Penn State as anything more than a trade school. But even as an undergraduate at Dartmouth I had known that the foundations of the old-regime education had been criticised as unsound. Charles Francis Adams's Phi Beta Kappa address, "A College Fetich," a condemnation of the Greek and Latin curriculum, had been delivered at Harvard the year before I entered Dartmouth. I had heard echoes of it all through my college course, and without exception I had heard the address sneered at and condemned as Harvard smartness, educational sensationalism to attract attention. As viewed from the Dartmouth classrooms it seemed as radical a proposal as would be the removal of the four Gospels from the Biblical canon. Dartmouth, especially its student body, never rated Harvard high. As seen from the college campus, they were "Little Willies," crammed with "the quality of Boston." The student body was with Yale, a "he-man" college, Yale, *alma mater* of Eleazer Wheelock who had gone into the wilderness

> With a Gradus ad Parnassum
> And a Bible and a drum
> And five-hundred gallons
> Of New England rum.

Yale they remembered had been founded as an antidote for Harvard. Let me add that we of the Greek and Latin majority were inclined to look with high-hat disdain at our own Chandler Scientific School, which was trying, and succeeding, in giving a college education without the classical languages.

Now at Penn State I found myself in a college wholly in accord with the Chandler Scientific School and beyond it in its new educational ideals, and the feeling everywhere growing that its type of training was rapidly becoming a dominating force. When in 1894 I arrived at Penn State I found the Mechanics Arts Department dominating the college. Of the 178 students enrolled in all courses 123 were in the Electrical, the Mechanical, the Civil Engineering Departments.

The first speech I ever heard General Beaver of the Penn State Board of Trustees make before the student body started with a description of a railroad train *de luxe* he had been riding on a few nights before. Suddenly, he said, something had gone wrong, and he had heard an anxious voice sounding through the train, "Where's the electrician?" "That call," he declared, "is ringing now through the whole United States of America and the world: 'Where's the electrician? Where's the engineer?' Fellows, the future of the world is in the hands now of the engineers, and we have only begun to furnish them. You are to be engineers and the world is going to be in your hands. For the first time we are beginning to train men for jobs as well as for the learned professions. Every one of you has in you the makings of a captain of industry. Get ready. The world is waiting eagerly for you."

How revolutionary all this was, as seen from the standpoint of the orthodox old colleges, may be shown by a note from my journal of 1903: "Took a long walk with Dr. Runkle.* We discussed the trend that technical education was taking. Is the present demand for technically trained men a merely temporary phenomenon that will die down when the balance of supply and demand is reached or is it the beginning of a new era? Applied electricity is new, not over 20 years old. There has come a sudden avalanche of demand. Will it last? Dr. Runkle had his doubts. He said there was a parallel in early Roman history. The dominating question then was: Shall Greece rule education or shall education go Roman? Greece won and she educated Rome. For 20 years now we have been in an era of organization. As yet nothing is settled, but Greece again will win. The humanities, even Greek and Latin, will return."

But the agricultural end of the college was restive. The institution had been started as a "Farmer's High School" with agriculture the dominating subject, all students being required to work on the school farm. But with the reorganization of the school into a land-grant college the "farm" element was being slighted. The clause in the land grant bill defining the curricu-

---

*Professor of Philosophy and part-time Librarian.

lum courses was being made to read, so the farmers of the state complained, "including agriculture and THE MECHANIC ARTS." They had grounds for their complaint. In 1894 there were in the student body only 34 "Aggies" and 11 of these were "short-horns," as winter course students were called.

President Atherton was inclined to compromise between the two educational ideals. Before a little group of liberal arts professors at his house in November 1903, I note from a jotting I made at the time, that he put the matter before us with suc-cinctness: "He told us that when he first came to State College in 1882, he had to make efforts solely in the direction of agricul-ture. Then when he had got a good start in this direction, he had a basis on which to ask for mechanic arts. Now, he said, things were beginning to look toward the general side. He said he was delighted to have us come and that he would do all he could for the general side, but he was not ready to recommend required French and German for entrance, and he saw little hope for the Latin and Greek."

Dr. Atherton undoubtedly did all that he could for the lib-eral arts side of the college. Realizing the cultural value of the courses he himself had taken at Yale, he thought that the same cultural effect could be found in the study of the English lan-guage and literature. He directed me to use all my ingenuity as an educator in the experiment of making an exhaustive drill in the elements of the English language take the place of the train-ing that had been given in the Greek and Latin courses. He asked me to teach early English and from it to lead up to mod-ern English, using always the methods by which the classics had been taught in the older education. Accordingly I taught not only English composition to the engineers and the agricul-turalists and the chemists, but I inaugurated courses in the *Ormulum* of the Middle English period and in Chaucer. My students, even the best of the upperclassmen, I found were tot-ally unprepared for such work. Their vocabularies were surpris-ingly limited. Never have I worked harder than I worked on this experiment ordered by President Atherton, and never have I more dismally failed in anything I have since undertaken.

It was quickly evident that the freshmen had had no training in language, even their own tongue. The schools of Pennsylvania were sending their graduates to us ludicrously unprepared in English. I was forced to teach them eighth grade English and call it college work. There were no adequate text books for such a class. I began with the highly recommended rhetoric which had been used at Harvard by Professor Hill. This book, as all know, seeks to correct faulty English by having the student correct incorrect sentences, and all of these sentences I soon found had been taken from the writings of classic authors. Macaulay once in his life, it seems, had split an infinitive, and here it was presented to the poor freshman as a horrible mistake he must correct. I was getting nowhere. The student might quote, if he knew his Bible, "If the righteous scarcely are saved, where shall the ungodly and the sinner appear?" More and more it was coming to me that the student must face his own mistakes, and must be made to understand why correction is necessary. This could be effective only by means of personal interviews, but what could I do with only two men teaching a freshman class of 100? I had far more to learn than any of my students. To teach English to a class that has had several years of Latin and Greek is one thing; to teach English to technical students who have had no language training at all is quite another matter.

In every way I was handicapped. The whole atmosphere of the college was charged with criticism of everything that had been in the old college curriculum. The technical instructors were outspoken and emphatic. Education should look only at the end for which it was a preparation. It should be intensely practical. One prominent professor, Dr. Diemer of the Engineering Department, phrased the problem in this way:

"Students are not here for service or for culture, but for the selfish end of preparing for salary to come. They think only of jobs. Constantly I hear them asking, 'If I change over to your course what kind of a job will it help me to get when I graduate?' Students are weighing every subject they take on the scales of jobs to come. What jobs will Latin and Greek bring to a young man save teaching Latin and Greek, the most effeminate of all jobs a man can take? There may be a few professors idealistic enough to live above this atmosphere today, but not many."

That was in 1894. Before the decade was over, Dean Reber of the Engineering School had on the wall of his office framed pictures of his most successful graduates, and under each picture in large figures the amount of salary each was now receiving.

Distinctly I remember that in one of the early faculty meetings a petition was received signed by all the sophomore civil engineers asking that a required course in history be dropped and that there be substituted for it a course in concrete structures. In vain did the liberal arts minority on the faculty argue that the two subjects were in utterly different worlds and that a course in history was even more practical for the men than the technical subject, for a contractor hiring a young graduate would teach him more concerning concrete while he was working on the job than he could get in any class room. In vain. The petition was granted. I immediately made notes for an article to be entitled "The Concrete in American Education."

I now added a new word to my educational vocabulary, "practicum." By faculty enactment all students must be scheduled for a weekly load of 15 hours of recitation and 10 of practicum, or as it often was explained, 15 hours of theory and 10 of application. For credit purposes one hour of recitation counted the same as two hours of practicum. All the students were required to take carpentry courses and other laboratory work, but what practicums could be found for liberal arts juniors and seniors? Here I found the president inflexible: they too must have practicums in the courses they were pursuing. I told them it was impossible to mix the two varieties; technical education with its laboratories and liberal arts work not done in laboratories did not mix. He yielded not in the least. "You can do it if you really want to do it," he said. "I have noticed that when you see a spook and run from it, it chases you, but when you run for it, it flees."

As a result I began to experiment. I could have my liberal arts students for 10 hours of practicum each week. But what laboratory work could be devised for a student who was signed for a B.A. course or any other courses after the old order? Struggling with the problem, I at length thought of research as a solution. I could give the students the kind of work given those preparing for a graduate degree. I at once introduced what I called research courses in English, but with the library the college possessed I was handicapped on every side. I gave them work in library classification, had them make bibliographies on specified subjects, and lists of books needed by the library. One senior class under my direction dug out all the printed matter in the college archives pertaining to the history of the college and after classifying it in a scholarly way, wrote a history of Penn State College, each student doing an assigned part. Only the seniors were ready for such work, and in the lower classes reading courses were for the most part all that I could require.

Living now in the very center of the greatest producing state of the Union, with the rich anthracite coal fields to the east and the great petroleum areas to the west, and not far away the limitless soft coal mines with their coke ovens, their natural gas wells, and their iron ore, all of it feeding the Pittsburgh mills, I saw in process an evolution of which I had never dreamed. In my class rooms when I first arrived at the college I found approximately one half of the students, judging only by their names, were of English-speaking descent. The other half, still judging only by their names, were manifestly from Pennsylvania Dutch ancestry, the "Dutch" in their speech all but obliterated by the public schools.

But during the 34 years of my residence at the college other elements began to appear in numbers, lads from the oil fields and the mining regions and the mill towns, especially Pittsburgh. More and more there came individuals from the second and third generations of the eastern European stock that had been brought into the State during the period following our Civil War. In the days before the importing of contract laborers had been stopped by federal enactment, ship-loads of men— Czechs, Pollacks, Lithuanians, Bohemians and others—had been imported with numbers sewn upon their backs instead of names, herded from the ships into freight cars and fed into the Pittsburgh mills, where they were used as puddlers and machine tenders in places wholly without safety appliances, and were required to work with no limits as to hours of labor. The fit survived, and the fittest prospered and sent their children to the public schools where they became Americans, and in the land of unlimited opportunity at last went to college like the other Americans among whom they lived. Some of them had shorn the "sky" and "ski" and the unpronounceable elements from their names and had become even Smiths and Joneses. Others had not, but numbers of them now were coming to Penn State to fit themselves for leadership in the industrial environment which was the only world they knew. I remember well a homesick Czech freshman who, despite all of our efforts, returned home after a week at the college. "There aren't oil wells here," he moaned. "I can't stand it not to see oil derricks."

That many of these boys actually did become "captains of industry" is evident to me every time I open the *Alumni News*. Now these once-foreign elements come in numbers, making up a considerable part of the 6000 students now (1928) annually on the college rolls. Before I left Penn State I served as faculty adviser for a Czech fraternity that had its own chapter house, the college home of 20 or 30 students, who in speech and appearance and ideals differed not at all from the groups in other fraternity houses, and yet for the most part they were the grandchildren of the men who, with numbers for names, had been herded in freight-car loads into the iron mills that were to take such a grim toll of their numbers.

It was now that I began to wonder about the quality of my education at Dartmouth; now I began to understand why my predecessor Professor Emery had been willing to exchange a Penn State professorship and department headship for an instructorship at Dartmouth. As yet I had not fully realized that a revolution was in process before my very eyes. My generation, as I later realized, was cast between two forces, one dying— the other struggling to be born—and I was on the fence between the two.

Only three girls were in the upper three classes when I arrived at Penn State. It was as monastic an institution as was the Dartmouth of my day. The college, supported as it was by the tax-payers of the State, was perforce co-educational. The individual tax-payer had as much right to send his daughter to the institution that his money was supporting as he had to send his son. The tide, however, once it turned, became at length a flood. In every class more co-eds, until at last the masculine student body rebelled. Penn State, they argued, had always been a he-man's college. Once in high indignation over the increasing percentage of the femininity admitted, the students held a mass meeting and had a petition drawn which was sent to the trustees. One fiery senior orator at this meeting declared that there was now "too much soprano in the college yell. Admit calico into a college and the college becomes a tea party and a dress parade. Look at the colleges in the West which are now completely wound up in calico. Penn State's a he-man's college, not a nunnery." The trustees could only set a percentage beyond which feminine students would not be enrolled.

As late as 1901, when I wrote the *Alma Mater* song for the college, it had not come to my consciousness that Penn State was not as masculine a student body as was Dartmouth. To me then a college was for the education of *men*. Thus, not realizing what it would mean in later years, I wrote this stanza:

> When we stood at boyhood's gate
> Shapeless in the hands of fate,
> Thou didst mold us, dear old State,
> Into Men.

Think of the student body today, nearly a third of it feminine, singing this stanza. Surely in this world nothing is permanent save only change. If change must be, I suggest this:

> When we stood at childhood's gate,
> Shapeless in the hands of fate,
> Thou didst mold us, dear old State,
> Dear old State.

But looking back at the Penn State I knew, the 30 years that made the alumni roll which is a dominating force today, it does seem to me its mission has been to mold *men* for the major jobs of the world during a generation that has molded the physical world more than any other in all history. I hesitate to change the stanza. Let someone with the forward look do it.

Alma Mater

For the glory of old State,
For her founders strong and great,
For the future that we wait,
    Raise the song.

Sing our love and loyalty,
Sing our hopes that bright and free
Rest, O mother dear with thee,
    All with thee.

When we stood at boyhood's gate,
Shapeless in the hands of fate,
Thou didst mold us, dear old State,
    Into men.

May no act of ours bring shame
To one heart that loves thy name
May our lives but swell thy fame
    Dear old State.

Written March, 1901   Fred Lewis Pattee.

CHAPTER IX

Is There an American Literature?

ℜOT LONG WERE WE in the center of the Keystone before we had the sensations that Franklin tells about when he arrived in the Quaker City from Boston. For the first time in our lives we came into contact with the "Pennsylvania Dutch." I never had heard of them before, but now on the street men and women were speaking what seemed like German but which conveyed no meaning to me though I had taught German for four years. A strange survival it was surely, German still spoken as the prevailing language in many sections of Pennsylvania after nearly two centuries in America. Meeting each other, people said, "How gehts?" instead of "Wie gehts?" Even among the speakers of English in the region there was an abundance of German idioms. If you failed to buy the butter your cook had asked for, then she might say on the following morning: "The butter is all still." Once I saw this notice upon a front door: "The bell don't make. Bump." At every gathering of faculty people there was always presented a new string of funny "Dutch" localisms.

I had not been long in Pennsylvania before I realized that I was viewed by the natives with disfavor. I became conscious of a whispered campaign of criticism directed at President Atherton. He was filling the faculty with New England Yankees. Benjamin Gill, a graduate of Connecticut Wesleyan, had just been appointed professor of Greek and Latin, and Joseph Willard, a fraternity mate of mine at Dartmouth, had been made professor of mathematics. Now the new professor of English was a New England Yankee. Criticism was not outspoken, but everywhere I was told about the way I handled my Yankee "Rs." In vain I countered with the local pronunciation of "V" and "W." When asked to say, "Venus was very vain," they would say "Wenus vas werry wain." One of my greatest labors as a teacher of public speaking was my attempts to get the "Ws" out of the students' spoken work. And yet they laughed at me constantly for saying "idear" and "deah."

As my Pennsylvania years increased I began more and more to admire the Pennsylvania Germans. They were more American than I, for they were permanent settlers before the first pioneer of my own line had left England. They were a sifted people. I was told that there were few individuals among the Amish and the Mennonite sects who had not an ancestor who had died as a martyr for his adherence to his religious beliefs. The Amish were strange-looking, with their shovel beards, their plain black garments without buttons, and their broad-brimmed hats, but they were thoroughly honest and reliable, untiring as farmers, and law-abiding as citizens. They were genuinely religious, fundamentalists in their interpretation of the Bible. Some of the sects had no professional clergy: When a preacher in one of their churches died, a "preacher-picking" meeting was called. To each male adult member was given a Bible and in one Bible was a slip reading, "Thou art the man." Without dropping any of his usual work this man became the preacher. Once I questioned this method as an Amish student told me of it. Might not an ignoramus be chosen, one with no talent for the work? His answer was, "How was Matthias chosen? Read Acts I:26."

It was my good fortune to know a literary Pennsylvania Dutchman of Bellefonte, Thomas H. Harter. In the newspaper of which he was editor he published during a long period what he called his "Boonastiel" papers in the dialect which was his mother tongue. They were republished in a volume still in print, a volume valuable since it preserves a rapidly disappearing dialect. It is rich with humor. The old editor as I knew him in his latter days was somewhat doleful of mood. He had expected more from his sketches than had been realized. They are native and original and realistic, but few people can read them.

was uncompromising in his views of the subject. "I wish we might find some writer and publisher with the courage to entitle such a book 'A History of English Literature in America'—the only expression for the thing which is not absolutely false and misleading." Thirty years later he was of the same mind. In a letter to me written from Rome, Italy, dated January, 1924, he said:

> I do not feel that I have changed in my old opinion that, however general usage may sanction it, it is small and provincial for us to think of American literature as a something distinctive and apart from the great sea of English literature of which it is but one arm. I like to feel Shakespeare, Milton and the rest are not alien writers but as much ours as Longfellow and Whitman. I like to think of the solidarity of the English speaking race and I repudiate Mr. Mencken with his "American Language" and all his works. In a smaller way I object to the use of the word American delimited to the English speaking people of the United States, as it is bumptious and arrogant, which is only another word for narrow and provincial. Let's be big, not small about literature.
>
> On the other hand I by no means decry what we have done on our side of the water and I welcome every manifestation of an independent spirit. Our chief bane has been following English or rather British writers. Let us be ourselves, but not by attitudinizing or assuming an importance not really ours.
>
> As to our catalogues, I should like to have all courses in American writers given under the head of English Literature in America, that is literature in the English tongue in America, and I feel that it should be peculiarly our function to study and work up more fully such writers as have happened to be on this side of the water, always provided that we do not lose our sense of proportion in so doing. Perhaps this will give you somewhat my point of view.
>
> Sincerely yours,
>
> F. E. SCHELLING

As late as 1941, when I was introduced to H. G. Wells as a "Professor of American Literature," he came back sharply with,

"What do you mean by that? What's *American* literature?" I told him, and my explanation seemed to nettle him.

"Ridiculous!" he said.

"Then you must think that America is ridiculous. All America is in it. It could have been produced nowhere else."

"But the stuff is in the English language and therefore is in the descent from Shakespeare and Milton. A literature is the writing in a given language."

"Could Mark Twain or Whitman be called an Englishman? Could their literature be called English? Twain was as American as Hannibal, Missouri, and what he wrote is as American as the buffalo. So with dozens of our writers. We have expressed America not England."

He was not convinced. Like all Englishmen, he seemed to think of America as a father thinks of his son who has left home and is on his own.

"By the same argument," he said, "why not a professorship in Bronx literature?"

"Bronx literature is a chapter in American literature."

At that moment another professor was introduced and the debate ended.

It was but a skirmish in the battle I have been fighting for years. My first written line of defense I published in the Chicago *Dial*, November 1, 1896. This was my conclusion:

> It seems to me that it may be laid down almost as an axiom that when a distinct nation has acquired a distinct individuality and has produced writers and writings *sui generis*, reflecting the soil, the spirit, the individuality of that people, then that nation has a distinct literature, no matter what may be the language in which it is written.

Criticism of this paper was instant and devastating. The New York *Evening Post*, in a caustic column, classified it as "fussy anxiety about how our literature is to be classified." Most of the criticisms were tinged with rancor, as if I had profaned sacred ground. All the academic criticism seemed to imply that the American literary product was not old enough yet to be classified by critics. The calmest and most sensible of the attacks upon the *Dial* article was that of the London *Author*, January 1897:

> No one has ever claimed Lowell, Longfellow, Holmes, Emerson, Washington Irving, Edgar Allan Poe, or any other

great American writer, as belonging to the literary history of this country. On the contrary, we are ready to acknowledge all that Mr. Pattee claims for them—that they are distinctively American; their atmosphere, their conditions are American; no Englishman would have written quite in their way: their speech betrayeth them. But what is the language in which they write? It is English, the language that grew up in this island, which is called after the name of that southern part; the language which is spoken by five great Republics and one Kingdom; or, if you please, the language spoken by two great and powerful confederations. Unless, therefore, one of these confederations changes its language, its literature will continue to be, first and above all things, that of its language. Cannot American literature be content not to be tied by apron strings, as Mr. Pattee puts it, to its mother, but to be an independent branch; perhaps destined to be the greater of two branches, perhaps destined to be one of five or six branches of the noble literature which we call English? There are no more illustrious ancestors that the American poet can desire than those which he possesses. They do not make him dependent on the place where they flourished; they are his possession, while Byron, Tennyson, Browning, are in no sense his possession, any more than Lowell and Longfellow are the possessions of Swinburne and Austin Dobson.

3

One day while this battle was in progress I was startled to receive a note calling me in on the college presidential carpet. Dr. Atherton desired to see me. As usual, he wasted no time on preliminaries. "I have been told," he said, "that the New York *Nation*, a scurrilous sheet, has severely criticised something that you have written. Don't let that trouble you for one moment. Abuse is its whole stock in trade." I assured him that the attack had not annoyed me; on the contrary it had pleased me. "The quality of the apples on a tree can often be judged by the number of clubs and stones lying under it," I said.

"No one ever gains anything from being assaulted by a skunk," he came back at me testily. "The *Nation* is a journal of opposition. It attacks for the mere sake of conflict. I have refused to allow it in our college library. It is not fit reading for maturing minds. Never become embittered by what the *Nation* does to you. Remember the literary life is a fight without armistice or ending and that neither party wins in the end. Don't lose your temper, that's all."

I had long known the president's antipathy to the *Nation*. Once before he had condemned it in my presence. In my diary I had made this record: "Had a conference with the president about books and magazines to be added to the library. He condemned the *Arena* as cranky and uncertain, full of materials not fit to put before any growing mind. It discussed with all seriousness occultism and other insane isms. He also had no patience with the *Nation*. It was freaky, he said. He never picked up a copy of it that he did not find something that made him angry. He condemned several books on my list as too trivial for a college library, but finally said, 'If you need them in your English work, then get them.' "

What had given the president his anger against the *Nation* I never knew. In my own critical work I have always found the magazine vigorous and original. Its book reviews always voiced more nearly the final verdicts rendered by time than did any other literary review of the period. Under Godkin the *Nation* was a voice and a creative force.

As a summary of what in my own estimation I accomplished during the early period when American literature was not presented to college students, or else was grudgingly doled out in brief appendix treatments of the early nine whose work for years constituted American literature (Irving, Bryant, Emerson, Longfellow, Whittier, Hawthorne, Lowell, Holmes, Poe) allow me to reproduce a letter that I wrote in 1939 to the editor of the weekly New York *Herald Tribune* review, *Books:*

> I wish you would bring this letter to the attention of the editor who wrote the department 'Reprints, New Editions' review in the August 6 issue of *Books*. Reviewing the one-volume edition of Parrington's *Main Currents in American Thought*, he declares that Parrington 'set out to interpret American literature in its relation to American life in general.' With this statement I agree, of course, but not with the statement that follows: 'Nobody had yet studied American literature in that way.' The *Main Currents* was published in 1927. Parrington's article in the *Cambridge History of American Literature* you list as pioneer work. That appeared in 1917. My own *History of American Literature* for schools and col-

leges appeared in 1896 and its key note, as everybody knows who has read it or who has read any of the reviews of it, was the relation of American literature to American life. Everywhere was it hailed as a new note, and by many scholars it was attacked because of this point of view. I can say the same thing of my own contribution to the *Cambridge History of American Literature* and also of my treatment of our literature in the article I furnished in 1897 for the *Encyclopaedia Britannica*. Then in 1915 came my *History of American Literature since 1870*, a book that all agreed influenced the current of American literature history. In 1896 there was only one text-book in the subject, Smythe's, a minor affair, and mine went through 20 large editions. I have always had as my thesis that literature must be interpreted as an evolution from American life and that it has become now an independent entity.

I received no reply.

4

Class scraps were an important part of campus life. Each spring freshmen tried to raise their class flag on a pole somewhere on the campus, against the opposition of the sophomores. In the cider scrap the freshmen tried to outwit the sophomores and to bring a barrel of cider on campus for their friends, the juniors. The class-supper scrap came when freshmen, at a signal of three shots, would rush to a hotel in the vicinity for a secretly planned dinner before the sophomores could discover the rendezvous and kidnap the toastmaster. One freshman class put its toastmaster in a box and sent him by express 60 miles away to Sunbury where the banquet was held. Every fall compulsory parades of freshmen, routed out of their lodgings, ended in baths of soot or molasses and feathers.

The early football teams, though often defeated by their better coached opponents, were usually strongly supported. I still recall the telegram sent by our student football manager from New Haven one year: "Yale 78; Penn State 0. The team played well."

When victories came, parades and bonfires automatically followed. The whitewashed fence that ran along the front campus, the shocks of corn in the experimental plot and the board sidewalks of the town, all went to feed the flames, along with miscellaneous small sheds and loose lumber. After one unusually good season, students were given a free half-day to build a bonfire. The structure rose to the height of two stories, and a barrel of gasoline was poured around to give the fire a good start. The president of the senior class had the doubtful honor of applying the match. He escaped with singed hair and clothing and body burns. Nearby spectators were thrown to the ground and windows at some distance were smashed.

A sinister rumor spread over the college a few days later. One of the students had disappeared, and there had been no trace of him since the day of the fire. Then came the report that human bones had been found in the ashes and that the college authorities had sent them away for an expert report. When later rumors said the experts had called the bones bovine, not human, the students were not convinced. The father and mother of the missing boy knew nothing of his whereabouts, and for weeks lived in an agony of doubt. Finally after some two months, a letter came from the boy saying that, below grade in his studies, he had run away and had found a job in Pittsburgh.

Penn State, almost a hundred years younger than Dartmouth, had relatively few traditions. There were the usual senseless college yells and some football songs adapted from those of other schools, but there was no official Alma Mater.

In April 1901, I published an article in the student *Free Lance* deploring the fact that we had no college song, and I wrote a sample song, setting it to the music of a hymn, *Travelling to a Better Land*, which had also been used as the tune of the class song of '95. It was first sung at the commencement of 1901, and President Beaver of the Board of Trustees pronounced it the official Alma Mater without waiting for other proposals. Dr. Atherton had written, or later did write, what I considered a better Alma Mater, but it was set to the music of *The Watch on the Rhine* and had no chance of later success.

CHAPTER X

Around England on a Bicycle

C AN ONE CLIMB out of the rut that has been worn ages deep by one's ancestors? It is easier in America, but to break from one's tribe even here brings inevitable penalties. Leave behind you the old totem poles, begin to doubt in your heart the worth of the old rituals, and there is no return possible. One makes of himself an Ishmael, at home nowhere.

When from time to time during my college years I came back for a vacation in my native town, I noticed a growing difference. In some of my old schoolmates I detected a half concealed bitterness. I was "getting high hat," I was "feeling my college oats and looking down on them." Their democratic blood simmered a bit and then boiled. "By God, I'm just as good a man as he is!" Others deplored their luck. "He's had the breaks and I've had the hard knocks." "I han't never had no show." Very little of this actually came to my ears, but I felt it and it hurt.

In time the gulf became wider. I was not understood even by my own near relatives. I had become, all unknowingly and all unwillingly, estranged from my tribe, uncomprehended by my kin. I remembered what Supt. Nathan Schaeffer of Pennsylvania once told me. In his boyhood home only Pennsylvania German was spoken. Later he went to school, to college, and to a German university. When he and his educated brother visited the old home they lapsed at once into the dialect of their youth and talked of family health, of neighborhood doings, of crops and cattle and the like, but when he and his brother turned to each other and spoke of their work in the larger world in which they now lived they turned at once to the English not spoken by their parents, and so were uncomprehended.

I note that John Burroughs had a similar experience. In his own words, " I was like a graft from some other tree. And this is always a disadvantage to a man—not to be the logical outcome of what went before him, not to be backed up by his family and inheritance—to be of the nature of a sport."

But to me, oversensitive perhaps, there was another five-barred barrier: somehow I felt that I was not wholly akin to the tribe in which I had fitted myself to live. I was like a white man gone Indian and living in a tepee the Indian life, but yet a white man. Was there not a gulf impassable between the world of my first two decades and the world in which Oliver Wendell Holmes had been reared with books and culture heaped upon his very cradle? I wonder if Mark Twain's inferiority complex when he broke from his tribe and moved with his cultured wife into the heart of New England Brahminism, there to make his home, was not responsible for some of his later depression and pessimism.

2

My vacations during all of the years I was at The Pennsylvania State College I spent on my father's farm which I had purchased in 1902, and in a camp which I had built on the west shore of Newfound Lake near the spot where Sugar Loaf Mountain ends in a precipice with a sheer drop of a thousand feet into the lake. Three months every summer kept me in touch with my native New England and the region I had explored so thoroughly as a boy.

There was no vacation for us during our first year at Penn State. For several months my wife had been critically ill. In May a daughter was born, Sarah Lewis, soon a sprightly little thing who put new color and new purpose into our lives. But the budget! and the bills! Fortune seemed to favor me, however. The doctor, whose bill had grown to appalling proportions, had in college a son who, fallen below in all his subjects, seemed about to take the "flunk-out" degree. The doctor came to me for help and agreed to my proposal that for $2 an hour during a period to be determined by the son's response to my tutoring, I would fit him to pass his examinations, "provided only that it was in the wood." Time proved that it was. He passed, and so did my doctor's bill.

But the house we had rented had to be furnished, and a long grocery bill and other bills had mounted high during the months of illness. And again fortune seemed to favor me. I had sent a copy of my American literature text-book to Moses Coit Tyler of Cornell, a scholar whom I considered then, and consider now, the first real historian of early American literature. His volume dealing with the colonial period, 1607-1765, had been an inspiration to me. I have considered it a classic in its field and I so wrote him. His response pleased me:

Cornell University, Ithaca, N. Y.
15 December, 1896

My dear Professor Pattee:

I am almost unkind enough to wish that you may have had some such experience of limited bodily health and strength, as would enable you to understand why I have not sooner acknowledged your most courteous letter of last March, which accompanied the gift of your book on American Literature. The truth is, that for the past two years I have been obliged to do day by day the work resting upon me in connection with my college duties and with the finishing of a large manuscript which I have long had in hand, and to be content to let nearly all other things—including my correspondence—go undone: I simply had not the vital power to do more. On the other side of this room now is a drawer full of letters, unanswered, many of them more ancient than this of yours.

I was much touched by the generous and manly words of your letter; and when I glanced over your book, I saw that it was a genuine piece of work, which I did not wish to write about until I had carefully read it. Not long after it came, I had an enquiry for the best text-book on the subject, and I did not hesitate, even from a slight reading, to recommend your book to my correspondent, who accordingly introduced it into the courses at Bay View Assembly, Michigan.

I have several times since then had your book in my hands, and have read here and there, with respect for your discrimination and independence; and with a general sympathy with your method. Of course, we could discuss details of critical opinion for days, if there were the days to spare.

I am glad you have done this book,—for it cannot fail to help in putting our literature in the right light before the young scholars, and in pointing them to the true lines of approach to it.

Hoping that I may sometime have the privilege of meeting you personally, and of comparing notes at greater length on subjects of great interest to us both, I remain

Sincerely your friend,

MOSES COIT TYLER

Tyler turned his *Bay View Magazine* work over to me at once. My *American Literature* was adopted as the text book to be used by the Assembly during the spring session. I made out the programs and directed the work. Then had come another helpful assignment: for the Werner Company's edition of the *Encyclopaedia Britannica* I was asked to furnish the section on the history of American literature during the 20 years since the last edition of the work, 7,500 words. In addition I was to furnish a section covering Canadian literature. The last sentence in the Werner Company's letter pleased me: "Mr. Williams of Philadelphia and Mr. Stedman of New York have both said in recent correspondence with us on other subjects, 'Professor Pattee should do your work on American literature.' "

3

All this in addition to my college work left me no leisure time. When I began my work at Penn State I was the entire English Department and also the entire Public Speaking Department. Later an assistant in English who signed his letters "Ass. in English," was added, a "last year's senior" who had done brilliant work in his specialty which was chemistry. Departing with the year to take up chemical work in Washington, where he made good, his place was filled by a well-trained worker, H. K. Munroe, a graduate of Wesleyan in Connecticut and an ardent admirer of Professor C. T. Winchester, professor there of English literature. Even with him added to the department, the work required was overwhelming. Work in college English must be measured not in class hours, but in hours required for labor on student themes.

It has always been my contention that five minutes of personal conference with a student over his theme teaches him far more than he could get from having a dozen of his themes merely proof-read and marked with red ink. The Harvard daily theme for freshmen courses was then the new fashion and it was widely adopted by the colleges. To administer this plan, however, requires a large force of instructors, and with my minimum of helpers I was forced to require only one each week —one theme for every three class periods. That meant 100 themes a week, not to speak of much written work required of upper classes, and only two of us to do it. I who in my undergraduate courses at Dartmouth had been asked to write but a single theme and who in all my four undergraduate years had not had a single page of my written work corrected, was now devoting many hours each day to the written work of students. Did it pay?

Never in the whole history of literature was so much composition demanded of students, never so many courses even in the lower schools with emphasis on creative work, never so much literary advice given the young. And yet with all this multiplicity of instruction no period of distinctive literature has followed. Journalism of increased quality, yes, and of ocean-like quantity, yes. Never has there been a time when so many Americans could write correct and forceful newspaper English, but has not literature according to the old definitions suffered? Are not even our fiction and our poetry presented to us in newspaperese? Has not the daily theme in the colleges—I ask it in all seriousness—been a damage to our literature? To subject all students to the same goose-step drill, to regiment our writing youth with rules and patterns and to frown on all who are out of step and original, is it not to pollute at the source the springs of original literature? Because they were allowed to be themselves and to create their own instruments of expression the older writers became the makers of permanent classics. Call the roll of the supreme writers of a nation and you will also call the roll of the literary rebels of their generations. What would Whitman have been had he gone as a youth to Harvard and been subjected for a year to the regime of the daily theme?

In an autobiographical fragment written by Donald Culross Peattie I have found this pregnant statement: In college, "I signed for no English courses that fall, or ever. 'Themes' I knew to be the opposite of what editors want, and mine was a house where publication was considered the initial criterion of worth."

During all of my teaching life, however, themes have been an unavoidable part of my work. I began work as an instructor in the flood-tide of what may be called the "theme era" of American college English teaching. How many of my precious hours have been given to these themes which, however dreary, must be read and corrected! I have known of only one instructor in all my experience who professed to enjoy theme correcting. His room was near my residence and one night I heard his convulsed laughter for more than an hour. "You must have had a jolly visitor," I remarked to him the next morning. "Why, I had no visitor," he said. "I was alone all the evening. I was correcting my freshman themes." After 40 years of theme correcting that man is still sane.

In Cornell the picturesque Professor Hiram Corson, who wore an Abrahamic beard and who taught Anglo-Saxon punctuated with bon mots that students remembered after they had completely forgotten everything in the lessons, became even before his death a Cornell tradition. Once when I was visiting the college which is perched like an eyrie "high above Cayuga's waters," they told me this bit of college history: "One evening out for a walk on the campus he met three lark-hunting students. 'Good evening, Father Abraham,' said one. 'Good evening, Father Isaac,' said the second, and 'Good evening, Father Jacob,' said the third. Thereupon the Professor responded, "You are wrong. I am neither Abraham, Isaac, nor Jacob. I am Saul, the son of Kish, and I am seeking my father's asses, and lo, I have found them."

Vacations from my work came to me often because debating and public speaking were administered by my department. I accompanied teams and the dramatic club on trips and often I was called by other colleges to serve as judge in their contests, my expenses being paid by the college served. Such trips often allowed me privileges denied me when I was interned at the college. In Philadelphia on one of these trips I saw presented the old morality play *Everyman*, then the most popular play of the season. Never have I been able to account for the mystic feeling that this play wrought in me and in the audience as well. Certainly it was a unique experience. The theater was packed with an audience that sat in total silence as if at a church communion. And so, they told me, it was night after night. There was no curtain, no scenery to speak of, no theatricality of any kind, and there was no break in the action to the end. The actors entered from the audience, seemingly from spontaneous impulse. No explanations were given and no final lecture. No play could be more simple, more bare, or more unthespianic, and yet night after night all the seats in the theater were full.

Soon I was voluntarily adding to my work schedule. With "Jack" Leete, then a member of the Mathematics Department, I helped to organize a student dramatic club, naming it The Thespians. In 1898 I think it was, we put on *The School for Scandal*, following it the next year with *She Stoops to Conquer*. Penn State then was in reality a masculine college. The feminine students were largely the daughters of faculty members or of residents in the vicinity; for years there were only one or two co-eds in each graduating class. As a result we had to use boys for the feminine parts, a necessity that added rather than detracted from the popularity of the presentations. The faculty wives took a huge delight in fitting out these masculine femininities. One actress, it was said, looked the part perfectly if he shaved between acts. Soon the Thespians sought wider audiences and yearly "took to the road," presenting their play at Bellefonte, Williamsport, and two or three other places. I not only coached these plays but accompanied the troupes on their barnstorming trips. Always the masculine ladies got great applause. Once when the leading lady's elaborate wig slipped off when she was exhibiting violent emotion, the play had to stop for several moments to allow the audience to laugh. That audience got its money's worth.

The success of my American literature text book suggested to my publisher in Boston, Silver, Burdett & Co., the preparation of other books for use in schools. I accordingly edited for them a reading course in American Literature, a school edition of *Macbeth*, and at their request began to collect materials for a history of English literature. To prepare for this volume, my assistant, Mr. Munroe, suggested a summer in England to follow the literary tour made by his Wesleyan professor, C. F. Winchester. Instead of walking, however, we could make the tour on bicycles inexpensively and independently. It was at the high noon of the bicycle period when women in surprising numbers found the new "safety-low bike" both usable and proper. Everywhere now cyclist associations. The automobile was as yet a mere dream, but one could go on "joy rides" all the same. Bicycle tours on the public roads rapidly grew into a fad. All in a moment swarms of eager "wheelers," old men and youngsters, girls and women. The venerable President Atherton acquired a "bike," mastered it, and with groups of faculty members and their wives was often to be seen of pleasant afternoons on the Bellefonte road. And what a jouncy, bog-holed, stone-strewn road it was when compared with the road today. So everywhere. The 30 years after the advent of the automobile saw the most amazing road-building operations the world had ever seen. To one who lived in the day before the coming of the "tin Lizzie" the change in the road system of the country is as remarkable and as seemingly impossible as the flying machine and the radio.

It was quickly found that bicycle touring could be extended to the British Isles and to Europe beyond them. With a "bike" at his command a tourist could break away from the conventional routes,—the "grand tour"—avoid the show places, and find the real England never seen by the "tripper swarms." It seemed to me an ideal preparation for the English literature volume asked for by my publishers. What better way to get the atmosphere such a book should have? I confess that when I started on my tour in 1897 I knew England only as I had visited it in the works of the English poets and romancers, and with such travellers with rose-tinted glasses as Irving and Willis and Longfellow. It was an ivory-towered England that I was to visit, a mirage that I feared would vanish into clouds when actually I set foot on its shores. In this I was happily disappointed. The land exceeded my dreams of it. When I stood in a field near old Chester and saw the skylarks in heaven or near it pouring down torrents of excited song, a strange exhilaration came upon me, as again there came on the heather moors of the Lorna Doone country, or the flint roads of Hardy's Wessex, or the mountain-rimmed lakes in the Wordsworth country, the roads about them fringed with hedges of foxglove.

Three "bikers" made up our party: Professor Munroe, a friend of his, William J. Benners, and myself, all of us registered members of the English Cyclist Club and freely furnished with their maps and instructions. Benners was a Philadelphian and to us both a unique personality. He described himself as a novelist, with many books to his credit (or discredit), but in modern terms he would be listed as a "pulpster," maker of lurid serials to be read by housemaids. He assured us that he had written no less than 30 novels with Bertha Clay on their title pages as their author. A veritable specialist we found him in a literary world of which we knew nothing, a literary world whose output in quantity amazed me. Long afterward I learned that the real "Bertha Clay" was a woman, Charlotte M. Braeme.

During our stay in London, Benners toured the submerged publishing houses, emerging often with files of unheard-of periodicals which he immediately shipped home to serve as a quarry from which to dig new Bertha Clay stories. They could be given new titles and sold as new materials to American publishers. Once in high glee he emerged with a pamphlet edition of one of his own stories, *Madeline's Mystery*, an English reprint of which he knew nothing. He presented it to me.

He was a kindly soul, in every way helpful to us on our tour. His laugh was contagious and his cheek was colossal. He told us that one can get what one wants and go where one wants to go if one only knows how to laugh. This bit of wisdom he illustrated to us on shipboard: "We are going down now," he announced one day, "into the engine room and see the stokers." "Impossible. It is strictly forbidden," we countered in startled surprise. "No one ever goes there without special permission." "Pshaw!" he answered. "They can't any more than fire us out. Come on," and we followed him. Before we were observed we had seen the engines and the grimy stokers and were talking to one of them when an official swept down upon us with a torrent of profanity. Benners acted as if it were a joke, and argued laughingly with the man, and so good naturedly answered his arguments that the official began to smile. He was firm, however, and we complied with his demand that we at once go above. Benners did not seem to hear orders well, and remained below joking and asking questions radiant with good nature for some 20 minutes. "Do you know," he said, "you can get anything you want in this world, if you only know how to smile? A good laugh will kill even the devil."

Our summer's tour I shall record but briefly; "everybody" has been in England. To paraphrase what has been said about another world wonder: "My God, who can describe London, let alone *all* England?" Even if it could be done who would read the stuff? Many have *seen* the actual England and nearly every soul who has been there has raised his pen to describe it. Not everyone, however, has toured the unvisited areas of the little island on a "bike." We made the entire circuit from Cornwall to upper Scotland and back, a trip of nearly a thousand miles. Landing at Liverpool, we visited Chester, then turned southward, traversed the Valley of the Wye, lingering at Tintern Abbey, then Bath, Bridgewater, Minehead, the Lorna Doone country, Lynton, Ilfracombe, Clovelly, the Hardy country, Stonehenge, London. Then to Oxford, the cathedral district, Durham, Dryburgh, Melrose, Abbottsford, the northern moors.

On the whole, the trip brought disillusion. I had gone to England as to a Holy Land. I had already lived richly in this old home of my ancestry, but I had journeyed only through books: Irving's *Bracebridge Hall*, Addison's *The Roger de Coverley*

Papers, Shakespeare, Wordsworth, Scott, Charles Lamb, Dickens, Tennyson, George Eliot, Thackeray, Hardy, and the rest of the galaxy of British writers. Let me quote from letters written at English inns between cyclings:

"I was disappointed in Stratford-on-Avon. I had idealized the place largely because of my readings in Irving and I am half inclined to be sorry that I included the town in my itinerary. We got there on a bank holiday and the place was packed with people. The Shakespeare House was packed with sight-seers at a shilling a head. Attendants kept the crowd moving briskly. It seemed to me like a circus side-show. An attendant in every room with a little speech said over and over, "This is the room in which Shakespeare was born. On the window is Lord Byron's autograph written with a diamond. This is the room in which Shakespeare was born,"—and so on and on and on in room after room. It took not long to rush us through. The house might have impressed us, but the people! and the guides! It did not thrill me; it angered and disgusted me. So did the whole town. At every point of historical interest there was a charge of sixpence. I had pictured a quiet little hamlet on a river bank with ancient trees and green meadows; we found nothing of the kind. A modern city it is of 6000 inhabitants who live in glaring new red brick houses. I said to Munroe, "I'll bet if I stopped the first man we meet on the next street and give him a sixpence, he'll touch his hat and say, 'Thank yeh, suh!' " We had not nerve enough to try it.

Over and over we were insulted because, being Americans, we did not bestow tips of American size. One historic old castle ruin had as custodian a broken-down old soldier who said he had fought in the Crimea and in India. We gave him what we thought was an adequate tip and he said we had insulted him. We had given him the tip that is thrown at a "bloody beggar" and he was an English soldier who had given his life to his country. As we left the grounds he poured upon us a flood of barrack-room curses until we were out of hearing.

Asked what I considered the major industry of Scotland, I at once answered: "Robert Burns." Probably no other mortal

in human history has been so advertised. On every wall one finds him: "Drink the Bobby Burns Whisky." "Drink the Whisky that made Burns Great." "Use the Bobby Burns Soap." Everywhere "Bobby Burns" from Kilmarnock to Dumfries and beyond. One is powerless to escape. From the magnificent monument that crowns like a temple the acropolis at Edinburgh, to the costly mausoleum above his grave at Dumfries there is a succession of monuments such as honor no other poet of modern times. There are statues of Burns in Glasgow, Ayr, Kilmarnock, and Dumfries and there are monuments of massive size, with museums of Burns relics within them, in Kilmarnock, Mossgill and Alloway. The Mecca of the Burns pilgrim, however, is Ayer, his birthplace. Still standing is Alloway Kirk, the Tam O'Shanter Inn and the thatched cottage where the poet was born. Again disillusionment. A large addition in the rear of the cottage has been built for a restaurant, there is a large department for souvenirs, and to enter one must pay a fee of twopence. Iron turn-gates count and control the crowds which always exceed those seeking the birthplace of Shakespeare.

England,—the land of England—however, satisfied us even beyond our expectations. The skylarks, the hedges and lawns, the rural dwellings embowered in shrubbery, the wild flowers along the roads, the heather, the lakes and the moors continually thrilled us. Our enthusiasm reached its climax at Stoke Poges. I reproduce in full my letter written near Oxford:

Maidenhead, 8 Miles from Oxford

I am sitting under a hedge waiting for Munroe to get his wind. Have made 32 miles this morning easily over excellent roads. Yesterday we spent the forenoon packing up and getting ready, and we left London on the train for Windsor, where we arrived at 4, the time everything shuts up. We saw the castle, however, and had the pleasure of wandering about inside the walls. It is a magnificent place. The Queen was not at home, so we made no call on her. Left Windsor about 6 and wheeled through Eton, the seat of Eton college, and out to Stoke Poges where we arrived at just the right hour. The "lowing herds," "the weary ploughman," and the old churchyard were all there, and "now fades the glimmering landscape." It was beautiful. The old church and yard are just as when Gray wrote

The Elegy. The yew tree and the ivy-mantled tower were just what readers of the poem would expect. I send a slip from the former and an ivy leaf from the latter. Gray is buried in the church yard within ten feet of the church, and near by is an elaborate monument to his memory. This church and yard were one of the few things that did not disappoint us. I shall never forget my visit there.

We pressed on and reached Maidenhead about dark, and as my wheel needed certain repairs we stopped over for the night. Started out this morning at eight and have been going ever since. Went through Reading, a large place, and took dinner at Wallingford. Bread, butter, tomatoes, and canned tongue, 1 s., 3 d. Shall be glad to get home and get something cooked as I like it. Have had no decent green things yet. They cook their peas with mint or curry and I hate them. No string beans and no other things good. Ham and eggs, chops, and beef are all you can get and they are not cooked so I like them. My appetite is good and I eat like the dickens, but it is not because things are good. For breakfast had boiled eggs, bread, butter and jam. It is well that I got an appetite for marmalade that time you were sick for we have had it on the table every meal since I landed.

Benners stayed in London so as to be able to go to the theatre more. He will meet us in Oxford Monday noon and wheel on with us to Stratford on Avon. I am afraid this will not get into the mail in time, but I am going to try it. Will now arise.

Yours from under a hedge,

Not always is it safe to try to reduce to actuality romances and poems that have kindled our imaginations and emotions. Fresh from a reading of *Lorna Doone*, we wheeled on a mid-July day over Yarner Moor from the summit of which as far as the eye could see stretched the wild Exmoor moors, purple with heather and dotted everywhere with grazing sheep. Descending, we came to the tiny village of Oare, a half-dozen farm houses bowered in green hedges and reached by lanes such as one finds only in England. Here is the centre of Doone land made classic ground by Blackmore's romance. From it one enters the bridle path which leads after some miles into the Doone Valley, central in the story. Before exploring it, we interviewed some of the villagers. First we asked an old farmer if he knew of the John Ridd of the story. In a dialect which was almost like a foreign tongue he made us understand vaguely that there were in Dev-

onshire families by the name of Ridd, but he did not know them. Others we asked knew nothing of *Lorna Doone* and only vaguely of the Doones once said to have lived in the valley. One young man advised us to see the sexton's wife. We found her and repeated our questions. Though an intelligent woman who was fond of books, she had never heard of the novel, and as for the Doones, "There were, so I have been told, some very wicked people there once. I've heard of them ever since I was a little girl, but John Ridd, law, sir, I never expect there was such a man."

Securing horses, we journeyed horseback into what we expected to find, in terms of romance, "a deep green valley, carved out of the mountains in a perfect oval with a fence of sheer rock standing around it 80 feet or 100 feet high, from whose brink black wooded hills swept up to the skyline." We found nothing of the kind. A tiny brook, gentle slopes purple with heather, no trees in any direction. Where was that tremendous Doone Gate "with a portcullis of rock above it" in the jaws of the pass that successfully defied the king's army? A tiny house occupied by a shepherd was the only building in sight. We asked him how we could get to Glen Doone. "You're there now," he said. "And the ruined huts of the Doones?" "Must be them stones," he said. A vivid imagination might turn the scattered rocks into foundation ruins, we could not. Nor could we turn the tiny trickling stream with barely fall enough for a ripple into the John Ridd water slide so nearly fatal to him: "For lo! I stood at the foot of a long pale slide of water, coming smoothly to me, without any break or hindrance, for a hundred yards or so and fenced on either side with cliff, sheer and straight and shining." And this sluggish valley brook in a moor devoid of rocks and guiltless of precipices was the John Ridd water slide he had climbed up to find his Lorna Doone. We laughed but with no joy in our laughter. Visit not the scenes of romance if you wish not to rid your soul of romance and dreams.

CHAPTER XI

The Yellow Nineties and Beyond

T HE JUNE, 1903, COMMENCEMENT may be taken as the high-water mark of the technology inundation that had swept the college into publicity. Dr. Lawrence Colfelt, who delivered the baccalaureate sermon, took as his text Ezekiel I:20, "And the spirit of the living creature was in the wheels." Centering his address in the thesis that the wheel is the symbol of the modern age, he made four demands: "Put dignity into the wheels; put grace into the wheels; put optimism into the wheels; put religion into the wheels."

On Wednesday came the dedication of the hardly-finished auditorium building, the gift of Charles M. Schwab, a leading industrialist of his era. The building from the first had stirred the soul of Dr. Atherton as nothing else had done during his administration. So eager had he been to have it ready for commencement that he had caused extraordinary methods to be used in its construction. In his own words, "During the entire winter, when the elements without would have prevented work, they, as many of you know, actually enhoused this whole building in a temporary structure, so that it might be heated and lighted and the work go on."

At one time the bricklayers struck refusing to work on a foundation that had been laid by non-union workers, but competent local masons were soon found and there was no delay. Johnny Corrigan, Irish superintendent of the college grounds and buildings, a convivial wag now a college tradition, nearly found his match in the Teutonic superintending architect of the new building. Never did the two meet without combats of wit, always good natured. Finally Johnny conceded a moot point: yes, he would admit, once a year the Germans did get ahead of the Irish, but even then it was only a rod or two. On St. Patrick's Day the procession was usually headed by a little German band, hired by the Irish.

At the request of the president, I had prepared an ode which I read at the dedication service. Recognizing the part that enginery was to play in the age that was opening, I stressed the demand made by Dr. Colfelt to "put religion into the wheels." We were dedicating a college chapel which was to be the centre of an institution devoted to industrial education and activity, but

> Who enters here
> Leaves shaft and gear;
> Leaves far behind, like thunders of the sea,
>   The restless soul of piston and of wheel,
>   The fierce wild heart that throbs in steam and steel,
> And all the bellowing of the enginery . . .
>   Who enters here comes to the unseen near;
> Comes from the din and darkness into light,
> Comes for the stars to set himself aright,
>   As mariners upon the ocean tossed,
>   All landmarks lost,
> Look out at noon of every toilful day
> From ship and wave away,
>   Up to the silent sun
>   To guide their run;
> Fixing their goal, the distant harbor bar,
> By worlds afar.

Poetry had changed its meaning for me since the early days when, inspired by Whittier, I had written of Nature. At college I had fallen under the debilitating influence of Aldrich, Taylor, H. C. Bunner and the makers of old French forms. Now I was making and judging poetry in terms of message contained, and less and less I found myself in poetic mood.

"There was a time,"—I quote from Wordsworth—"when meadow, grove and stream" seemed to me "apparelled in celestial light," especially when I viewed them in my early days through the medium of poetry. Whittier's early lyrics dealing with the White Hills of New Hampshire once created for me a poetic realm that stirred something within impossible for me to describe. In lines like these there was for me almost a hypnotic quality:

> No sound save the lapse of the waves on thy shores,
> The plunging of otters, the light dip of oars.

But the daily correcting of student themes for years turns

a poet into a critic, into a scientist armed with established laws
and ascertained facts. Gradually the poet dies. In the couplet
from Whittier I began to see fatal errors of fact. Whittier was a
poet of imagination all compact, not a realist observer. He used
his feelings more than he did his eyes. An obscure poet, Marie
de L. Welch, in 1934, did use her eyes, and in doing so revealed the false note in Whittier's poem, though doubtless she
had never read a word of it:

> Nothing breaks when the otter plunges
> Into the river, nothing changes;
> Nothing shatters when he parts the crisp silver;
> He knows the still way into the river.

And the upper Merrimack River in the early days pictured in the
poem had never heard the sound of oars, though familiar the
waters may have been to the sound of paddles. I fear that had a
student written Wordsworth's lyric *The Solitary Reaper*, a
poem that once so charmed me that I committed it to memory,
I might have returned to him the manuscript with four words
underlined in the opening stanza:

> Behold her *single* in the field,
> Yon *solitary* Highland Lass!
> Reaping and singing *by herself*;
> Stop here, or gently pass!
> *Alone* she cuts and binds the grain . . .

All my teaching life I have fought the schoolmaster that
was evolving within me. For a long time I devoted my Sunday
afternoons to poetry, reading it, revising my own earlier efforts,
and attempting new work, but despite all this effort—Wordsworth again—"it is not now as it hath been of yore." Is not
poetry a phenomenon of adolescence, and are there not some
who, like Peter Pan, never grew up at all? Lately in a story I
was reading I marked this sentence: "Maybe that I am an incurable romantic—which is another way of saying that I have
never grown up."

Unquestionably poetry and romanticism live in their most
glorious reaches in the atmosphere of youth. Irvin Cobb, for a
single instance, is sure that his first work was his inspired work
and that it was so because "I wrote out of homesickness for

things that were gone from us . . . Don't think Dickens didn't use all the homesickness there was, because he did . . . When Mark Twain wrote *Huckleberry Finn* he was homesick—he was hungry for fried catfish, and he dipped his pen into the innards of a l'il tough-footed boy." I wish I had written that, for it tells the story of *me* completely. All my best poetry is youthful dreams and homesickness—a vain striving to win back the gleam. Alone of all my fiction *Mary Garvin*, my first novel, has *me* in it. I wonder if I have ever shaken from me the romanticism instilled into my early years. I wonder if I have really grown up.

My poem, delivered at the dedication of the Schwab auditorium, I published as a booklet with the title *The Message of the West* in an edition limited to 75 numbered copies. One of these I sent to the Poet Laureate, Alfred Austin, when I was in London. That he acknowledged my gift in a letter beginning "Dear Madam" is doubtless a criticism of my penmanship. His misquotation of my title, however, cannot be so easily explained:

> Swinford Old Manor, Ashford, Kent
> October 10, 1903
>
> Dear Madam:
>
> I thank you for sending me a copy of "The Message From the West." I have read it with much interest and no little admiration. It is expressive, for the most part, in elevated language, of most generous thoughts. I wish I could share your hopeful views as to the power of the more Spiritual forces resident in men to cope with the colossal Materialism of the Age & their present attitude and tendency. But I am disposed to fear that the prevailing Quest for Gold and Luxury will culminate in disaster & collapse & not till then will the nobler elements of Life again have a chance of asserting themselves successfully.
>
> There is a misprint in the penultimate line of your poem where "that" is substituted for "than."
>
> Believe me your faithfully
>
> ALFRED AUSTIN

The isolation of the college was for me a handicap. The location in the Seven Mountains had been chosen when the State accepted the Land Grant appropriation, first because of the farm acres that had been offered as an inducement and second because of its location in the exact centre of the state. Isolation in the mountains might be good for students in the days before the automobile allowed them to make easy escapes into the outlying world, but it tended to make a concentration-camp-like internment place for the faculty. Perforce they were thrown in upon themselves for entertainment. The theater, distinctive lectures, the opera, adequate library advantages, and urban contacts generally, were far away. Research was for me a difficult matter. I was out of contact with the literary world generally. The Penn State library gave me little help. It was largely technical. Two literary societies there had been in earlier days, "The Washington" and "The Cresson," each possessing a small library made up largely of eighteenth century English classics, but the coming of the Greek letter fraternities had killed them even as it had done at Dartmouth and the other old colleges. The Liberal Arts Department, however, was growing and so steadily that at length it became a school with a supervising dean. The liberal arts end of the library was growing also, but until recent years it made no effort to add materials for research work in literature.

But in the literary world outside newness was in the air: even in the Seven Mountains one could not be unconscious of it. The decade of the nineties seemed yellow to us who entered it with the music of the Tennyson-Longfellow era still ringing in our ears. As the dying century approached its end it seemed like a dying year to clothe itself in mauve and yellow. The phrase, now all too common, "the gay nineties," is ridiculous. The nineties were not gay. They were yellow, they were disillusioned, they looked back at the "gilded age" from which America was emerging, though not completely escaping as yet. They were doubtless reckless, but not whole-heartedly were they gay. Everywhere one heard the word "decadence." Max Nordau had started it: despite Darwin, the race was degenerating, not moving upward toward perfection. "Decadent" became overworked. There was decadence in art—Aubrey Beardsleyism; like the peach-tree, literature was found to be subject to "the yellows," a fatal disease we all thought then. I bought copies of the English *Yellow Book*, and felt like apologising when visitors found it on my parlor table. To be found reading it labelled and classified one. In later years I have leafed through the entire 12 volumes of the thing, and, viewing it through the present-day atmosphere, I have pronounced it vapid, timid, lifeless: a Methodist minister's son swaggering into his father's study smoking a cigarette. I bought also the Chicago echo of the yellow newness, *The Chap Book*, and then pluckings by the score of the amazing toadstool crop of periodical chap-books that sprang up around the dying trunk of the old century, fungi with spores like *The Lark*, and Elbert Hubbard's *The Philistine*. Were these merely night-growths which would perish with the century, or were they the apprentice work of the new generation in the world of letters to come? Gloom there was undoubtedly, but are not all year-ends and century-ends disheartening affairs as one looks back over the accomplished past?

With the new year comes always hope: "the year is dying in the night," but a new morning is coming! But the beginning of a new century! Who could think of decadence and despondency when came that amazing midnight when 1899 became 1900 in Time's cyclometer? No one alive had ever felt the thrill of a newly born century, with all chimes pealing, "Ring out the old, ring in the new; ring out the false, ring in the true." Marvellous and moving the ceremony held in Boston that memorable midnight. Margaret Deland has recorded it better than ever I could do it:

> At exactly 15 minutes before 12 o'clock the chorus master gave a signal: Instantly the cornets sounded 'taps.' The nineteenth century was descending into the grave of the past. When the notes ceased, Dr. Hale, standing at the top of the great steps, slowly lifted his arms and a tidal wave of voices swept over us:
>
> Praise God from whom all blessing flow . . .
>
> The stillness could be felt. It seemed as if we scarcely breathed! Dr. Hale, his shaggy hair falling to his shoulders, stood looking out over the listening thousands. Then with the majesty of age and holiness he began to read the Ninetieth Psalm.

Every soul there felt as if standing at the moment when a new era was opening. A new era indeed *was* opening.

In the literary world a revolution was gathering. We had felt it coming all through the nineties, though as seen through the yellow haze it was indistinct in its outlines. Vividly there comes to me the remembrance of the thrill created by the first work of the young English-Indian writer Rudyard Kipling. Something new and tremendously moving awoke within me as I read his *Plain Tales from the Hills* and his *Barrack Room Ballads*. Who could read for the first time his vision of the new century without feeling his heart thumping in his throat, the golden new era now at hand, when

> Only the Master shall praise us,
> And only the Master shall blame,
> And no one shall work for money
> And no one shall work for fame,
> But each for the joy of the working,
> And each on a separate star
> Shall paint the thing as he sees it
> For the God of things as they are.

"The God of things as they are," how it echoed over America. Some called it realism, some veritism, some naturalism, but who cared for definitions? Literature was to come down from the clouds to the solid earth. Bret Harte had started the young East Indian, but he was not to dominate his work. *The Luck of Roaring Camp* had been a *tour de force* built around a sentimental *cliché* that had originated in the mining camps. There was in it no experience, no actuality. And now the new generation, born in the 1870s, was demanding TRUTH.

The century began as a new century should, in major key. In the national life it began with Theodore Roosevelt. Action now, "the strenuous life," "supermen" after the Nietzsche pattern, "men with the bark on" as Frederick Remington expressed it, men who had listened to the "Call of the Wild" like Jack London. From the national capitol there rang now such war-cries as "mollycoddle!" "Ananias Club members!" "nature fakir!"

"Joy was it in that dawn to be alive, but to be young was very heaven."

Now galloped in the cow-boy and the wilderness hunter. Garland depicted life in the raw on the Middle Border; London made graphic the actualities of the Klondike and then the South Seas; Frank Norris wrote *McTeague, The Octopus, The Pit;* and Mary E. Wilkins was exhibiting the human debris left after the new glacial age had swept over the New England farm lands.

The new century had indeed come in like an explosion. In New York City one day I overheard a group of men of my own age invited by one who had joined them to "come down and see the new cartoon, 'Teddy Bucking the Tammany Tiger.' It's a Lulu!" My curiosity aroused, I followed them, and there it hung in the newspaper office window, full size as it had left the cartoonist's hand. Certainly the sinister old Tiger was having a hard fight, was doing his worst but was no match for Teddy. The air was full of the new champion. His glasses and his teeth were terrific. John L. Sullivan would not have lasted a minute before that he-man onslaught. And how those men roared! They could not get away from it. A new spirit was in the air: the "era of the strenuous life" was opening, soon to find literary voicing in *The Blazed Trail, The Biography of a Grizzly, Men with the Bark On, The Sea Wolf, The Jungle,* whole shelves of strenuosity. Even the surge of historical romance which had followed the swift closing of the war with Spain, a surge that gave to anaemic readers the heroes they had hoped to have had in the flesh as the result of romantic campaigns in Cuba, even this was in key. In Mary Johnston's romances of early Virginia life the super-man hero could engage in sword play with two and even three opponents and invariably slay them—one, two, three!

This new surge of romance touched me lightly in the summer of 1906 when I was in New Hampshire on my Sabine Farm. For the first time I saw this romance in veritable action. The American Winston Churchill after a series of war romances highly successful, had himself taken a lance and was charging wind-mills in a headlong *blitz-krieg*. He was campaigning for nomination as governor of New Hampshire and was pledging himself to fight with all his powers Teddy Roosevelt-style, against the domination of the Boston and Maine Railroad. Cer-

tainly he was putting up a vigorous fight, and though no longer
a voter in New Hampshire, I volunteered for a brief moment to
serve him as a Sancho Panza. I even presided at one of his rallies, making a speech that, thank God, never got into print. The
campaign was vigorous and picturesque but he lost the nomination. He had charged the wind-mill and the wind-mill had won.

During this period I read for the first time Churchill's romances and was distressed to find them carefully tempered to
the winds of their era. *Coniston* I found strong in episodes and
climaxes, but diffuse. Worth reading, however, it is even now.
At State College in the fall I read a paper before our Literary
Club on the historical romance vogue, on the whole condemning
it. I took Churchill's *The Crisis* as a type and found it for the
most part a hasty work, littered with lumber. The author, I
thought, had been eager to bring into his story all the famous
characters of the time—Grant, Sherman, Lincoln, and others—
merely to exhibit them. The love story peters out and the ending
of the romance is sprawly. The best parts of the book are the
picturings here and there of the old South before the war.

And now I must confess that during this period of tremendous sales of "When Knighthood was in Flower" fiction, I
was for a time myself infected by the literary "flu" that was in
the air. I planned a romance that was to be entitled *Old Second
Street*, a tale of the British occupation of Philadelphia. I collected
much material and I brought the thing to completion. I was too
late.

It was impossible not to feel the strenuosity that blew in
all the winds, but it seemed to me that I had nothing to give. I
had lived a life of scholarly seclusion and had had no headlong
adventures such as I felt readers must now have. I was like
Stewart E. White before Brander Matthews had advised him.
"You say you want to write, but have nothing to write about,"
Brander had said. "Then get something. You are from Michigan,
the lumber state, go into the woods this winter as a lumber jack,
live the life of an axe-man, and ride out in the spring on the
river drive. You'll have a subject then." That started something;
that was good teaching.

Now all at once the college enrollment began to increase by leaps and bounds. Technology was in the air and for a time liberal arts courses seemed like old-fashioned stuff soon to be extinct.

With the greatly increased enrollment, many students now found it impossible to secure rooms. The "Old Main Rats" filled to overflowing the one masculine dormitory possessed by the college, and the fraternities had not then begun that feverish building era that soon was to fill the town with fraternity houses. The first attempt at dormitory extension was an improvised shack in front of the armory, a long hemlock board structure with some 10 rooms which General Beaver, fresh from a visit to the Grand Canyon, christened "The Bright Angel." Like the mushroom it was, it lasted not long.

New buildings of every kind were urgently needed. Classrooms and laboratories were overcrowded, and as a result the Appropriation Committee of the State Legislature on its annual visit was greeted by expedients of every variety for impressing the college needs. Classes in agriculture were removed for the day to a tumble-down old shed called Hemlock Hall; classes were required to be found reciting their lessons on the stairways of Old Main; long-ago abandoned apparatus was resurrected for the day and used in the dairy and in other departments. In all directions the college extended its worst foot.

Once we all but lost our appropriation because of a deed done by a dozen or so of the "hell-raising element" of the student body. The Committee came that year in a railroad coach which had a well-stocked refrigerator and a kitchen and a cook. The students while the Committee was busy inspecting the college, rushed the car, overpowered the cook and porter, raided the icebox, leaving not a drop of the benign fluid so necessary for legislators, and made large inroads on the "eats." The tempest that followed colored black the report the Committee made to the assembled law-makers in Harrisburg.

In my college work I found myself under fire from two opposite batteries. The Engineering departments demanded that I teach their students "engineering English." "Cut out your literary stuff," they demanded, "and teach the students to dope out the reports they will have to make as engineers. They are not going to write poetry; Shakespeare did not know anything about engineering." A similar demand came from the other end of the campus: "Teach agricultural English. Cut out the embroidery and frills and teach them to write as farmers have to write." In vain I argued that English is English; that their graduates were going out into the world as college educated men, "to mingle and compete with college educated men." I was teaching no frills, I told them. I was endeavoring to make them able to write correct, clear, properly spelled and punctuated sentences. But this made no impression upon my critics, and finally I compromised: I made the punishment fit the crime, I gave out theme subjects in the student's specialty. To Aggies I assigned as theme subjects "Barnyard Manure vs. Commercial Fertilizers," "Problems in Cow Culture," and "Trap Nests for Hens." Greek Professor Gill's comment was brief: "Education once was man; now it is manure."

At length I awoke to the fact that I had had in my early life experiences that could be used for fiction even in the present era of the strenuous life. Garland had not seen the fictional possibilities of his prairie days until he had experienced life in other localities. Returning to it he now saw its realities. So with me. The result was my novel *Mary Garvin*. Notebook jottings played no part in that book. I wrote it, dialect and all, out of myself. Asa Garvin and his wife were my own parents and the pathetic old man "Gransur" was my own grandfather, Moses Pattee. Squire Zeb was a Bristol actuality. The rest were combinations of personalities I had actually known. Joel Green was a concentrate of half a dozen Yankee characters with whom I had passed my boyhood. The book was no best-seller, and it was, after the colossal success of *David Harum*, nothing new. It did, however, sell 3500 copies, netting me at 15 per cent, enough to pay half the amount asked for the old farm of my boyhood depicted in the novel. It made possible the earnest desire of father and mother to take up their residence in Bristol where life in their period of growing feebleness would not be so hard.

For the most part the reviews of the novel were very favorable and I received many personal letters such as please young authors and even old ones. I shall reproduce only one of these:

115 East 16th Street, New York
March 24, 1902

My dear Mr. Pattee,

In spite of your considerateness, you see that I resolve to give you a fairly prompt acknowledgement of *this* book (your novel), especially as I chanced to have a work-dodging spell on the day of its arrival, and therefore refreshed myself by reading it straight through that evening. To most people I scarcely dare to say a word, even when I like a book received, since I am no longer able to write reviews, and since I have of late declared that I can 'make no exceptions' as to citations of what I may say. But to you, who have taken so friendly a view of my own work, and who are quite able to let your book go on its merits, I need have no reserve in this private letter.

Well, I congratulate you on being able to do a thing of this sort, since it is the mode of the time, and that is what an imaginative author must adopt or starve! And I have to thank you for taking me out of my troubles while I read *Mary Garvin*. It is true 'realism,' true to American up-country life—a life which I well knew—and speech—in fact a genuine New Hampshire idyl, and, I trust, the forerunner of future inventive efforts on your part. If I were to find a technical fault, it would relate to the too summary 'lightning change' (or reversion) back of the hero's defection from the town love to the country love. You don't exactly know how to restore the proper status, and so there seems to be a good deal to be imagined between the last two chapters. But *Mary Garvin* is a remarkable first novel by a critical university scholar.

I have followed your writings from the date of your first publication, and I wish I had had a teacher of English like you in my blundering long-ago student days.

Sincerely yours,

EDMUND C. STEDMAN

Had I been wise in my literary work? Had I not lost time doing text books and such hack-work as I had furnished Seymour Eaton? The whole summer of 1901 I had given in Philadelphia to the Booklovers Reading Courses, an office having been assigned to me in the Witherspoon Building. Four complete courses I had edited during the summer and so acceptably to Mr. Eaton that he had offered me the editorship of the projected *Booklovers Magazine*. Professor Richardson of Dartmouth had advised me to accept the offer and I was strongly tempted. Certain weaknesses, however, that I had noted in the organization and in the project gave me pause. President Atherton who visited me at my office in Philadelphia advised me to continue the work I had begun at the college and I took his advice to my great satisfaction now. The publishers of my American literature text book had kept me at work for a year on the history of English literature that they issued in 1900 under the title *The Foundations of English Literature*. And for another publisher I had edited Lowell's *Conversations on the Old Poets*.

But was I on the right track?

The great success of my novel *Mary Garvin* upset me completely and started me on what I dreamed was to be my real life-work—fiction. As I have already noted, I began a novel dealing with the Revolution. I worked eagerly and thoroughly and accomplished what even now I consider as good a piece of historical fiction as was issued during the brief summer the *genre* was in vogue. But I was too late.

My next novel, *The House of the Black Ring*, was in a totally different realm. It depicted the "Pennsylvania Dutch," of which until my residence at State College I had known nothing. It was a *tour de force* made from note-book jottings and research. The editing of my edition of Philip Freneau delayed the volume, but I grubbed steadily for materials, jotting down dialect even as did Mary N. Murfree for her Tennessee Mountain tales. One of my sources I think I can pronounce unique. I worked my composition classes for materials. For a year I asked them to write their weekly themes on such topics as these: "Strange Nooks in the Pennsylvania Mountains"; "Queer Dishes Served by Pennsylvania Housewives"; "Some Dutch Superstitions"; "Queer People I have Known"; "Dutch Weather Signs"; "A Funny Happening in My Home Neighborhood"; "Dutch Localisms," and dozens like them. Henry Holt and Company published the novel, and it has since run through two other editions.

Hamlin Garland I think voiced the final verdict concerning the novel. In a letter to me he wrote: "I read your story on the train and was interested in it. It has many good points, and I can't tell exactly why it did not please me in a higher degree. I think it may be that I found it too detailed in places—too much insistence on local color for local color's sake. You can write a novel. Tackle your White Mountain Country. Why don't you try it? I think you'd make a go of it."

The editing of the *Poems of Philip Freneau* took most of my spare time for several years. It brought me from the first into unexplored literary regions. I found most of my materials in Philadelphia where I spent many week-ends and between-term vacations, and I made exploring trips to New York and to New Jersey. No one had done research work on Freneau's literary product and I had to rescue masses of it from contemporary papers. Princeton University published the work, the first volume in 1902 and the third in 1907. The picturesque old sea dog grew on me as I worked, and I did all I could with the scanty materials then available to make him recognized as the pioneer poet of our literature. Professor Richardson pronounced the edition the most distinctive one that had been given to any eighteenth century American writer.

I have had adventures as a result of work with Freneau. One of them I think is worthy of record. In the *Freeman's Journal* of August, 1788, I discovered an unknown letter written by Freneau to Francis Bailey, editor of the paper, and by him thought worthy of publication in his columns. It was an account of "one of the hardest gales that ever blew upon this coast." Freneau's ship was demasted and stripped of all its gear. Most of the crew went overboard and the captain was saved almost by a miracle. In his spirited account of the wreck he wrote, "Captain William Cannon, who I think you know, was going passenger with me to Charleston, and Mr. Joseph Stillwell, a lad of a reputable family in New Jersey, were both washed overboard and drowned, notwithstanding every effort to save them."

I record these details because of a curious sequel. I reproduced this letter in my edition of Freneau 100 years after it was written, and some years later I received a letter from the descendants of Captain Cannon saying that they had seen my edition and had read the letter and had learned for the first time in all the years what had become of their nautical ancestor. He had disappeared without trace.

3

After 1903 the old farm on which I had passed my boyhood became our summer home. I made it more comfortable by putting in running water and a bathroom, and by making the old "sap house" in the yard and the adjoining wagon house into a neat cottage to be used by me as a library and study for 25 years. Here I did much of my literary work. Joyous escape periods those rural summers. In time we owned a horse and a cow, both of them taken care of by farmers during the winter and we had always a productive garden that made our summer table distinctive. Potatoes and apples raised on the farm we shipped to Pennsylvania for winter use.

Every summer had its adventure: some calls upon us by the wild. The summer nights were populous with porcupines,— "hedgehogs," or "quillpigs" we natives always called them. They haunt old buildings and gnaw at them all night long. One summer a horrendous old fellow gnawed a hole a foot in diameter through the hemlock sill of our house and took up his abode in our cellar.

One weird voice of the wilds, a quavering cry like a banshee note on autumn nights, I had heard ever since I was a boy and had never found its source. Heard in the far away, over the moonlit mountain, it had an uncanny mystery about it that seemed to be a part of the mystery that haunts all forests. I asked about it and the general opinion among the native hunters was that it was the cry of the raccoon. I recalled a poem, an autumn dirge, by the prairie poet Ellen P. Allerton, one stanza of which was this:

But I hear the owlet's cry,
>   Forlorn, forlorn;
> I hear the owlet's cry,
> When the waning moon is high,
>   And the raccoon's greedy call among the corn.

I consulted John Burroughs, the leading authority then on the ways of nature, and he wrote me: "I have no proof that the raccoon makes the sound or call that is usually attributed to him. Sportsmen and others say the plaintive whinnying call we hear of autumn nights is made by him, and I have little doubt that it is. I have heard it. It is not a bird or an owl. The little screech owl makes quite a different cry. I should think that the keeper of any zoo could answer definitely. Write to Frank Ballou of Washington or Mr. Horneday of the Bronx Park."

I wrote to the latter who told me that he had never heard raccoons utter cries at night. I wrote to Thompson Seton and was told by him that what I had heard was the autumn note of the screech owl. That very autumn I proved that he was right. I heard the identical note from the top of an oak near my home at the college, and was able to see the owl that uttered it.

One summer was rendered tragic for some by the invasion of the so-called "kissing bug." The ravages of this vampire-like creature were recorded in the local papers. Every winged thing that invaded a room at night brought terror to a nervous few. People who lived near us told us with shaky voices that one of the creatures, "as big as a swallow," had sailed into the room the night before and had headed straight toward the lips of the woman. Again and again it had made for her lips but had been beaten off by the man and killed. I saw the defunct thing and pronounced it a hellgrammite in the butterfly stage, an insect perfectly harmless. Totally out of patience with the kissing bug myth that was frightening so many, *The Manchester Union* offered $10 for a specimen of the bug. The next day a highly excited group of street boys captured a specimen, put it into a tin can, and sent their leader in with it to get the $10. A few moments later the boy returned somewhat crestfallen to the group.

"Have you got the money?" they demanded eagerly.

"No. He said that ain't no kissing bug."

"What was it then?"

"I didn't jest get what he said it was. I made him say it over, but I still ain't sure jest what he did call it. I think he called it "a-hell-of-a-bug."

My purchase of the family farm, as I see it now, was a part of a new movement of populations in New Hampshire. The Old Home Day innovation by Governor Rollins at the opening of the century started something. The initial Old Home Day celebration, "ushered in," to quote the Governor, "with bonfires and beacon lights on mountain tops and high hills, flashing a welcome from Coos to the sea," had been celebrated in the summer of 1899. "New Hampshire," said the Governor, "has suffered greatly from the drifting away of its best-bred stock to build up and open up the more arable lands of the West," and he exhorted all *emigres*, wherever they might be, "to turn their steps once more to the open fields and pastures of their childhood." Many came; the day was an unqualified success, so much so that it started a movement that in some communities has not died. I attended these Old Home Days often as a speaker, and I studied attentively those who came. Unquestionably the tide that had drained the hill lands would never turn and bring back the lost population, but it did have one note-worthy effect. Many returned as summer residents, bought, as I had done, old farm buildings, and so swelled the summer tide that has grown steadily in volume. Many an abandoned farm house in the hills has been taken now and furnished with modern conveniences and often with antiques that are growing more and more hard to find in the hill towns.

The antique craze indeed had swept over the region like a thunder gust. Old bureaus were hunted out and purchased at prices that made old farmers whose attics had been explored conclude that the world had "gone plumb crazy." Most of the old farms still had agricultural possibilities. A neighboring farmer in the spring could start a garden for you and a potato patch which in August would be a boon indeed.

A few came back permanently. There was Robert Frost,

born in California, later a farmer in Franconia, and there was Dorothy Canfield Fisher, born in Kansas of New England stock, but preferring to spend her last years at Arlington, Vermont, the home of her ancestors. This she wrote in a letter to me:

"I never felt, as a child, that our family life was uprooted, although we moved from one town to another in the West when I was a little girl. The point was that I never felt that was our home at all, but that this particular piece of the globe where I now live, and where all the Canfields have kept their footing since they settled here in 1764, was our home, which never changed at all. Our travels here and there, were like travels to me, always. Arlington—no, not even Arlington, but this very side of Red Mountain, was the stable thing in life."

My own experience was similar. For 25 years the old farm where I resided for three months of the year, was my home. I never took root in Pennsylvania though I lived there more than 30 years. I never destroyed the packing boxes that I used when I went to State College, and in some of them were my goods when I left. No longer was the farm possible after my wife died, and since then I have been transplanted into another and an alien soil, but with no deep rootage.

Stone Walls

Great grandsire built this wall
Of rocks from off the farm he cleared
When roads were few and all was wilderness.
Great bowlders first, then small and smaller stones
Clear to the top. "Sheep high" he said it was,
"Bull strong" and everywhere "hog tight."
What toil it took,
What shouts at heaving oxen, "Gee!" and "Haw!"
What digging, lifting, crowbar-prying work,
What hauling out of bowlders from their beds!
What straining, rolling, hoisting toil on toil!
Back-aching toil to make a rod a day.
But joy was in it all:
Not for himself alone he built that wall:
For sons and sons of sons that grinding toil.
Their sheep and bulls and lusty swine
For centuries to come
Would need that wall.

But now for mile on mile its moss-grown length
Runs through the utter wild,
A forest dense as when the land was cleared
A century and a half ago.
The sons went west or city-ward they went,
And sons of sons have left the farm to die.
The cellar-hole where once the farmhouse stood
Holds now an ancient oak.
The well that grandsire dug,
And stoned with weeks of toil
Is full of rubbish now and wholly lost.
The fertile fields once billowy with rye,
And heavy with their crops of corn and hay,
Are forest now with heavy oaks and pine.

Some day a hunter-man of alien breed
With gun alert,
Will stop before this wall within the wood
And wonder what it means.
"Why this must be a wall, a hand-built wall,
A massive wall that giants must have made.
What race of men once lived within these wilds,
And why should they have made this heavy wall,
These miles of wall?"

4

I saw the rise of another migration back to the mountain
lands. The summer boarder was arriving in increasing numbers.
Vacations for the many are comparatively recent innovations.
Sarah Orne Jewett wrote her first novel *Deephaven*, as a protest
against many evils attendant upon the new invasion. "When I
was fifteen," she wrote (1864, perhaps), "the first summer
boarders began to make their appearance near Berwick, (Maine)
and the way they misconstrued the country people and made
game of their peculiarities fired me with indignation. I determined to teach the world that country people are not the awkward, ignorant set those people seemed to think. I wanted the
world to know their grand simple lives; and, so far as I had a
mission, when I first began to write, I think that was it."

The White Mountains of New Hampshire had long been a
sight-seer's wonderland and many like Whittier had found inspiration and rest in farm-houses overhung by Mount Washing-

ton or Chicorua. Thoreau had toured the mountains often, Hawthorne had bathed the region in his weird romance, and Starr King had written his classic volume in poetic prose. "The Switzerland of America" the mountain land was, as all knew, and all Boston and beyond at one time or another saw the Old Man of the Mountain and the Presidential Range. It was largely on account of the mountains that New Hampshire became more and more a vacation centre. Along a veritable grand tour trail there had been erected dozens of summer hotels, some of them great wooden structures like the Profile House, advertised as the largest hotel in New England. Each served an unvarying clientele, the same in number the entire season. The region was ruled by horse-drawn vehicles, Concord Tally-ho coaches in the lead, and every pleasant summer morning coaching parties swept merrily along the roads to dine at a sister hotel and return in the cool of the day.

My first tour of the mountains was in 1880 when I was working in the printing office. With two weeks of vacation before us a fellow workman, Charles H. Sawyer, and I started to do the Wonderland on foot each with a 27 pound pack on his back. It was 40 miles to the Profile House, but we were at North Woodstock 10 miles below it by noon the next day. The road we traversed up the Pemigewasset Valley was as beautiful a winding trail as one could find anywhere in New England. Mountains on all sides wooded to the top, clear water streams, and in the distance, ever more distinct as we approached them, the bare ledges of the Franconias. Time and again there passed us Concord coaches with eight and ten on the top, the four horses at full speed, and the driver time and again raising the echoes with his alpine horn. Romance indeed, how it thrilled us! Summer boarders everywhere. My journal of the trip records that every little hotel and boarding place along the route was alive with summer people.

Then we took a side trip of four days into the wilds of the East Branch from North Woodstock. Starting at the farm house made famous by F. Hopkinson Smith in his sketch entitled *Jonathan*, an actual personage who helped us dig worms for bait and who provided us with a never-to-be-forgotten meal of bread and milk, we plunged into the primitive wilderness and after 10 terrific miles camped on the Old Pork Barrel Pond under Mount Willard. As tradition had it, the pond was packed with trout as a barrel is packed with pork. We did not find this literally true, but we caught trout to our heart's content and ate surprising numbers of what we caught. Here nature had been undisturbed since the days of creation. Civilization here was only a dream. As a footnote let me add that years afterward I again visited this East Branch valley and found it slashed from end to end. A dinkey railroad had traversed it and great mills at North Woodstock had made interminable lumber of the virgin trees.

Out on the road again we found the Old Man of the Mountain, that impressive face on the granite crag, wondered at the vastness of the Profile House and started for the Mount Washington area down the ten miles of narrow gauge road to Bethlehem. Miles of this road ran through land just cleared and never have I seen raspberries in such abundance.

We camped wherever night overtook us, lived largely on Indian meal hasty-pudding with molasses on it, and boiled eggs. Never did we go hungry, and yet—"believe it or not"—all our expenses for two weeks totalled three dollars apiece. Puritanic I was in those days and strictly brought up as to Sabbath observance. When Sunday came I refused to travel, lay in camp all day, and as a result missed being on Mount Washington on the most perfect day of the whole summer. We walked up the cog railroad in a dense fog, saw everything except the landscape when we reached the top, bought copies of *Among the Clouds*, the only mountain-top newspaper in America, and rode down the track about as Garland and his brother had done as recorded in *A Son of the Middle Border*. Reaching the end of the cog road just at dark, we spent a rainy night snug and dry, curled up in an overturned water tank by the railroad.

Not at all did I realize that the end of an era was passing before my eyes. The tally-ho coaches with their galloping horses, the Alpine horn notes echoing from the near peaks, the great hotels with their crowds of permanents were to disappear with the new century like the night mists that vanish of a morning.

CHAPTER XII

In a German University

EW COLLEGES OF COMMANDING RANK have been more isolated from the world than was Penn State during the years I knew it. It was a secluded nook in the Seven Mountains, and before the automobile age it could be reached only after a prolonged journey. One might approach it, as I had done in 1894, from the East up the shaky, sharp-curved dinkey railroad through the mountains from Lewisburg, alighting at Lemont for a two-mile drive up the Nittany Valley, or one might go to Bellefonte and traverse a never-to-be-forgotten 20 miles on "Parker's Boat," as the train that daily ran through the "Barrens" had been dubbed by students of the college. Stories of "Parker's Boat" greeted newcomers on the day of their arrival and they were the last stories heard when they departed from the town. Some of the stories became local classics:

A passenger asks at Wolf's Run, "Conductor, how long have you been on this train?"

"Twelve years," replies Parker.

"Then you must have got on the station before I did."
And again:

"Hey, Parker! What are you stopping the train for?"

"Calves on the track. Got to shoo 'em off."

Then a half hour later: "Say, Parker, what are we stopping again for?"

"Them damn calves have got back onto the track again."

Dozens of similar tales accumulated until a veritable "Parker's Boat" mythology was created. It became one of the college traditions. Speakers who were to address the students were often tipped off in advance with, "If you want to get a laugh, tell about how you arrived in town on 'Parker's Boat.' "

A lecture trip to the college in the early days, especially if it came in the winter, was often an adventure well worth recording. F. Hopkinson Smith might have made of his State College visit, February 7, 1908, a story even better than his graphically told sketch, "A Night Out." He fought his way from the East through a veritable blizzard with all the odds against his arrival on time, if at all. Finally after a wild night ride through the Seven Mountains he reached Lemont where he found no conveyance save an old "Dutch" farmer with a load of wood drawn by mules. Smith mounted the load, and the mules, struck sharply by the farmer, were suddenly off, and so was Smith. Rolling in the snow, he lost his hat and his glasses, both of which, with the farmer's aid, he recovered. Arrived on time at the college he was given a royal reception. In the evening lecture he completely won his audience. He was himself Colonel Carter of Cartersville as he read; he looked the part, he talked the part. "Chad" was inimitable as he represented him, so was the story of the "One-legged Goose," and so was Yankee "Jonathan" whom I had myself known at North Woodstock, New Hampshire.

But the storm grew even as he read to us, and it increased in volume all night, until next morning the town was as completely snow-bound as the farmhouse in Whittier's classic. A hardy native for a double fee fought him through the drifts to Lemont only to find that no trains were running. Back at the college he was told that "Parker's Boat" had been shoveled out and Parker was saying nothing ever had stopped him yet and wouldn't now. But after sitting in the Boat's cold car most of the forenoon Smith was told that the engine had jumped the track at the Y and Parker had given up. Wallowing back to town the original of Colonel Carter, told that the trip by horse and sleigh to Bellefonte was impossible, declared that he specialized in the impossible, and, walking most of the way sometimes on rail fences, he made it before night, reaching the main line where trains still ran.

Ten years earlier George W. Cable had visited the college. It was May and the town and the region were at their best, all the hills white with dogwood. He had offered us two programs and we had chosen his *Dr. Sevier* even though he had written me, "I do not believe you can choose better than to take the programme of 'Posson Jone.' After years of experience with all of them, it is my favorite." On his arrival I took dinner with him at President Atherton's and got the impression of a retiring and even timid personality. He did not lead the conversation at all, though when he did join it was with a flash of twinkling eyes, as when he said apropos of a recently deceased nonentity whose name for the moment was in all the newspapers, "It reminds me of an old ox we once owned, the laziest and most worthless beast in the whole county, but folks far and wide came to see the big hole in the pasture he made when he died."

We enjoyed his readings from *Dr. Sevier*, but were disappointed because he gave us nothing that had a Creole or even a southern flavor. When first he had come North as a reader from his tales and novels he had impersonated characters in *Old Creole Days*, and had even sung Creole songs. But residence in the North had seemed to arouse in him an inferiority complex. He had taken elocution lessons and was no longer his unstudied self. From his *Dr. Sevier* volume he had selected for his program humorous episodes in the conjugal relations between the Italian Ristofalo and his Irish wife—a foreshadowing, as we see it now, of the later New York hit, *Abie's Irish Rose*.

In later years Cable told me much about himself. "My mother," he wrote me, "was born in Indiana of New England stock. She married there, and in 1837 my father and she went South, seeking to mend a fortune broken by the crash of that year. There is no French or Creole strain in either my father's or my mother's family. My father was a Virginian, but of German descent. My production of the stories which make up *Old Creole Days* was as slow as you say of it, because I could not lay down counting-room work and make literature my profession but by degrees."

In 1914 he wrote me:

> Edward King came to New Orleans almost at the beginning of his tour of the South and we became acquainted and friends. I askt him where to send some stories—two or three—which I had just written, and he himself read, and sent two to Doctor Holland, editor of *Scribner's Monthly*. Then Gilder, assistant editor, wrote me and my lifetime acquaintance with both the *Century* and Charles Scribner's Sons began. I cannot

say that King's Great South papers affected the Southern literary awakening. I think the two were merely coincidental. I don't think Joel Chandler Harris ever knew King, or that Thomas Nelson Page ever met him, or that Richard Malcolm Johnston met him or felt an influence from him.

Yes, I read some French literature and believe it had its influence on me, tho not as much as Dickens, Thackeray, Poe, or Irving. My Frenchmen were Hugo, Merimee, and About. I also read many of the old *Relations* of the priest-explorers and much other French matter of early historical value.

It would give me pleasure to tell you just how I came to drop into the writing of romances, but I cannot; I just dropt. Money, fame, didactic or controversial impulse I scarcely felt a throb of. I just wanted to do it because it seemed a pity for the stuff to go so to waste.

2

In addition to the time-consuming miscellany of my regular work during my first eight years at the college, I had written or edited a book each year and in addition had produced a steady stream of magazine articles and reviews. I felt that I needed a vacation, and in 1902 I was granted my first sabbatical leave of absence on the usual terms: a year on half salary or half a year on full salary. I chose the latter and in mid-February with my wife and seven-years-old daughter sailed for Southhampton. Graduate work at that time meant Germany, and as several of our friends on the faculty had studied at Göttingen and could give us helpful advice, we headed for that ancient city "für Bier und Bildung berühmt."

We were in holiday mood, and during the whole half-year we simply enjoyed Europe, with university lectures a necessary evil. No vacation I have ever taken has over it in my memory so Indian-summer-like a haze of romance. The mediaeval city surrounded by its great wall on the broad top of which all took their daily walks, was in every way a relic of earlier centuries. Only one bath tub in the entire province and that not connected with any plumbing, but hung on a wall as a curiosity. No sewers in the entire city, no water-flushed toilets, no septic tanks. And the city was large, extending in all directions beyond the primitive wall. We found, however, a comfortable room at Fräulein

Schlote's *pension*, a resort known and highly esteemed by many American scholars who had resided there, and in her we found a very helpful teacher of the German language.

A walk about the old town always had its thrills. Everywhere on the ancient houses we found the names of prominent scholars who had resided in them during their university days. We found Longfellow's quarters, and Edward Everett's, and Bancroft's and Motley's. A much-pointed-out place was the picturesque cottage on the Leine where Bismarck had resided when a student. The spring was opening; Schlüsselblumen—key flowers—were in blossom in the woods about the Bismarck Türme. Within short walking distances were romantic castle ruins so old that we could find no one who could tell us of their history, and primitive *Dörfer* unchanged seemingly since mediaeval times, peasant workers in the fields who seemed as antique as their dwellings. We left Germany when the semester was over as one leaves a pleasant romance.

The university lectures were hard to follow at first. Printed German I could read, but spoken German seemed almost like another language from that found in books. I took two courses with Professor Morsbach, one of them entitled "A Reading of Chaucer's Prologue" and the other a seminar course in Marlowe's *Doctor Faustus*. My first impression in all the courses I attended was the same. In the Chaucer course, for instance, pronunciation of the text came first. Just how did Chaucer pronounce his words? The first scholar in Germany—no other scholars, especially the English Skeat, were worth mentioning —to formulate the laws for pronunciation of the Chaucerian vocabulary was—let us say—Professor X at Halle years before. Some years later Professor Y, say of Heidelberg, had shown the scientific fallacy of these laws and had constructed a new approach. Some years later another professor, say at Leipzig, had destroyed the Heidelberg theory and introduced another series of laws. Now he, Morsbach, was to show the fallacy of this last attempt and was to propose a theory that he felt would settle the matter forever. All of this took weeks of time. One entire lecture hour he devoted to the sound of "k" in words of

French origin borrowed by Chaucer. Actually he read to us but 90 lines of the Prologue; the rest of the time he spent in getting ready to read the classic. I got from the course very little Chaucer, yet I considered the course very valuable. I learned critical methods, a sort of literary detective work, useful for a critic to know.

In the same way the Marlowe seminar gave me nothing save an insight into German thoroughness and German seminar methods. "Take nothing for granted," was dinned into the ears of the class again and again. At the beginning of the semester two lines of the play were assigned to each student, and each was given a seminar hour in which to present his findings in the lines. Questions from the class always flew thick and fast and also criticisms. I remember a battle that raged for an entire seminar period over the phrase "go tell German Valdes." Who was this Spanish-named German? Each student had his theory, often darting to the shelves which were filled with volumes, pulling out an authority and reading it in triumphant tone, to be greeted with a roar by the professor, "Childish, childish! Sit down!" Condemning every attempt at solution, he would finally give his own theory carefully backed up with references and the battle would be over. During the entire semester we covered but 60 lines of the drama.

From Professor Roethe's course in Goethe's *Faust* I got nothing at all, but Professor Heyne's "Geschichte der Sturm und Drangperiode" I considered, and still consider, the most distinctive course I ever listened to. It was, it proved, his last lecture course. His hair was snow white and abundant; he was evidently feeble with age, but mentally he was alert and in full mastery of his brilliant powers. Commencing with Bürger and the Göttinger Dichterbund, he traced the origins of the Romantic movement in Germany, and followed it as it spread over Europe. The shuttle-like give and take between Great Britain and Germany, involving *Percy's Reliques* and *Ossian* which had been read by the Hainbund under the oak tree by moonlight near Göttingen, resulting in Bürger's "Lenore," which had started Scott who in turn started English romantic fiction, all this was presented with scholarly accuracy and fairness. I can still hear his frequently-interjected "Ar-r-r-ber," opening the other side of a proposition.

In her dining room Fräulein Schlote seated me at a table of students, and as a result I got an insight into many academic customs. I was finally allowed by my table-mates to sit as a spectator of a series of *mensurs*, bloody affairs that could hardly be called duels since the unskilled Fuchs, or freshman, is carved at leisure by a skilled upperclass swordsman. The outsider permitted in the spectator's gallery is compelled to look at the butchery no matter how much it may shock his sensibilities. A Scotchman sitting by me refused to look, and was first bawled out and then led from the room by a guard. At the table at mealtime, *mensurs* were discussed much as football is in American colleges. Beautiful cuts were gloated over, especially cuts on the right cheek, for the swordsman being right-handed naturally cuts the left cheek of his antagonist.

The opera was cheap and abundant and we attended often. Wagner was everywhere the favorite. I heard a professor in his room singing lustily bars from *Tristan*. I felt myself the sinister lure of the Wagner music and even now, knowing fully its baleful meaning, I am thrilled by many of its thunderous rhythms. I consider that Wagner exalts physical force and animalistic love, and destroys all the finer sentiments. His triumphs are all of them materialistic, and his atmospheres are tragic. Listening to his music now I am able to see how it helped train Teutonic Germany into Hitlerism. Bill Nye's comment that "Wagner's music is better than it sounds," should now, it seems to me, be changed to read, "Wagner's music is worse than it sounds," substituting fact for humor.

I was early impressed by the position of women in the German economy. Women were treated not only as man's inferiors, but as man's slaves. Often have I seen a farmer and his wife returning from market, she loaded to the staggering point with groceries, and he swinging his cane. Time and again I have seen the farmer working as driver of the horses, sitting idly on his cart, while his wife and daughters shovelled in manure. Every morning I saw garden products and milk drawn to market by a team consisting of a woman on one side and a dog or a cow on the other. While I was there a friend took a snapshot of a peasant holding the plow handles with four women yoked up as motive power.

That Germany was a military camp was everywhere evident. Every morning we were awakened by goose-stepping soldiers. The influence of the Kaiser was like an atmosphere, everywhere felt, though his name was never spoken. Once when walking with a German who was giving me lessons in the spoken vernacular, I asked about the Kaiser and was instantly hushed. "German walls have ears," he whispered. "Pronounce that name and every ear in the vicinity opens wide." Forty-two men were languishing in prison for *lese majeste*, the most of them newspaper editors. Military discipline was iron-bound and pitiless. Just before our arrival, a new recruit was sent to town from the barracks on an errand. Meeting the commandant of the battalion on the street he greeted him familiarly with, "Fine day, isn't it, General?" He had not saluted and instantly the officer whipped out his sword and ran the boy through. Called to account after the boy died, the general appealed the case to the Kaiser who justified the action. The commandant represented the Kaiser in Göttingen, therefore it had been the Kaiser who had been insulted and the Kaiser was above all common law.

War was smoldering all over Germany, but we did not suspect it. The British were at war in South Africa and the Germans sympathized strongly with the Boers. I remember the fierce joy of Fräulein Schlote when she heard of the death of Cecil Rhodes—"Gott sei dank!" Bismarck was then the German superman, worshipped almost as a god. On his birthday, fires were burned all night on the Bismarck Türme of the empire.

Once, at Göttingen, I asked the chancellor in his office if my wife and her sister would be permitted to sit as visitors in the lecture room where a course was being given in English. He asked if they had been admitted formally to the university. I said, "No." "*Dann ist Erlaubnis nicht gegeben.*" It was not the words he said, it was the tone and the look. I, an ignorant

American, had insulted the representative of the Kaiser by thinking such a thing was possible. It makes me angry even now as I think of it. He was Herr Roethe and I was taking his course in Goethe, and always as I listened to his lectures I felt repulsion in my bones. As he day by day interpreted the poet, I said to myself: "His Goethe is not the Goethe that I read and admired in college. He is building up his ideal of the Teutonic superman as poet. He is lecturing on Odin and Thor, not Goethe." One lecture he devoted to foreign estimates of the poet, holding up to laughter and scorn every English critic who had ever attempted to interpret him. It was as if he was telling of small children's descriptions and conceptions of the personality of God.

Twelve years later when stories of German atrocities began to circulate I chided the tellers, sometimes with heat. In both of my residences in the Reich I had found the common people kindly and helpful. Had it been the French about whom these stories were told I could have believed them, for I had not been pleased with my visits to France. But the greater number of the Germans I had lived with seemed to me to be sincerely religious, even sentimentally so, neighborly and home-loving. When I had asked, "Why do you need so many soldiers?" the answer always was the same. "We are peace-lovers, but we have bad neighbors." But more and more as the tales of atrocities poured in there came to me the brutal voice of Herr Professor Roethe, Chancellor of the Kaiser's University at Göttingen, and I understood. It was the Kaiser who had spoken. Every officer in all Germany represented the Kaiser and in his appointed place *was* the Kaiser.

3

During the autumn of 1905 President Atherton was ill, so ill indeed that he was unable to attend the Pennsylvania Day exercises. The faculty presided over by its senior member, Dr. Buckhout, relieved him of work and responsibility, but they were unable to continue the discipline that had so easily been maintained by the president. To realize the handicap under which the faculty had to work one must realize the Athertonian conception of college administration. Commencing in 1882 with the college almost at zero mark, he had built it into prominence and after nearly a quarter of a century of intense effort he had made what seemed to him a personal possession. He had held all power and authority in his own hands. It was a town joke that the agricultural department could not buy a bull until he had inspected it and passed on it. As a result the illness of the president all but stopped the college. Nothing new and positive could be attempted. The students grew restive under faculty rule. A relatively minor action, a rule passed making the 24 hours before and after a holiday not subject to cuts, exasperated the classes. The faculty refusing to rescind the rule, the students called a general strike which continued for eight days. A committee of the trustees then settled the matter, neither side feeling that it had won, and work went on. The president had left the matter in the hands of the faculty and did not interfere.

I did not realize how ill he was until on December 16, he called me to his sickroom to have me read to him a paper I had prepared for the Woman's Club on "The Educational Value of the Novel." He did not agree with my estimates of fictional values and presented his opinions with positiveness, but his appearance alarmed me. He was wan and feeble. A week later he asked to be relieved of the presidency. By faculty action I was one of a committee of three to frame a petition to the trustees asking that the president be retained in office even in the face of his expressed wish to be relieved of the work. Later we learned that the president had not spoken of the matter in terms of resignation.

He spent the winter in California, returning late in April, and after making several attempts to resume his work, suffered a collapse that was all but fatal. For a week no one expected him to live. He rallied, however, and on June 13 insisted on giving the graduating class their degrees. No one who saw his entrance upon the stage and his ten minutes with the class will ever forget it. Haggard, emaciated, really a dying man, he entered without support, erect and masterful as always. His brief address to the class had in it all of his old-time convincingness and sincerity.

Education, he said, is "the learning how best to adapt oneself to one's environment." With his physician close at hand to watch his every movement, with trembling hands he gave the graduates their diplomas, and marched out erect and masterful. Six weeks later, July 24, he was dead. His grave is at the side of the Schwab Auditorium that had meant so much to him.

The year or more that followed must be counted as a "doldrums" period in which the college came near to shipwreck. There began now what may be called in modern terms "a war of nerves." In the fall, General Beaver, chairman of the Board of Trustees, called a meeting of the entire teaching force a full week before the college opening, and laid down laws for the new regime. He did not hesitate to tell the faculty that they were incompetent, almost totally so. They had caused the strike by not giving the boys a square deal. Too many students, he declared, were being flunked. After he and other real friends of the college had worked hard to win a member of the state appropriation committee and had induced him to send his boy to Penn State, the faculty invariably flunked the boy and angered the father, and by that endangered the appropriation. "Let the faculty understand this," he roared, "the teacher who flunks a boy proves by that one fact his inability to teach. The real teacher wins his student, interests him, finds a point of contact, and makes his problems so clear that the boy cannot fail to understand and so passes his examinations. I shall watch the grade sheets to find out the good teachers, and let it be known that we are not going to tolerate any but good teachers."

At the opening exercises a week later he characterized Dr. Atherton as "the most skilful manipulator of men I ever knew," a characterization that angered me and many others. Telling the students that he had been unable to sleep on account of the hazing, he called for good conduct. "Unless you behave yourselves it will affect our appropriation,"—a whole world away from Dr. Atherton's conception of character.

Dr. Judson P. Welsh, once a normal school principal, now was appointed vice-president in active charge of the college, and in the opinion of many, and of Dr. Welsh himself, he was in due time to assume the presidency. To him a college administration was a dictatorship. My first experience with him came early. By telephone he informed me that he had chosen a new instructor for my department. I made him repeat the statement.

"You mean that he has been elected?" I gasped.

"He surely has."

"Without consulting me."

"Yes."

"Did you not know of the section in the trustees' regulations ruling that nominations for members of a department must be made by the head of that department?"

"Wholly unnecessary. The man has been elected. Goodbye." In my journal I wrote, "This is sheer tyranny. He turns down Bidelspacher whom I recommended and without consulting me elects another man."

For a year or more the college was governed by a dictator. My diary is full of entries like this: "Welsh without consulting any one informed the student body that Saturday was to be a holiday." On November 29, 1907, I made this entry:

> The situation here has been exceedingly unsatisfactory for a year. Dr. Welsh has taken the entire government of the college into his own hands. There has not been a council meeting this fall and few faculty meetings. All discipline has been taken over by Dr. Welsh. He has been everything. The departure of Professor Reber was largely due to him. There is no doubt that a whole swarm of presidential bees buzzed in his hat. It is now settled that he has no chance, and he is a very disappointed man. He made his mistake in not "sizing up" the situation. He bowed to Beaver. He considered the faculty incompetent. Like Beaver, he had contempt for them. As a result, the faculty stirred up the alumni and the younger trustees and "the young men arose, wound him up, carried him out and buried him."

The students seemed to look upon the faculty much as Dr. Welsh did. Led by a brilliant youngster, an anonymous group of seniors published an attractively-bound little magazine called *The Lemon*. Dozens of its numbers were sold during the year, and in them the faculty was lampooned without mercy. At times an anti-Lemon periodical would be issued entitled *The Lemon*

Squeezer, playing havoc with the older volume, but quickly it was discovered that the same board edited both magazines.

Everywhere restlessness. Several heads of departments found chairs in other colleges. I am free to confess that could I have found a position that appealed to me I should have followed this group. Then came the news that Dr. E. E. Sparks of the University of Chicago had been elected to the presidency, and I was content to stay. I knew him well. He had been Principal of the Sub-Freshman Department of the college during my first two years at Penn State. He was to assume the presidency in June, 1908.

CHAPTER XIII

Penn State Under President Sparks

THE ELECTION TO THE PRESIDENCY of the college of Dr. E. E. Sparks of the University of Chicago, a man who in the early nineties had served as principal of its sub-freshman class, ended a long-standing war of nerves. In April, Professor Willard of the Mathematics Department had said to me, "A man asked me lately why my hair had grown so white of late and I told him that if any Penn State man's hair had not turned white during the past two years that man had not been doing his duty."

The president-elect visited the college in January, and addressing the student body in chapel said, "I am coming back as no educational reformer. I have no theories. I am planning no revolution. The college is to go on just as it *has* gone on, performing its duties to the *people* of Pennsylvania, for this is the people's college. Some aid comes from the general government, but the people of Pennsylvania support it." At a Pittsburgh alumni banquet a few nights before this, as reported by Professor Foss, who was just leaving the college for another position, Dr. Sparks had made a good impression. The standard of scholarship, he had declared, was to be kept high. No diploma would be given that would cheapen any diploma now held. There would be no politics. One man was to be as good as another, and no better. He had then deplored the loss of good men from the faculty during the recent years. Turning to his old friend Professor Foss, he had said, "If any magnetism or corkscrew work can bring you back, you are coming back. You can tear a college down in a year, but it takes years to build it up again."

In reality Dr. Sparks began his administration May 11, though, as his wife complained, he was to receive no salary until he was inaugurated in June. He at once met the students in a mass-meeting "without the faculty," and there "talked turkey." He said a townsman had told him that "Everything is all sweet and beautiful now, but wait till you say *No* for the first time." "No" would be said, however, when "no" was needed to be said, he had told them, and he would begin by saying that the college would no longer tolerate an anonymous publication (meaning *The Lemon*), nor would it tolerate hazing.

On the twelfth he presided over his first faculty meeting, doing the unprecedented thing of having the chaplain offer a prayer. I had been chosen by the faculty to make the welcoming speech, which I then did, assuring him of our loyalty and our spirit of cooperation. In response he read to us, with comments and additions, the letter he had sent to the trustees when he had accepted the presidency. In it he had outlined his policy.

A few jarring notes there were. General Beaver and Dr. Welsh had evidently been in session with the new president, telling him of faculty inefficiency and departmental discords. This condition he would not tolerate, he said, and he was determined to end it, even if it took surgery. Moreover, he classified the faculty as "the hired men of the trustees." But on the whole I expressed the feelings of the faculty in the jotting I made that night in my diary: "We are all greatly pleased with Dr. Sparks. He took us into his confidence and talked to us as if we were fellow workers. It cleared up the atmosphere greatly. Under him we can now, I am sure, work as a unit, and with enthusiasm."

One thing he said pleased us mightily. Heretofore salaries had been paid only twice a year: January 1 and June 1. To all who needed more frequent payments notes were given which the banks would discount at 6%. I had been forced to submit to this discount monthly, a process that reduced my salary appreciably. Dr. Sparks now told us the old regime had ended. That had been one of his requirements before accepting his office. Payment of salaries would now come the first of every month.

The inauguration passed off without incident: the usual long procession in academic robes, the presidential address, shortened to fifteen minutes, and then in the afternoon a brilliant address on classical studies by Paul Shorey of Chicago, and an address by President Humphries of Stevens Institute. Dr. Sparks was at his best. He told of an experience he had recently at a sister college where a long list of honorary degrees had been awarded. Following these awards, the president had read the list of benefactions that had come to the college during the year. "Mr. Blank," he said, "to whom we have just given the degree, has given $1000; Mr. Noman, who also has received the degree, gave $1000." Governor Stuart, called upon to speak at this point, made what Dr. Sparks considered a remarkable speech for a politician. He had opened with a story. He had been reminded, he said, of the Western college president who announced that he must have $50,000. "Do you mean we must raise that great sum at once?" asked a trustee. "No," answered the president, "We had better raise it by degrees."

Once in the work, the president found no easy sailing. One day in his office I found him with work in heaps on his desk. "I feel," he said "like a mastodon in the mud. With each struggle I get deeper. At times I am tempted to roll over on my side and give up and turn into a fossil." The two years of maladministration had left all the college waters muddy and uncertain.

Professor Diemer of the faculty considered student insubordination in colleges a disease nation wide. "Never," he declared, "has there been so much disrespect for authority among college men. Dr. Angell of Ann Arbor is having an unprecedented lot of trouble. There are strikes everywhere among student bodies. And at the same time it can be said that there never has been more demand for men who know how to obey. That is the first question asked by employers? Always it is, 'Can the man obey and keep time and live up to rules?' " He deplored the fact that young men in the Engineering Building had to smoke a cigarette about once an hour, although in all manufacturing establishments men are turned off if they are found stealing off into a corner now and then to smoke.

The reorganization put in action by the new administration made all the faculty heads, even as did the new president, feel like bogged mastodons, floundering ineffectively and getting ever deeper. The president wanted student government and in due time he got it; he wanted the freshman class divided into small groups each with a father-like adviser, and he wanted frequent meetings of these advisers where individual cases could be discussed and final action taken. And it was done. Slowly other reforms came, most of them long needed.

My share of all this added work came upon me after I had obligated myself to do a piece of educational work not at all connected with the college. Sheer chance had brought it upon me. I had a vigorous Sunday school class at the local Methodist Church and I had long been dissatisfied with the "Lesson Helps" in the Monthly Journal issued by the educational department of the denomination. I found them superficial, hastily made, and, as I saw it, inadequate. Once of a Saturday night, after I had prepared my lesson for the morrow's Sunday school class, by an impulse I wrote a treatment of the current lesson as I thought it should be and sent it to the Sunday School Board. The reception it received amazed me. I was asked to go to New York as soon as possible to confer with the Board. I went, and when I returned I was in charge of the pedagogical department of the new *Teacher Training Magazine* soon to be issued, and was listed as one of a committee to work out the new graded work. For a year this kept every moment of my spare time full. In the summer of 1908 I gave a long course of lectures on Sunday School Teacher Training before a summer convention at Braddock Heights, Maryland. The final result of all this work was published by the Church in 1909 under the title *The Elements of Religious Pedagogy*, a book widely circulated.

I had no idea, however, of making a profession of this work, as I might easily have done. I finished my contract and quit, though it troubled me, I confess, to do it. I had been wandering from the track I had planned to take and I felt lost. Had

I not been a desultory worker? Had I stuck to anything? I felt that I had not said, "This one thing I do," even in the most cherished field of my ambition, fiction. I had been always a belated follower not a leader. I had brought nothing new. Was it not now too late? Was I not about to drop into the Serbonian Bog where armies (of once ambitious professors) whole have sunk?

This jotting I find in the notebook I then kept: "I get discouraged at times. I write interminably; I revise and re-revise and I pay no attention to rejection slips. What else can a writer do? I wrote to the Scribners when they had held a manuscript of mine for three months and still were silent: 'Authors are a feeble folk and like the conies they dwell among the rocks none of which they are able to hurl.' Am I on the right track? I have been rejection-slipped more than any other writer in America and I have with infinite patience rewritten and tried again. If my *Old Second Street* novel fails, I shall drop fiction. After a man has had five novels killed under him, it is time to seek another mount."

This I did, but not at once. Discouragement might cloud a day, but never did it stop my work. Whatever of success I have won has come from strict obedience to a life plan that once I threw into a quatrain, a bit of verse that I have written dozens of times when my autograph has been asked for:

> Be not dismayed when worsted in the fight,
>   Arise and yet arise and face the field;
> Fight on; though in the dust think not of flight,
>   The laurel comes to him who will not yield.

Like politics, the teaching profession sometimes brings strange bed-fellows. I represented the college at one time at the annual meeting of the Association of Colleges of the Middle States and Maryland. The meeting was at Poughkeepsie, New York, and I had neglected to make a reservation for a room. Hotel after hotel reported all rooms taken. Finally I found a place where a room could be had if I would share it with another teacher. This I was glad to do, and tired out I retired early. When I awoke it was broad daylight and a man was in bed with me sleeping noisily. An hour later he arose on his elbow and said, "Who are you?" I told him and then echoed his question. I found he was Dr. Joseph Henry Dubbs, Professor of Theology at Franklin and Marshall College, as I remember it, and author of *The Reformed Church of Pennsylvania*, 1902. I found him delightful. Some years later at a church meeting at Baltimore I found myself in a similar predicament. The man compelled to share my room, though not my bed, was an old presiding elder from New Jersey. He looked at me doubtfully, but there was no other room. In the morning he was serene. "I had looked to him," he said, "like a man who would sleep with his cut-out open," but I had slept as noiselessly as a baby.

3

Strange birds at times fluttered into our seclusion. When Jerome K. Jerome made his American tour we considered ourselves fortunate to get him to appear at the college. It was arranged that he was to be entertained in our house on the campus, since we were fellow writers and the hotel of the town was inadequate. It startled us. We were at something like a loss to know "upon what meat" the man did feed, "that he had grown so great." We were not quite sure, for the newspapers had made much of his epicurean whimsies. I said, "He is an Englishman, and no Englishman was ever known to refuse beef." I remembered English hotels where I had seen whole sides of beef wheeled in at breakfast time for guests to choose the cuts they wished for dinner. He was a beefsteak-eater I had heard, and therefore we got for him the finest steak money could buy in the best market in the region, and cooked it after his own demands on a grill over a charcoal fire. My wife with foresight, however, cooked a chicken in addition to the steak.

A student committee had been appointed to meet the humorist at the station and conduct him to our home, and judge of our consternation when they brought with him a woman whom he introduced as his wife. We had heard nothing of any wife. He demanded to be taken immediately to his room. Several hours later we called them to dinner. We had brought in as a guest the one native Englishman on the faculty, Professor Benjamin Gill, of infinite wit and geniality.

In due time came the steak which we considered a masterpiece. He examined it critically, cut it open, and then pushed it aside. (A week later, talking to the beef-steak club of New York, as we read in the papers, he said no civilized man would eat a steak that was not cooked on a silver grill.) He deigned to help himself to chicken however. Then a student came from the post office with his mail—a half a dozen letters which, oblivious of us all, he proceeded to open and read, picking now and then at a shred of chicken. His wife, a very human soul, sought to rescue the situation by animated conversation, but he at once interrupted her to read to her bits here and there from the letters.

After dinner, in the drawing room, I asked him where he had lectured the evening before. "Oh, I've forgotten the name. Where they make something—where was it, dear?" he asked, turning to his wife. "Cash registers—Dayton, Ohio." "Oh yes." I asked him how long he was to stay in America, and he said, "As long as I can stand it and I pray God it won't be long." Bored to the limit he seemed, until I showed him some snapshots I had taken in the region where he lived. One he recognized as within a half mile of his home, and standing before the open fire as only an Englishman can stand, he rubbed his hands together and fairly beamed on me. I wanted his autograph on my copy of *Three Men in a Boat*, but he would not touch the book until assured that it was what he termed "that rare thing in America, an English book not pirated."

A large audience greeted him in the auditorium. With him on his tour went the American entertainer, C. B. Loomis, whom I asked before I introduced the speaker how to pronounce "Jerome." I had read that he pronounced it himself "Jerum K. Jerum," but Loomis said, "Forget it. Pronounce it the way it is spelled."

The reading was a complete failure so far as Jerome was concerned. It was not easy to understand his British intonations and the students were not familiar with the English accent. His type of humor also was unfamiliar. The most of the audience had attended to hear a great English humorist. Because of the man's fame a special train had been run from Bellefonte, but from the audience came not a single ripple of laughter. It was not American humor, and it touched the students not at all. When Loomis, however, came out and ran his fingers through his hair causing it to stand on end and began a volley of American jokes, the boys roared with delight. Again and again they called him back. As the students expressed it, "The Englishman was a flop, but Loomis saved the day." The Jeromes, learning of the special train, abruptly left us and spent the night in Bellefonte.

How it struck the Bellefonte contingent let George Meek, a local editor, explain years later:

Some years ago, Jerome K. Jerome, English, and author of "Three Men in a Boat" and Charles B. Loomis made a lecture tour of 'the Stoits.' State College was just then becoming ambitious to emerge from the pupa stage of 'agriculture and the mechanic arts' and soar into realms cultural. The distinguished, perigrinating literati were offered good money to spout their stuff at State. The engagement caused a furore in Bellefonte. We consulted the late 'Pop' Thomas and contracted for a 'boat' via The Bellefonte Central to take the local literati to State College to hear this Jerome and Loomis combination. No need for saying anything about the joys of the ride up on 'the rattler.' This story has only to do with the trip home. Being in charge of the 'special' we hustled down to the station without waiting to tell Prof. Pattee what we had heard of Jerome's comment on the way a steak should be broiled. Seated in the smoker, next to the stove—for then there was segregation for those who used the weed—was someone in a 'great coat' whom we thought to be Tommy Eadon. We took the seat directly behind him. After all had gotten on board and the train had started backing out to the Y at Struble's, Francie Speer asked us what we thought of the lecture. We asked what he thought of it. Shouting loud enough to be heard above the roar of the train, he said, 'Jerome might be all right sittin' in a chair writin' books, but he ain't worth a continental damn standin' up and talkin'.' Then Parker, Admiral of the Boat, rushed up to us and whispered, "that's Jerome right in front of you." Talking about denouements: that was one. It was too good to keep, so we rushed to the back car where all the ladies were and started to spill the joke. As we progressed in stentorian tones that rose above the roar of the 'rattler,' we saw two ladies rushing frantically toward us. We paid no attention. Then came the deluge. They said "Why George, that was Mrs. Jerome sitting right beside you when you were telling of Francie's faux pas." And there we were covered with confusion for we had made Francie's 'break' look trifling when compared with the one we had just spilled.

4

In 1909 the Reverend Frank N. Buchman applied in person for the secretaryship of the Y. M. C. A. at the college, and Professor Willard and I were appointed to interview him and report. The interview was at my home on the campus. We found that he was 31 years old, a graduate of Muhlenberg, an ordained Lutheran minister who had served a three years' pastorate at Overbrook, and a mission worker who had been connected with several city organizations. His earnestness and evident sincerity and the dynamic program he presented pleased us, and we reported favorably.

His initial year at the college I know only from hearsay. I was in Europe, but I was in close contact with him during the five remaining years of his Penn State sojourn. At once the "Y" became intensely active. It began to be a dominating force in the college. With every year the fame of the work echoed through the colleges of the nation. Sooner or later there appeared on the campus every "Y" official and every college religious leader in the nation to study Buchman's methods.

It was found that he was at his best always when organizing and conducting student gatherings, but few realized that behind these gatherings there had been preparations made with German thoroughness. For months one by one he would gather delegates to summer conventions and one by one he would instruct them and inspire them with enthusiasm. As a result the Penn State delegations were always large. I attended as an instructor in Bible some of these "All-Eastern" summer conferences. One at Eaglesmere I especially remember. At the close of the convention Buchman gathered all his men late in the evening in a cottage lighted only by a flickering fire-place fire, the men seated in rows on the floor. After prayer and Scripture, both impressively rendered, Buchman asked them one by one to tell what the conference had done for them. It was near morning when we adjourned and before the closing many confessions had come and many high resolves. This was always his method. Often "Y" meetings at the college after adjournment would reassemble in some isolated cabin in the near mountains.

His "Y" week every year was a big event, dominating toward the last all the college activities. Mass meetings every night and sometimes every forenoon, addressed by speakers everybody had heard about. The town would be running over with notables and how he paid for such usually-high-priced men was everywhere a question. Asked about it, his reply was always the same: "When you are working for the Lord, the Lord pays expenses." Somehow or other money always did come. At every critical moment, he said, someone always came forward with an adequate check. He told me that once he had felt a sudden call to go to London, for what or why he had no idea. He was totally without money, but at once he started for the first boat sailing for Southampton. As he was walking up the gang-plank, a stranger had hailed him. "I know your work," he had said, "and I want to help it on. Here's a check." It was just enough to pay the expense of the trip.

Among the townspeople at that time was William Gilliland, familiarly known as "Bill Pickle." His nickname came from the legend that he had once opened a keg expecting to find alcoholic spirits, only to discover that it contained pickles. Buchman devoted part of his off-campus evangelism to improving or "changing" Bill, with some success. From that time on Buchman publicized him as the first convert, and paid his expenses to many meetings of the Oxford Group, as it was later called, in this country and abroad where he retold the story of his conversion. When Gilliland died a few years ago, this organization held memorial services in London and New York, and Dr. Buchman attended the State College funeral.

5

One other strenuous religionist visited the campus during this period, Billy Sunday who preached to overflow meetings for nearly a week. Dr. Sparks had known him personally in Chicago, and once when Sunday was conducting a campaign in Pittsburgh had slipped into one of his meetings to hear him. Billy saw him in the audience and at the opening moment called out, "I see in our audience Dr. Edwin Earle Sparks, President of The Pennsylvania State College. He will now lead us in prayer." Dr. Sparks greatly surprised, did so. When he had finished his prayer, Sunday had shouted, "You pray, Dr. Sparks, as if the Lord was seven million miles away," and the president had instantly countered with "I haven't got a short circuit on the Lord the way you have, Billy."

Before the Sunday meetings began at Penn State the president, knowing what was coming, took precautions. He had the college carpenter anchor the pulpit. In every possible way he bolted it down, and the bolts surely were needed. During every sermon the pulpit was rushed and shaken and pounded as if it were the center of all sin, and every sermon ended with the preacher perched victoriously on the top of it. Preaching with Billy Sunday was an athletic exercise. At the close of every sermon the college athletic department took possession of the preacher and rubbed him down as if he had just finished a marathon run. "Red" Bebout of the football squad, who helped with the work, declared that Billy had muscles "as hard as nails." He had never seen a more perfect athletic specimen.

CHAPTER XIV

The Ph.D. Mirage

𝒥 T TAKES THE YOUNG ASPIRANT for a professor's chair not long to learn that this coveted piece of furniture is locked in an Aladdin's Cave, not to be entered without a password. Its outer gate will yield to the mystic symbols A.B. or A.M., but its inner shrines are guarded by a door that swings only to the "open sesame," *mot de passe*, "Ph.D.," a hard word to learn. By rare good luck I had hypnotized the gate-keeper by means of books of poetry and prose that I had written, and, all innocent of the mystic insignia, had been made a full professor in a growing college and the head of an important academic department. What use then for me to grub for years for three letters now of no consequence to me save for decorative purposes? But I had elected to live my life with scholars, and would not my academic career be one long apology for entering the shrine not by the door but by some other way? Could I keep my self-respect when with the leaders of my profession? I am free to confess that, being human, I coveted the degree, and took my first sabbatical leave from the college intent upon winning it.

Germany at that time, 1902, was standing in the scholastic world in a leading position. It had evolved research methods well worth studying. Accordingly I had gone to Germany and had been matriculated in the University of Göttingen. Once there I had gone over the matter of a German degree with Professor Morsbach of the university, and later had talked much with perspiring candidates that I found in residence. I corresponded with Heidelberg and Leipzig. As a result I found that to secure a degree I must be interned in Germany for three years, must master several languages including mediaeval Latin, and then prepare a thesis on some such subject as "The use of *but* in the plays of Shakespeare," this final grind ruining perhaps a year. As a result I had gone home disillusioned. The game was not worth the candle. It would, I felt sure, destroy in me the creative and make me a mere "gerund grinder." Was not this Ph.D. mania the dry rot that of late had all but destroyed the old college curriculum? The demand for the degree seemed to be a fairly new phenomenon. I remembered that when I entered Dartmouth in 1884 only two of the faculty were Ph.D.s, and that faculty certainly was a distinctive one, able to turn out men of the heroic type sung by Richard Hovey in his "Men of Dartmouth" Ode. Later I was refreshed by a vigorous pronouncement by Stuart P. Sherman, himself a winner of the degree: "The very best men do not enter upon graduate study at all; the next best drop out after a year's experiment; the mediocre men at the end of two years; the most unfit survive and become Doctors of Philosophy, who go forth and reproduce their kind."

Granted a second sabbatical in 1909, I set out for Europe *cum uxore liberisque*, but now with no thought of a degree. I would go now as an academic free-lance intent only on self improvement, on fitting myself as completely as possible for the work I had set out to do. We sailed for Liverpool by the Montreal route, an unusual voyage since two days of it were on the river. The passenger list was largely Canadian and to my surprise somewhat anti-American. Passing the Quebec rock, I was told by a burly Britisher where to look for the Chateau Frontenac. Learning my nationality he made the comment, "Yes, yes, I was a day or two once in New York and Boston and it was quite enough."

As a fellow passenger I thereupon found him delightful and indeed enlightening. It seemed that my sabbatical attendance upon lectures was to begin even while we were on the river. By chance I found myself seated at table with a professor, one Dr. George Bryce, Professor of English in the University of Winnipeg, and, in his own words, "the supreme authority on the history of Western Canada." He was in fact reading the proof of a history of the region soon to be published. Each meal time therefore, and sometimes for hours afterward I listened to his lectures on Canadian history. Everything connected with the "States" seemed to exasperate him. "You have run wild on higher education," he growled. "Your State of Missouri alone has 60 colleges which grant degrees. In Winnipeg Province we have but one central university—*one*." Never did I meet him without encountering a burst of criticism. "In the United States the residuum of authority is the State; in Canada it is the direct opposite. You pose as a world power, and yet you can't compel your own States," and he went off into a tirade about the Fenian insurrection which the government had advised New York State to settle with the help of Canada. He said Montgomery was an Irishman and some of the United States Irish wanted to erect a monument for him, "but we stopped that. We do not admire United States Irishmen."

He was good company though. He knew his England thoroughly and entertained us with delightful *mots*. "There is an inn in London," he said, "called 'The Goat and Compasses.' It had been established by an old Puritan who gave it the name 'God Encompasses Us.' As the years went by the name was corrupted into its present form."

2

Arrived at Liverpool, we found a home-like *pension* and for a week or more settled down to rest. We found to our delight that all unknowingly we had during a month or more been following the crest of the strawberry harvest. The Pennsylvania season was at its height when we left in June; two weeks later it was at its best when we were in New Hampshire; and now the season was just opening in England; two weeks later it opened in Scotland. The British berries we found exceptionally fine.

One side-trip I insisted on taking, the trip I had so greatly enjoyed in 1897: to Chester and down the River Dee in a boat to Eton Hall. Again I found it ideal, England at its best. But I found at Chester a jarring note: it was a city antique, a city of relics and all of them for sale. Even the relics of the Romans who had given the city its name, relics in the municipal museum, had prices affixed.

Then Edinburgh, where a man with a push cart took our

baggage to a *pension* that was to serve as temporary quarters. House-hunting next, an ordeal luckily soon over. We found quite by accident an apartment on Great King Street that seemed ideal: three rooms and a bath for 35 shillings a week, and board for three at two guineas. Later we found that the house had belonged to David Masson, biographer of Milton, and that the living room assigned to us had been the study in which he had done his great work. The walls were still covered with the bookshelves of his day, but the volumes now filling them had not been a part of his library.

Then in due order came the exploration of Edinburgh which 12 years before I had been compelled to do in tourist fashion. Now we could do it with thoroughness, as it deserved. We had all summer for exploration. Of all the Grand Tour features Holyrood most attracted me. Three or four times during the summer I visited it, remaining sometimes for hours. What fascinated me was not the Palace, but the American tourists that one always found there in swarms. Oil cloth on the castle floors kills at the start all feelings of antiquity. Walls hung with paintings of long lines of Scottish kings are impressive only till one learns that one painter painted them all, using only his imagination. The show bored me, but the long rows of awe-struck Americans! I couldn't keep away. I lingered always longest in what seemed to be the climactic spot in the Holyrood tour, the bedroom of Queen Mary of Scots. At that time there was a red spot on the floor supposed to be the blood of the murdered Rizzio, and often there were gentle shrieks.

Everywhere in Edinburgh one finds evidences that Americans go there in droves, and that Americans pay. All the hotels while I was there flew the American flag. One saw few British flags. Princess Street seemed like an avenue in a World's Fair. Along the Grand Tour routes, boys ran before you turning handsprings and then begging for "a penny to buy a scone." One cannot take a seat in a park without being swarmed over by youngsters who lecture on Edinburgh "sights," point out famous landmarks, offer to act as guides, or thrust into your hands guide-books for you to buy. Yet, nowhere else in Europe can one find a city where scenery, history, and romance more perfectly blend.

No city more religious. Our landlady informed us that the churches one sees on every street are not well filled in summer, but in winter they are full. On Sunday there is nowhere else to go. On the Holy Sabbath Day everything closes, even the restaurants. Another thing she told us: drunkenness is everywhere in the city. It is not safe, she said, for a woman to be out at night unaccompanied by a man. Warningly she told us this the first thing after our arrival. Yet it is the City of Churches. One Sunday morning what seemed like a fully equipped military band marched along our street under our very windows playing with great volume, "For you I am praying; I'm praying for you."

During the summer I read aloud to Anna and Sarah *The Heart of Midlothian*, and afternoons, when there were no lectures, we visited one by one every locality touched in the novel. We found Dumbredyke's Cottage, we climbed the Salisbury Crags, explored Arthur's seat, and Castle Cliff. We tried every bus line out of the city, rode to the end, and then returned. I think we exhausted the guidebook lists of sights to see.

Nor was all our reading Scotch. I revelled in the treasures I found in old book stores. I picked up a life of Queen Anne, 1721, and read it aloud all one evening. One single sentence paid me for the book. Quoting Bishop Kennet, the author wrote: "The death of the young Duke of Gloucester was in a great measure occasioned by the over-heating of himself in the solemn observance of his birthday."

We had chosen Edinburgh for our summer residence largely because of the "vacation courses" in the university, the fifth summer they had been given. The inaugural meeting was on July 28, a dull occasion as such meetings always are,—mostly conventional welcomes and responses. I was not at all interested until I found beside me an unusual youngster who announced himself as H. Peveril Turnbull, 17 South Castle Street. He said he was poet, musical composer, writer on political subjects, and teacher of English. He prided himself, he said, on his accent which he considered unusually fine for Edinburgh. He recited to me with resonant voice a poem which he said he had just written on the political situation. He was not a Socialist; he was an original reformer, he said. "The American tariff is beastly. You get big wages, then spend it all for a pair of breeches. England's greatness depends on her navy and now her navy is a thing of the past. Flying machines will be dropping in here soon like locusts. The first passage of the channel the other day by a Frenchman is the beginning of the end. England and America must come together. Not an Englishman in the world to-day but boils with indignation over the treatment of the 13 colonies. The two must work together; that's the remedy. It's the duty of Americans, as men of English blood, to rally to the old fatherland." His cock-sureness nettled me. I told him that like every other Englishman he had the wrong perspective: "England, as seen from any part of the United States looks to be about the size of a two-penny postage stamp. We in the United States started as Englishmen, but we have improved on the breed and are now Americans." He countered hotly in kind and we had a wonderful time, voted the day a success, and exchanged cards for another meeting.

Two of the courses interested me greatly, though for very different reasons. A. A. Jack of the University of Aberdeen treated critically the English writers of the nineteenth century, and so interestingly that I missed not a lecture. George Saintsbury also lectured but I do not remember now even the subject of his course. It fascinated me however to see how dull a lecturer can actually be and "get away with it."

He would saunter leisurely in, precisely on the hour, hang up his hat and cane, open his desk drawer, pull out a large manuscript, run his finger down till he found a pencil mark, and then read droningly without expression of enthusiasm for the full hour. Then the bell would ring, he would stop abruptly, take out his pencil and make a check at the stopping place, return the manuscript to the drawer, take hat and cane and leave the room. The phenomenon interested me. I had handled many of Saintsbury's books, and once had remarked that I could not think of him as an individual, he must be a syndicate. His studies of French literature I had once found very stimulating, and I wished to talk with him.

In reply to my note he invited me to his home, 2 Eton Terrace. I was surprised to find it just at the end of Dean's Bridge, overlooking the chasm, an ideal spot. He received me in his study and then invited me up to take tea with Mrs. Saintsbury. I judged him to be about 65. She was a motherly woman with a sweet smile and few words. Her husband gave little chance for any one to get a word into the torrent of his talk. He began at once on Whitman, declaring that he, Saintsbury, had been the first English writer to point out the real values in *Leaves of Grass*. He had reviewed the book at length before anyone in England had noticed it. The Pre-Raphaelite discovery of the poet had come because of his review. He pointed to a large picture of Whitman hanging in a conspicuous part of the room, the only portrait in sight.

"And isn't it strange," he said, "that you, an American, come to me on the very day I get a letter from my son travelling in America with the news that he has just made a journey to Camden, Maine, where Whitman lived."

"Camden, New Jersey," I gently corrected.

"Oh no, no, no! Camden, Maine. As I was saying, this very day I receive a letter from my son saying he has visited the Whitman home in Camden, Maine, and the very day I receive it you, an American, come."

"But, Mr. Saintsbury,"— the schoolmaster within me would not down—"Whitman spent his last years in Camden, New Jersey, just across from Philadelphia. I have been there myself, and . . ."

"Oh, no, no, no. My son says Camden, Maine, is wonderfully interesting, just where you'd expect to have a poet like Whitman born, and . . ." he bubbled on and on.

I did not interrupt again. He asked me how I liked Edinburgh and before I could answer he was off pell-mell telling how he liked it himself, his tea cup dancing in his hand. "A noisy city, isn't it? Particularly did it distress my friend Professor Gayley of America. The stones have a particularly resonant character. I think fewer Americans are coming to Edinburgh than formerly, perhaps not because of the noise, but because London is now putting forth so many attractions." He said his work in the university touched only the undergraduates of which he had about 250. He read their examination papers himself, three examinations each year. Changing the subject quickly, he asked me if I did not deplore the advent of brick houses in Edinburgh. "Brown stone is the traditional material for Edinburgh buildings, but the old quarry has been exhausted. From the native stone they made houses that were enduring and comfortable. Bricks are not suited at all to the climate," and much he deplored their use.

Professor Jack I found stimulating and original. He seemed of the Scottish type,—sandy-haired, light of complexion, somewhat undersized. He lectured as if he were speaking from inspiration, his eyes always turned to the ceiling on the other side of the room, seldom upon his audience. Poetry he read as if it were something sacred, something not to be spoken in ordinary tones. I got much from the lectures.

In December following, I visited Professor and Mrs. Jack in their rooms at Durham Villas, Kensington, London, near the Holland House associated with memories of Sidney Smith, Macaulay and their circle. I found the professor in a study the walls of which were completely covered with book-shelves heavily loaded. He told me he did not go in for first editions; he sought merely for good working texts. He had Scott in 120 volumes and the essayists in about as many more. His father, he said, had read every word of Scott. He believed America and also England were in too prosperous a condition, too much taken up with trade and commerce to do anything with literature. It was the struggling countries that produced literature. He had as a boy had a passion for Hawthorne and had read him as a great classic. Of late, however, Hawthorne did not appeal. He was too moral: he gave one the impression all the time that he (Hawthorne) believed he was treading on the verge of a most serious impropriety, that he was handling most dangerous explosives. After one has read Tolstoi and Ibsen one sees how tawdry Hawthorne is. In answer to my question, he said in his opinion Emerson was undoubtedly our greatest author. He was of the opinion that the only man fitted to be a critic is the man who can feel the author's soul. Sydney Lee he classed as a mere scholar. "In all his life of Shakespeare he has not ventured a single opinion of his own." I told Professor Jack he should publish some of his lectures. He replied that he had no time. He had done something toward a volume of essays, he said, but people have got sick of the old talk about old poets. No afternoon visit being complete without tea, Mrs. Jack thereupon took charge of the remainder of the hour.

3

We were two weeks in Paris where we arrived August 31. The city bored me. It seemed unreal, like a colossal made-up feature at a World's Fair. One could spend a year there diligently sight-seeing and not see it all. Visitors intent on covering the Grand Tour of Europe see only the surface and many who remain longer see not much more. It is a worn-out saying that one finds in Paris what he brings to Paris, but it is still true.

The city as a work of art, as a collection of marvellous architectural masterpieces, monuments, vistas of beauty, interested and at times thrilled me, but always there were the French people and always there were the tourists. It was like viewing the Pyramids in a mosquito swarm. Never had I seen "tips" so insolently asked for and so often expected. When I shook my head at the collection bag at a cathedral service, the priest who was gathering the collections scowled at me. Thrusting the bag again at me and again meeting refusal, for an instant it seemed as if assault were imminent. On all the streets a furious snapping of whips as if an early Henry Ford "Tin Lizzie" was back-firing with American vim. Over the head of the plodding old cab horse explodes constantly a volley of shots that would make an American horse frantic. The old French nag, however, seems to enjoy the racket. I have never seen a cab horse actually hit by the lash. Never does it make him quicken his pace. For me it explained much that I saw in Paris. Whatever soul these Parisians may have it seems always to be theatric in its expression, temperamental, and dramatic like the coachman's whip. He is eloquent with his hands. When he talks, every particle of him seeks expression. One day I saw two bicycle riders collide on the street. Scramblingly they picked themselves up and simultaneously they assaulted the air with vocables and hands. Even I, with nothing to guide me but my hard-learned book French, could understand what they were saying. I expected murder and wondered if I would not be held as a witness, but never did they touch each other. A marvellous movie it would have made. I wondered how so perfect a piece of theatric art could have been created without rehearsal. The end was perfect in its art. As by a prearranged signal they stopped, shook hands, mounted their undamaged bikes and the act was over.

I have mentioned the tourists. One illustration is enough. Standing in the Louvre before the Venus of Milo, I heard two American women talking. Said one of them, "That's said to be the most beautiful woman in the world." Said the other, "Aw! Come off!"

Only one event of our stay needs recording. By appointment we took tea with Madame Plummer, the wife of the "Old Tiger" Clemenceau. A beautiful lady we found her, her age in the mid-sixties, almost wholly deaf. She had not, she said, been out of her rooms for six or seven years. Her life surely has been one of the leading romances of her generation. The young Clemenceau, for political misdoings, had been forced to flee to America, and, bare of funds, had secured a position as teacher of French in a fashionable Connecticut school for women. Here he had been captivated by the beauty of one of his students, Miss Mary Plummer, had married her, and had taken her to France where at length she had presided over the castle home which he had inherited. In later years she had left him, unable to endure his affairs with other women, but never was there a legal separation. She had lived with her children and, when they had married, had lived alone with a servant. My wife was her cousin and the Plummer family history was the topic of discussion.

Eagerly the now-French woman went over her youth, a part of it spent on the Pattee farm where I also had spent my youth. She said our call had come on a Plummer anniversary: 49 years ago this very day her father had died. She had a brother alive, she said, in Wisconsin. On the walls hung family pictures and among them one of the most beautiful portraits I had ever seen. "Who is that?" I asked. "That's my dead self," she said. No wonder Clemenceau married her. She told us she had three children, one boy, "a brave soldier," and two girls. There are now, she said, five grandchildren who visit her often. Since her marriage she had visited America twice. Few novels have ever surpassed in romance and tragedy the actual record of this woman's life.

We left Paris September 15, for Frankfort-on-the-Main, and we were glad to go. This I find in my journal written on the train leaving France: "We did not greatly like Paris. It is a city of art, or in other words it seems wholly artificial. There seems to be no soul. The buildings are marvellously beautiful and so are the monuments and boulevards and squares, but everything is glaring and unreal. We found no mellow and restful atmospheres as we found them everywhere in England. It is life dramatic, life at high pitch. There is no greensward, and the trees as we saw them seemed withered and struggling for life. The language is spoken explosively. It is more exciting than New York. The boulevards swarm with automobiles driven at high speed. It is dangerous to attempt a street crossing. Everywhere headlong rush, nervousness, excitement. We were glad to go."

The choice of Germany rather than France for the continuation of my studies came, I suppose, from the extreme difficulty I always found in mastering a spoken language. My eye had no great difficulty in acquiring a language, but my ear and tongue were always in trouble. I found that a winter in Paris would do little for me save to make me able to understand spoken French. Already I could understand German. Therefore we headed for Germany, and listening to the advice of a friend, we chose the University of Marburg. The winter climate was better there than in the North, we were told, and the scenery was inspiring. I confess that in the back of my mind lurked the knowledge that it was from Hesse-Cassel the Hessians had been drawn to aid the English during our Revolution. Here I could study the Hessians at first hand.

CHAPTER XV

Marburg on the Lahn

$\mathcal{F}$OR A DAY WE PAUSED at Frankfort-on-the-Main which we found in gala dress. It was September 16, 1909. All Germany seemed to have descended upon the city. The Great International Airship Exhibition in honor of Count Zeppelin was in progress, an affair with side-shows and refreshment stands like Coney Island. But the unique features of the show were the great balloon and airship sheds with their amazing contents pulled out by soldiers for the Germans to see. First came the great Luftschiff *Parseval* which in due time took off with nine passengers, two of them ladies. It was gone for two hours. Then had followed the Zeppelin III with 18 or 20. The noise from the engines was deafening, the great structures seemed under perfect control. The crowds roared their delight. All day one heard nothing but "Luftschiff." The Luftschiff age was opening, and it was opening in Germany. Transportation was to be revolutionized. Of heavier-than-air machines we heard nothing. The future was to be ruled by the Zeppelins, and looking at the great monsters so feather-light, so obedient, so graceful, so able with great loads to slip up into the clouds, we were thrilled, I confess it, almost as much as were the German crowds.

During the whole of our autumn in Germany we felt constantly the Luftschiff excitement that was covering the country like an atmosphere. Once in October a Zeppelin was advertised to alight on the Marburg meadow at 2:30 p.m., and immediately the area became a veritable mass-meeting—students, schoolboys, citizens, peasants, soldiers, tradesmen watching for hours, but the flying ship failed to appear. Once in November our landlady rushed into our room shouting as if the house were on fire, "Das Luftschiff, das Luftschiff ist hier!" and we found the whole town in the streets looking excitedly into the sky where rode the Parseval III so near the tree tops that we could see the dangling landing ropes and the flashing propellers.

We reached the quaint old city of Marburg September 16, and from the first found it highly interesting. It is a city set upon a hill at the apex of which is the castle, once the residence of the Landgrave of Oberhesse, but for many years unoccupied. Everywhere antiquity. The old church once preached in by Luther seems always to have been there. The peasants as I saw them in the fields everywhere seemed perfectly in keeping with the church. These were replicas, I let myself imagine, of the Hessians so picturesque in our Revolutionary War.

We found comfortable apartments kept by the widow of a missionary who had died at his post in Africa. Under our window flowed the river Lahn through a green meadow which day by day we were to find spread over with a veritable snowfall of sheets, pillow cases and the like which had been washed in the river and laid out to dry. In Marburg, we were to learn, washing day corresponds to the Yankee spring house-cleaning orgy. In cleanly families it comes every three months. For a long time I thought the meadow was the drying field of a public laundry. There were miles of clotheslines and acres of green grass all used to full capacity. A family whose turn had come to use the field would hire half a dozen peasant women to wash clothes all day in the river, each kneeling on a platform and spreading the clothes in every direction to dry. Madame Wickert thought it "awful" to let washing accumulate so long. She washed every two months.

She was, we found, an unusual character with a stirring history. In 1878 she had married a soldier who in the war of 1870 with France had been severely wounded with a sabre in the battle of Gravelotte. Later he had gone to Africa as a missionary, taking her with him, and there she had lived for 30 years, returning home only once. His eyesight failing, he had gone to Germany for treatment and while there the Boer War had broken out rendering his return impossible. She had been left with her seven children in the midst of the war area. Terrified, she had taken her children to camp after camp for refugees.

All she had had been stolen. Then her husband had broken through the blockade, only, however, to be stricken down with sickness. Without doctor or medicine he had died. Finally she had reached Germany, but her children, she said, were lost, "scattered over the whole world."

Settled now in Germany we began at once to brush up our German, a task highly necessary since so far as we were able to discover for weeks we were the only English speakers in the city. My German, I found, in the seven years of non-use had evaporated considerably, especially in the illogical areas of gender and sentence order and damnable idiom.

Seven years before, when I first began to struggle with a spoken German, these things had amused me, but not for long. At college I had taken all the German in the curriculum and I had taught German for four years at Coe's Academy, and I thought I knew German like a book. In short order I found that that was *just* how I knew it. Never had I heard German spoken, and at once I found myself in difficulties seemingly insuperable. Some of them indeed were, for Americans at least, insuperable. I defy anyone whose mother tongue is not German to vocalize this sentence so that it will satisfy a Teutonic tutor: "Die Köchin kocht in der Kirchenküche bei Kirchenhausen einen Kirschenkuchen."

To us the German type of sentence seems unnatural and illogical. To hold the verb to the end of a long sentence is a linguistic artificiality that requires an undue straining of a hearer's powers of attention and makes German style unwieldly and heavy. Here is a literal translation of a sentence I found in a Marburg newspaper: "We hope that the under-so-good-auspices-opened season of our theatre to the actors as also to the theatre-public right much joy bring will." Equally annoying are the verbal megatheriums, conglomerations made by pasting word upon word to form adjectives and nouns all but endless, like this, for instance: "der Doppelschraubenschellpostdampfer Deutschland." Difficult also is the task of learning the gender of nouns.

To write German if one has plenty of time and a good dictionary is not an impossibility even for an American college graduate, but to keep up one's end in a conversation is an exercise in mental gymnastics always highly amusing to Germans who know the awful possibilities of their language. It is a sorry sort of comfort to see them struggling with English pronunciations. But imagine yourself at a Kaffeeklatsch, and, as I have been, the only American present:

Hostess. "Will you not, I beg you, this cheese try?"

Learner. "It is to me somewhat afraid over German cheese. Is *he* strong?"

Hostess. "Ah, wholly otherwise. I beg you try. *He* may see not good out, but I am sure *he* will to you good smack."

Learner. "I will then prove. Ah royal! I eat *him* gladly."

Hostess. "Indeed, that does me joy. My servant girl has *him* this morning in the market bought."

Learner. "So? You have, I perceive, a wholly nice servant. Not?"

Hostess. "Yes. Much good. *It* has by me already only a pair of months been."

Learner. "How much must you *it* pay?"

Hostess. "Twenty marks the month. Very high, not? Shocking!"

Learner. "Certainly no. In America we often 80 marks pay."

Hostess. "Think you! Impossible! But then America!—Ah will you not try? (Passing what looks like thin slices of navy plug.)

Learner. "And what is this?"

Hostess. "Pumpernickel, bread of rye flour made. *He* is very wholesome."

Learner. "More so than blackbread?"

Hostess. "Blackbread? Ah *it* is by the soldiers altogether eaten. *It* is cheaper. Now yet one cup of chocolate. Yes?"

Learner. "I beg you with pleasure. I drink *her* far liever than coffee. *She* to me right capital smacks."

Hostess. "Ah right good. You should not coffee drink. *He* is unhealthful."

Learner. "And tea?"

Hostess. "*He* also is bad."

Learner. "And beer, is *he*, *she*, or *it* bad?"

Hostess. "Bier? ach, das ist ganz anders. Man kann nicht zu viel Bier trinken. Dass ist unmöglich."

In a store window I saw the outfit which that store had assembled for a prospective bride. It filled a large window. Every piece had the family initials embroidered in. There was a gross of towels, several dozens of sheets and pillow cases and everything else in proportion. There was even a complete outfit for a prospective baby. The bridegroom furnishes for the marriage outfit only his personal presence at the wedding, and even his dress suit and tie are sometimes hired for the occasion. Happy land of Germany, paradise for men. The woman does all the work in the home, brings her husband a handsome "dot" on the marriage day, a "dot" after the ceremony to be managed by him, and then is perfectly reconciled to being his devoted slave and ardent admirer all her life long. Her place is the home, and it is her duty to replenish the fatherland. She never had a dream of anything else in her whole life.

One day early in October we explored the little *Dorf* of Cappel, a village more primitive than any we had yet visited. As one approaches, one sees first a mass of red tiles through trees. As in all similar villages the church spire stands prominently, and the church, stone even to the tip of its spire, gives the impression that it is as much a part of the primitive landscape as the very rocks in the fields. Antiquity in every line. As one enters the main street, or rather, the central surface sewer, one's ears are saluted. The shrill twang of disturbed geese rings out in all directions. Next, the nose is assaulted. House and barn are a single unit and all refuse is thrown out in front. Manure heaps fill the front yards and a dark stream of water from sinks, barnyards, dung hills, and drainage ditches flows unhindered in the road. The swarming geese paddle in it, root their bills in it for choice morsels, and drink it seemingly as if it were rare liquor. The goose certainly is the national bird of Hesse: every house in the village must have at least a dozen. One must step carefully for nastiness of every variety is strewn everywhere.

The only persons in sight were women with huge tins as large as a door on their heads with dough cakes filled with damsons to be baked in the common oven. For it is the "Zwetschenzeit," the damson harvest time, when nothing else is talked about.

The village has architectural peculiarities that seem unbelievable at first. All houses are incredibly old, at least so they look. The criss-cross oak framing in front stands out black and weathered as by the storms of a thousand years. The triangular places left by the criss-crossing beams are bricked in and plastered over. Each house has its motto, and many of the more pretentious buildings are embellished with rude drawings or designs.

The men—what I saw of them—seemed to me illustrations from the history of the Revolution. These were the Hessians that were purchased by the English for soldiers, and who when they passed through Germany on their way to the embarkation port were made by Frederick to pay a cattle tax into his treasury. Undersized they seemed, vacant of expression, awkward and hulking of gait, sandy of complexion, sorry material it seemed to me for soldiers to fight in the forests of America.

With the month of October begins the "Michaelisferien" or "Kartoffelferien"—the Michaelmas or Potato Festival. A well-known painting by Joseph Jungwirth is entitled "Kaartoffel-ernte." It represents a peasant woman with her hoe leaning against her dress, both hands full of potatoes which she has picked up and is about to throw into her basket. In the Hesse area at least, the potato crop is harvested by women, and only women. Sometimes the potatoes are ploughed out for the women to pick up but oftener they are dug out with the crude heavy hoe represented in the picture of Millet's "Man with the Hoe." In one way the potato harvest became for me a personal matter: nowhere have I eaten better potatoes than those raised in Upper Hesse. Frau Wickert always served them boiled with their skins on.

The little Marburg newspaper the *Oberhessische Zeitung*, which I read every day made a quaint impression upon my Yankee sensibilities. It is vastly different from the bustling, news-gathering-from-all-the-world, yellow journal of America. It has no patent insides. Every particle of it you know is home-made and local-atmosphered. It is small as such a paper should be. In reporting news there is no telling the story twice over, to get two effects and there are no scare heads and no padding. It has a neighborly tone. The town is a great family and the paper is a home letter. It has diminutive editorials on locally timely subjects: the beginning of holidays, the opening of a season, or the opening day of a new month. What was the origin of October? What does it signify? and the like. It advises all to avoid sitting in cold rooms and going out without an overcoat. It begs parents to go into the woods with their children during the holidays, for the winter is at hand and the winter will be long. Such a paper makes one forget the bustle and the rush of modern life.

Intensely loyal was it to the little city that was its home. When the Hessenvolkslehrerverein chose the town for its convention the paper welcomed them with a poem that made lyric the charms of Marburg. The last of the eight stanzas reached this climax:

> Wo gibts in deutschen Lande eine Stadt,
> Die einen schoenren Kranz von Bergen hat,
> Als du, Mein Marburg, Koenigin der Lahn?
> Dir gilt mein Lied, o, nimm es freundlich an.

The first symptom of life in the university came in mid-October, a religious service held in the university church. The commencement sermon was preached by the scholarly Professor Archelis of the theological faculty, and to my surprise it was not analytic or in any way scholarly. Rather was it hortatory and evangelical. He took as his text "Meine Speise ist die, dass ich thue den Willen dess, der mich gesandt hat, und vollende sein Werk." At the opening of the new year, he said, it was well that they took a careful look at what they were working toward. Young men were constantly choosing their work: let them have as their first thought the bringing themselves into harmony with God. Work and pray: "Ora et labora." Remember that you are working not for self but in harmony with God. "Hausfrau, bei

Gottes Gnade bist du Hausfrau; Kaufman, bei Gottes Gnade bist du Kaufman," and so down a list ending with "student."

The audience had a Quaker look: the men were on one side and the women on the other. When the prayer was offered the men arose, but not the women.

During both of my residences in Germany I was impressed by the religious atmosphere everywhere evident. I attended prayer meetings that were as fervent and as spiritual as Methodist "love feasts." In one of them a serene old lady testified that she had but little to give to the Lord, but she had long given to the missionary work all the eggs her hens laid on Sunday.

On October 17 came the inauguration of the new rector of the university. The Aula was packed and there was plenty for all to see. First had come two stately beadles clad entirely in scarlet and holding sceptres. Then came the old rector in full regalia and with him the rector-to-be, quite plain. Following were the professors, some 45 of them, in evening dress. Academic costume it seemed was not worn in Marburg. Then came representatives of the various corps and "Burschenschaften," dressed most gorgeously and carrying their colors. After a chorus of voices had sung a song, the old rector made an address summing up the work of the past year. Among other things he said that for the first time women had been allowed to enter on equal terms with men. During the summer semester the enrollment of students had passed the 2000 mark. Then Doctor Maas, Professor of Klassischen Philologie was invested with the regalia of a rector and proceeded to read a scholarly dissertation on "Alt-Griechenland die Heimat der Klassischen Wissenchaften."

But the university even now was not open. Lectures would not begin for a week, and some of them not until November 1. The German university seems never to be in a hurry. The only iron-clad thing about it seems to be the examination which is in truth its center and soul. Germany is the land of the examination. A good part of every educated German's life has been spent in preparation for examinations. The goal of all study is the examination. You may attend classes at will, cut them all if you will, but you will at last be forced to face an examination in the subject.

I called early upon Professor H. Vietor in charge of the English courses. I had heard much of him in Edinburgh where in 1906 and again in 1907 he had delivered courses of lectures in the summer school. I had greatly admired his work. He was, I found, a modest, scholarly man of about 55 who spoke English like an Englishman. His first question was, "What was your object in coming to Marburg?" I said that I desired to learn German scholarly methods and to hear the lectures of Professor Vietor. It seemed to satisfy him and I had a delightful visit at the close of which he gave me tickets to the inaugural ceremony.

As a lecturer he was more human than most of the university scholars I had listened to. Once he even got his class into a burst of laughter, something seldom heard in German lecture rooms. He had read to the class Ascham's letter recording his journey up the Rhine. Then dropping the letter he had said, "When Ascham left England he feared that he could not get along without the English beer, but after he had been a time in Germany he hated to go home because he could not take with him the Rhenish wine. Tennyson in later years had much the same experience. Asked how he liked Venice, he said, 'It was abominable. I could get there no English tobacco.'"

Lectures at the university closed on the hour. The students began to shuffle their feet if the lecturer overran his time. The professor bolts out the instant he hears the bell and the students follow. In about 10 minutes the students for the next lecture begin to appear. The bell then strikes and there is a period of waiting, sometimes a prolonged one. Then like a kicked football the professor bounds in, usually out of breath, and begins his lecture before he reaches the desk with "Meine Herren." A ripple of applause greets his appearance and another at the close of the lecture. In one seminar I attended, the students arose when the professor came in.

I found Vietor's lectures valuable and I should have continued my work with him had not the illness of my wife taken so serious a turn that a further stay in Germany seemed impossible. She had been taken to the University Hospital and Dr. Brauer, their foremost specialist, advised me to take her home at once if her life was to be saved. He thought I had better go by way of England where she could rest before the long voyage to New York.

This note I find in my running comment on life as I lived it: "To-day I found a calendar leaf lying on the pavement and on it was this quatrain:

> Was ist das Leben?—Nur ein Tag!
> Wozu hier so viel Mueh' und Sorgen?
> Wer zaehlet aengstlich jeden Stundenschlag?
> Gleichviel, es end' am Abend oder Morgen.

And this was my translation:

> What is our life? A single day!
> Then wherefore all this care and sorrow?
> Why fearful count the hours that slip away?
> 'Twill end, perhaps, this evening or tomorrow."

It was the day I left Germany with my sick wife.

2

We left Germany with no inkling that war was in the German air and that within five years Europe was to be a flaming hell. Soldiers we had seen everywhere. As we passed the barracks grounds there were always squads in training. Once they were at rifle practice, and they were using as targets, so an old German told me, dummies dressed in French uniforms. "Why French uniforms?" I asked. "They make the shooting more accurate," he answered with a grin.

As I read the German newspapers I was impressed with the spirit of rampant Germanism found in all the columns. The verse published in these papers was highly patriotic. I clipped out a lyric by Freilegrath that stirred even me. This was the last stanza:

Auf, Deutschland, auf, und Gott mit dir!
Ins Feld! Der Wuerfel klirrt!
Wohl schnuert's die Brust uns, denken wir
Des Bluts, das fliessen wird!
Dennoch das Auge kuehn empor,
Denn siegen wirst du ja!
Gross, herrlich, frei, wie nie zuvor!
Hurra, Germania!
 Hurra, Viktoria!
 Hurra, Germania!

CHAPTER XVI

London

HE CHANNEL when we reached it was reasonably quiet, and at Dover my sick wife was removed to the London train with no serious upset. We had made arrangements to spend a few weeks in a guest home at Wandsworth Common, "Rushmere," which we were to discover had for many years been made a veritable *Bracebridge Hall* by Edwin Ransome, a leading member of the London Society of Friends. Reaching Rushmere was like getting home. Nowhere else in Europe had I found such genuine kindness and helpfulness. For years Mr. Ransome had been connected with London gas companies in his youthful days as a clerk, a most remarkable one it seemed to me. In those early days, he once told me, he could add the three columns of pounds, shillings and pence on the long pages of a daybook at a single reading, running up all three at once.

Though over 90 and physically feeble, the old Quaker was still lively, and intellectually as alert as ever he had been. With his white beard and his red Turkish skull-cap he looked like a Hebrew prophet, and he ruled his table like one. His seat, arranged with every conceivable device for comfort, was directly in front of the fireplace, and his plate sat always on a tray-like device filled with hot water to keep his helpings hot. Every evening after supper he read to us a chapter from the Bible and uttered a fervent prayer. His daughter, who presided at the other end of the table, was as able as her father ever had been, a skillful manager of the household, electric in repartee, a suffragette, and a leader among the Quakers. Half a dozen there were in the family circle and very often there were distinguished visitors. The old patriarch ruled the board like an autocrat. I wish I had taken down the table talk of the winter. A Doctor Holmes could have made a volume of it, though perforce it would have required the name *Autocrat of the Supper Table.* The old Quaker knew his London as Holmes had known Boston, and even better I think. Always the atmosphere was intensely English, save for now and then from me polite American objections. He had on all things very positive convictions. The so-called "higher criticism" of the Scriptures filled him with Quaker wrath. "We had a pet monkey once," he said, "and, finding a Bible one day, he tore out the whole Book of Revelations." As a young man he had for a time attended school on the continent and had been intimate with a fellow student who in later years became the writer George Meredith.

He was not in the least in sympathy with the suffragette notions of his daughter, and their debates amused us. "There are four irrefutable reasons against this 'votes for women' nonsense," he would lecture as if before a committee of Parliament. "First, a woman's chief duty is to repopulate the country. Her sphere is the home. Second, if woman had the suffrage it would make wranglings in the home. Third, woman is not the equal of man. As an employee she is not dependable; she is liable to be infatuated; she cannot be reprimanded, for she will always answer back and defend herself no matter how much she may realize that she is in the wrong; when called to task for remissness of any kind, she bursts into tears. A man takes his medicine and profits by it. And, fourth, in my youth I always believed that women are angels and I do not want to revise my ideal."

Here his middle-aged son, a Sunday visitor, put in a word, "Then too the suffrage would put too much power into the hands of the parsons; the women would run to them for advice."

In reality the daughter ruled the board. She argued but little, and when there was the slightest symptom of heat she skillfully turned the current of the conversation. Her flashes of wit kept everyone in laughing mood.

Another source of wit was an Irish lady, like ourselves a paying house guest for the winter. Enthusiasm, fiery dissent, wit, extempore puns thrown out to illustrate a story at the other end of the table came constantly like flashes from a broken electric wire. She was from Limerick and one night alluded to an ancient battle near her native city in which 400 kings were killed.

"You mean 400 soldiers," someone corrected.

"Not at all," she flashed, "400 kings. They were all Irish."

"Four hundred Irish kings. Ireland never had kings to that amount."

"You forget yourself," she flashed again. "Every man in Ireland is a king."

From the old Quaker's knowledge of his native England I got more during the winter than I got from any single course in a university. He lectured constantly like a college dean, opening up, perhaps, with a remark like this: "England is not one, but three. At least, the land like Gaul is divided into three parts. There is the North, as new almost as America. Its capitals are Sheffield, Leeds, Manchester, Bradford. From this section comes coal, iron, cotton and woolen goods. In the center lie the midlands, Birmingham the capital. It is the area of small, independent manufacturers. In the South lies *old* England, feudal England with its cathedrals and rotten boroughs and small farmers. The North went for free trade; the South did not."

His allusions to America often nettled me. When he declared one day that America had wrecked the English language, as completely as the "Pennsylvania Dutch" had wrecked the German language and the Canadian French the language of Paris, I answered him with a trace I fear of heat. "America," I declared, "speaks better English than England does. No two English counties speak the same language, but all the American States use the same English. The language we speak is the language of Shakespeare and the King James Bible. We left England when the language had reached the spacious heights of Queen Elizabeth. You have dragged the language through the mud of London and the dung heaps of peasant Cornwall and Yorkshire. In our public schools we have kept the language pure. In our southern mountains you can hear talk that sounds as it did around the table of Queen Elizabeth. Much of what you call American slang can be found in Shakespeare."

A young "medic" at the table asked me one night at table very gravely if I thought the United States would hold together any length of time now. I asked what there was to hinder its holding. "Why, your trusts, the corruption of your cities, the Negro problem, the iron rigidity of your written Constitution." I told him he read too much muckrake literature. We were by no means perfect, but we were honest enough to admit it. Indeed, we did not hesitate to hang out all our washing, rags and all, for the world to see, and foreigners saw only the rags. Mr. Ransome then took part:

"No republic has ever endured. It is not the right form of government for permanence. It is doomed."

Everywhere during the winter I found criticism and a little of what seemed to me fear. A little book I found in a London shop helped me to meet the English onslaught. It was entitled *Parables of Christopher Cobbleall*, and once I silenced criticism at the table by quoting from it. "What America is today England is to be tomorrow. In the forcing atmosphere of the New World the Englishman has been set ahead centuries. England in the not far future will be following America's lead."

The Englishman, as all know, speaks no language but English, and after a winter with Mr. Ransome I understood why. The born Briton has no need for any other language; other nations learn *his* language, and are anxious to do it. It is for their gain. Mr. Ransome told us once of a boy who refused to learn his French lessons in school. His father, not to be mastered by the boy, said, "I'll remedy that." Accordingly he sent the youngster to a small French village where not a soul knew a word of English, leaving him there for a year. Then he went after him, and to his amazement found that the boy still knew no French. But all the French boys in the village could speak English.

The garden at the Ransome House was surrounded by brick walls higher than one's head, walls covered with ivy or trained shrubs. Around it ran a gravel path beautifully sinuous, bordered with flower beds. Before the door was a fernery with rocks, beyond it a perfect lawn of English sward. Then behind all was the back garden with trees and shrubbery so arranged that no one in any neighboring building could look down into the garden at any point. For years he had planted and planned to secure this absolute seclusion. Everywhere one found curios: stone cupids, carvings from old pillars, lava, coral, and everywhere flower beds—fleur-de-lis, lilies of the valley, snapdragons, everything in its season. All the ivy in the garden had a history; one part had come from the grave of William Penn. Near the house was a fine holly tree, and in the back garden a huge sycamore which showed white among the other trees.

Everywhere were the whims and oddities of the master. The great dining room had been built so as to form in reality a part of the garden. The floor was but a step above its level and the side of the room near the garden was almost wholly of glass. There were no other windows in the room. One could sit in any part of the dining room and see the garden in its whole extent. A weather-cock in full view of the master's seat by the fireplace kept him perfectly informed of the weather—a peculiarly English convenience where the wind is studied carefully to determine the likelihood of a day's sport. The early crocuses and snow-drops and daffodils that sprang up everywhere among the rockeries and beds as early as February were in full view of the fireplace seat. Often he would ask that a chair might be moved from before the windows so that he could see the crocus bed. He had kept a record for many years of the first appearance of all the flowers of his garden, and at the first blooming of a flower he eagerly consulted his record. All through the winter the garden was visited by flocks of birds. Tomtits were his favorites. Baskets of food were hung near the window so the family might see the birds eating their breakfasts at the same time the family ate theirs. The stone bird-bath was alive with birds all winter no matter what was the weather, and they spattered the water out almost as fast as it could be renewed. There were starlings and thrushes (we called them robins), bullfinches and sparrows, and now and then an English robin.

Our Christmas at the Ransome home was a chapter out of *Bracebridge Hall*. Our daughter, Sarah, with the two children Olive and Edward, was called down early to find what Santa Claus had left in her stocking. They came to our door and all shouted in chorus, "We wish you a merry Christmas." The entire family was down to breakfast, the only morning in the year when Mr. Ransome eats with the rest. After breakfast he read the 103d Psalm and offered a fervent prayer. At 10 the drawing room was unlocked and on the centre table were found the presents for the family. For a long time with great merriment we undid our presents, the children highly excited. At two came the Christmas dinner. A 19-pound turkey festooned with a wreath of sausages was the central piece and then in came the great plum pudding which had on it a branch of holly. In this pudding, we were told, there was a ring, a thimble, a button, a sixpence, and a threepence. All were found except the thimble which would have indicated single blessedness on the part of the finder. Evidently the one who cut the cake knew the location of its contents and the proper receiver for each token. When all was over, Mr. Ransome said, "We now come to a custom which has been observed for many years in our family: To each one under our roof we give a new shilling of the current year." There were nine of us at the table and there were four servants in the kitchen. After tea the family got together and played charades and merry games and the children were allowed to sit up until 9:30.

The day after Christmas we found is known as "Boxing Day" and it is universally observed as a holiday. Formerly it was the custom to send boxes to all employees and servants. The custom is pretty well abandoned now, but the holiday still remains.

England to all Americans of British descent is full of experiences and scenes and expressions that come to one with surprise as if from an all-but-obliterated memory of a former life. One finds, too, traces everywhere of characters and objects become familiar through one's readings in English literature. Everywhere in London I caught glimpses of Dickens characters, and in Edinburgh I moved in the world created by Sir Walter Scott.

Everywhere I was told that English and American were two different languages day by day getting farther apart. It was useless to argue about it; argument only reinforces an Englishman's conviction that he is right and you wrong. One is ignorant of one's Americanisms until one tries them upon an Englishman. I remember once on a London street I saw a group gathered about a man lying unconscious in the gutter, no "bobby" as yet having arrived to take charge of the matter. A newcomer sidled up to me and said:

"What's the matter with him?"

"Full, I guess," I answered.

"Full of gas?" he questioned.

Only an American could see any humor in that brief exchange.

2

By great good fortune I had arrived in London in time to experience the closing weeks of a hotly contested general election. I was surprised that it differed little from an American campaign. Party propaganda covered the bulletin boards all over the city and propagandic circulars were everywhere. I remember one cartoon circular representing a red-coated John Bull member of the House of Lords roaring in aristocratic wrath, "What! Tax my land? Taxes are for the poor." Political rallies by the dozen were held every night, all of them addressed by prominent speakers. Mr. Ransome, a man of influence in many quarters, secured passes for me to many of these meetings often with the privilege of a seat on the platform.

One night I heard a Mr. Warren, candidate for Wandsworth, shout with all emphasis, "Those who are looking for a German war are like a blind man in a dark room looking for a black cat that isn't there." That, in 1910. He also scored with bitterness the nobility whose deer parks and land holdings had never been taxed. "Most dukes," he said, "have nothing in themselves that is valuable. They depend on their ancestors. They are like hills of potatoes: the only part worth anything at all is under ground."

One meeting held at Clapham Junction comes back to me with vividness. John Burns, his voice well-nigh gone because of much speaking, was the orator of the night. I had stood in line for an hour and a half, and 15 minutes before the speaking was to begin, the line was allowed to move into the hall between two solid rows of policemen. The line was cut off just behind me and the long line behind was conducted to another hall. As I entered, the great audience now finding seats, already was roaring a campaign song, each person having been given a sheet with the words to be sung. Led by a youngster who seemed like an American cheer-leader, the crowd was bellowing to the tune, "Tramp, Tramp, Tramp, the Boys are Marching":

> Vote, vote, vote for Mr. Warren;
> Turn old Kimber out of doors—

and so for four verses. Following it came another campaign screed, "The Land Song," sung to the tune "Marching through Georgia." To a purple-faced old John Bull jammed close to me on a platform seat, I said, "That's American music. Both of those tunes are American."

"Oh, you've got them over there already? You Yankees are cute. Those songs were made for this campaign, of course, and you say they are singing them in the States already? Just like you Americans."

"But," I replied, "both of those pieces of music were composed in America by native Americans way back in the 1860s, during our Civil War. The one they are singing now is our 'Marching Through Georgia.'"

"Nonsense. Made for this campaign. Rather fetching, don't you think?" And he drowned me out with a roaring "Hurrah! hurrah! We'll knock old Kimber Down," along with the bellowing audience.

Burns was hoarse but unquestionably effective. Much of his speech could have been spoken as appropriately on an American platform as on a British. He pleaded for the common people. "Are we going to be ruled by men who represent no one but themselves, who rule only because they are the sons of their fathers?" And the audience roared "NO!"

"England has reached a parting of the ways," he said, "and no man can foresee what is at the end," but to Burns the two roads where the parting began were free trade and tariffs.

He was emphatically for free trade. With the ports of England open without barrier to the commerce of the world the island would become the "nexus" over which would roll the goods of all the earth. England would take toll of it all, and what multitudes of "clarks" would be demanded to handle the accounts entailed. Burns knew his audience and they cheered him.

Never had I been in a meeting so full of the dramatic and the unexpected. The speakers were heckled at every point sometimes brutally, but heckling John Burns was hazardous business. At one point a voice shouted, " I wouldn't vote for you if you was the Angel Gabriel."

"My dear man," was the instant come-back, "if I was the Angel Gabriel you wouldn't be in the electorate."

Suddenly would come a falsetto voice, "Votes for Women! Votes for women!" repeated hysterically, until two policemen led out a woman who shrieked all the way to the door. Soon another screaming woman had to be removed.

Save for the suffragettes, the meeting made me feel strangely at home. It was like a "pep" mass-meeting held at an American college on the night before the big football game. The leader of the mass-singing was a veritable cheer-leader, dancing about the stage, every part of him in movement, and when the "Marching Through Georgia" series of "Hurrahs" came, he made the audience give them like college yells.

In my journal dated March 9, 1910, I find this: Today I visited the House of Commons with a letter of introduction to John Burns signed by Mr. Ransome. My card was sent in with the letter. At length Burns came stalking out very erect, his head held high, and I introduced myself. His response, shot out abruptly, startled me:

"What are you doing over here?" Then, "Where have you been?"

"For one semester in a German university," I answered. His response came out like an explosion:

"The illegitimacy in the German university towns is frightful." And he poured out statistics and instances ending suddenly with, "Where else have you been?"

"Scotland. All summer in Edinburgh," I said.

"Awfully drunken. Scotland is the only place in the world not affected by the recent temperance wave. London is a sober city." At this point we had come to the House of Lords and a guard came to tell us that it was not open, that the Lords were about to assemble.

"That's right. Do your duty," said Burns. "We'll go out." Then turning to me he said, "Well, you have seen it. Fine room." Suddenly as we entered the old Parliament room he paused, and said:

"See those brass nails in the floor? In that spot unfortunately for us, and far more unfortunately for you, we lost America. There sat the desk of the old house where Chatham and Pitt spoke for you." We went then into Westminster Hall, and into the little room where Cromwell signed the death warrant of Charles I, and then into Stephen's Chapel, where we sat and talked for half an hour. He told me that he considered America the greatest potentiality for evil in the world today. Germany he rated second and Russia third. The root of all our evils was the tariff. It blights the conscience and paralyzes the heart of a nation. "You, in America are ruled by the money kings."

"America," he said, "is the least free of all the nations. You professors dare not say your soul is your own. The university must be divorced from the state and be independent of the rich man or it is a farce."

I tried to defend America and the colleges, but it was not an easy thing to do since he thundered me down at every point. He said the political scandal in New York could not have happened in England. I countered by saying that the very fact that our political crimes are exposed is in our favor. In many lands, perhaps in England, they exist but are never exposed. He said all our evils came in the wake of protection. He had been in America three times and he knew what he was talking about. America had a stormy era ahead of it. He was so brutally severe that I mustered courage and said:

"The trouble with England is the fact that she considers herself eternally right and all the rest of the world wrong.

America and Germany are ready to adopt newnesses, to watch out for the best new thing the world has to offer, and throw the outworn stuff on the scrap heap, but England sticks eternally by the old simply because it is English, don't you know."

"You and Germany have scrapped altogether too much," he roared. "You turn out inferior work because you have no patience to do anything leisurely and well. You make locomotives too fast. Look at your wrecks."

"Yes," I said, "and look at our enormous railroad systems threading all kinds of territory. England is a mere pin-point and her engineering difficulties are small."

"But you have more level country for railroads than any other in the world,"— which avoided my point. Thereupon he opened fire at another angle. Our Negro problem would settle itself, he believed. The race would die out in the presence of the superior race just as the Indian had died out and as all savage nations die out. I replied that the Indian and the Negro were not to be compared for an instant. The Negro race was increasing faster than the white race. For an hour we argued. He impressed me as a man obsessed with a single theory. He has talked free trade until it is central in his thinking. He seizes upon all points that feed his theory and ignores all others. He was brutally positive; he damned the United States as if it were an enemy State; he contradicted me flatly at every point, and then presented his own side in an oratorical way as if he were on the stump. His vocabulary was filled with parliamentary terms. It was evident that he was self-educated with all the restrictions and prejudices that go with such an education. Yet he gave to me, a total stranger, an hour of his time and took pains to conduct me through the Houses of Parliament. He left me with a ticket to the stranger's gallery of the House of Commons and a hearty farewell: "Good luck to you."

As I entered the gallery, Winston Churchill was speaking on some phase of an army bill. He looked like a young man, and I would never take him for a statesman with such prominence as has since been his. He had a halting delivery. The whole debate which followed was far below what I had expected. The members had no desks but sat on benches apparently at random. There were no cries of "Mr. Speaker!" but at the close of a speech several would arise and one of them was recognized by the chair. In the lobby the members lounged about as if at the end of a dinner party, easy and luxurious. It seemed like a casual assembly of gentlemen whose talk had drifted to politics.

3

With the permission of the provost I was allowed the freedom of the London University lecture rooms during the whole winter and I missed but few lectures. The lectures of Professor I. Gollancz on Shakespeare's historical plays I found suggestive. He was a fat, very smiling little man with an effeminate voice and manner. His sentence ends were drawled out in a curiously flat way. Parts of his lectures could be described as "flowery." He lectured with a radiant, seraphic smile on his face, a smile like that of a susceptible old bachelor—which he was. He wore a gown while he lectured and once I saw him in the halls wearing a mortar-board cap. His lectures were attended largely by women.

In mid-February I took lunch with him. He was, I found, Dean of the Arts School of King's College. I waited in the main hall until he came at 1:10 and took me to the refectory which overlooked the Embankment. He talked very little, but sat and smiled and looked far off in an inspired sort of way. We had coffee in the reading room. Suddenly he turned to me his face aglow. "Is 'disgruntled' a good word? One of the professors found it in an American newspaper and asked me about it." I said, "It is not in Shakespeare, as you know, and it keeps in what you English would call bad company, but it has its uses. Most American slang originated in England." He then introduced me to the principal who told me of a case that had just gone wrong in the hospital. A patient had been operated on for a disease that the operation proved was not present, and the man had died. The authorities had made the excuse that every doctor is bound once in his life to make a fatal mistake. "I suppose," said the principal, "a surgeon after a period gets to thinking of his patients as mere 'cases' and treats them as wood to be sawed. Familiarity breeds contempt until some day he saws one wrongly and awakes, and just like the trainman who has wrecked a train, he is intensely careful ever after and should be retained, not discharged." In the evening I heard Mr. Hudson lecture on Ben Jonson, but was not greatly impressed even though I had heard him called the finest extension lecturer in England.

Dr. Gregory Kent, Provost of the University of London, at a meeting in his office February 8, 1910, told me that it was customary for those visiting college classes to leave their cards at the professor's desk at the close of the lecture and speak to him. I found him most cordial. He even invited me to take lunch with him the following Tuesday at 1:15. You may be sure I was there and on time. A man of about my own age, looking like a business man rather than a scholar, alert, quick of decision, I was attracted to him at once. He told me that as good lectures could be had in the University of London as could be had anywhere in Germany, especially in subjects pertaining to English literature. He considered Ker a better man than Brandl. My teacher at Göttingen, Professor Morsbach, had the reputation, he had heard, of gathering vast amounts of material and then digesting very little of it. A Frenchman once said that in Germany the professor lectured to improve himself; in England the professor lectured to improve his student. He asked me if I would like to attend the mass-meeting of the students to be held during the next hour for laying before them the need of a new chemistry laboratory. I said "yes" and soon found myself on a platform with six or eight others facing the student body. Dr. Foster told them that only three times before had there been a mass-meeting of the students and at each of these meetings the object aimed at had been accomplished. One of them had been a meeting of protest against the statue of the dog that had been killed by vivisectors—"the brown dog of Battersea."

I noticed on the bulletin board at University College the offer of £2/2 for a university song. $10 for a university song!

It aroused memories. Dartmouth College once advertised for a song, and I made a try for it. Dick Hovey won it with "Men of Dartmouth." When I read his thrilling song, with the soul of Dartmouth in it, I tore up my poor little try and burned it, lest it be seen.

I attended the lectures of Professor W. P. Ker. His exposition of the *Ancren Riwle* was scholarly and dry, but at times when he touched upon the lyric poetry of the period he was interesting. I liked better his lecture on the dictum of Dr. Johnson that the ending of *King Lear* is too sad. Ker was a man of 55, stiff, solemn, slow. He seemed incapable of smiling. He kept the same sad expression from the beginning to the end of his lecture and he spoke in a hesitating way. There were about 65 in his class, only 15 of them men. When I presented my card at the close of the lecture he seemed interested. We talked of our work and he invited me to take dinner with him March 2 at the New University Club in Suffolk Street. I found him the soul of courtesy, and once or twice he really smiled. For the most part he sat in pre-occupied silence, letting me do the talking, saying "uh," "uh," "uh" approvingly as I talked. He is, I found, unmarried and has been the head of the Department of English 21 years. He said, "Life plays practical jokes on us. I was to have dined three days ago with Professor Butler, and instead I went to his funeral." Of the American authors he would talk only of two, Charles Egbert Craddock and C. G. Leland. Craddock I think interested him because of the Elizabethan elements in the mountain dialect reported in her novels. He had just read a paper before the Royal Society on the early ballads. He believed that they were not created by the common people as generally believed, but by the upper classes who were more or less literate.

4

February 9 we saw *Peter Pan* at The Duke of York Theatre. For me a stage play has three elements: first and greatest, the play itself; second, the presentation by the actors; and third, the stage setting. I had read the play of course and had admired it greatly; the presentation was excellent, but the elaborateness of the stage settings spoiled everything, made it nothing but a marvellous show, a breath-taking spectacle. The introduction of electric light effects revolutionized the staging of plays. The play became no longer the thing; realistic backgrounds were now possible, and the effect on both producer and audience was like an intoxication. To me it was little short of legerdemain, the effects they were able to produce illustrating the Peter Pan world: mermaids on the rock sliding into the sea; the rising moon with its weird lighting effects; the starry heavens; the domain under the ground. Barrie's play disappeared and the stage mechanic's art ruled the hour. When the audience goes away discussing the marvellous scenery, the play has been a failure.

Miss Ransome was eager to have us hear J. H. Jowett of Birmingham who was to speak several times in London, February 13, at the East Hill Congregational Church. No sermon heard by me during my tour of Europe stirred me more deeply. His text was, "He that showeth mercy with cheerfulness." "Mercy to the man in the street means pity. According to the dictionary it means suspended judgment . . . Portia in the play pleaded for remittance from what was legally due . . . But the Mercy of the text is different. One must interpret it in the light of the whole Book of Romans. To take a fragment, a single passage, was like looking at a curlew in a museum. One does not know the curlew till one has heard him in the air over the misty moorlands. The Book of Romans must be looked at as a whole before we begin to interpret passages of it. Coleridge called it the most logical and compact piece of reasoning written by man. . . . Mercy then is a throwing of one's self into the gap in order to close it."

We heard him again in the evening. At that time nothing had been said about a call for Dr. Jowett by the Fifth Avenue Church of New York. Fourteen years earlier I had been greatly impressed in Edinburgh by Hugh Black, long before his call to America.

5

268 After three months in London, we ventured again on a move toward home. My sick wife had improved in the Ransome home, but still was seriously ill. We chose the *Mauritania*, sailing March 12, and were fortunate indeed in our choice, how fortunate I will let an expert, Sir Percy Scott of the British navy, a fellow passenger, tell, "In 32 years on the sea I never before saw 3000 miles where no gentleman was forced to give up his whiskey and soda and no lady forced to part with the roses in her beautiful cheeks."

I saw much of several noteworthy fellow passengers, among them Patten, the famous wheat pit broker who once all but cornered the market, and Vice President Fairbanks, returning from a tour of Europe. Once he gave an address to the passengers, and as he spoke I recalled what John Burns had said to me, "You make statesmen out of small timber in America judging from what I have been seeing of your Vice President Fairbanks."

On April 23 we arrived on the home farm in Bristol, and at once the sick one began to mend, until at the end of the summer she was quite herself again.

I spent several weeks during the spring getting acquainted with Harvard University. I visited classes of Barrett Wendell, Professor Kittredge and others and was bored rather than inspired. Everywhere education by the pouring-in process, the students sitting as passive buckets. In Copeland's classes there was humor enough and enthusiasm enough to keep the students awake, but I saw nowhere an awakening touch between the desk and the desks that impressed me. Education gone to lectures is education gone to seed. Words, words, words, and no human contacts.

The most memorable personage I met was Dean Briggs, who took me for a ride about the grounds. He kept his own horse at a stable and theoretically, as he expressed it, he rode it every day. I found him a delightful soul. He was free and even familiar with the students he met and it was very evident that they all loved him. His face had a way of lighting up most humorously and his retorts came instantly but with never a sting. He told me that aside from two years spent in Europe he had been at Harvard since he entered as a freshman in 1871. He considered the Harvard English Department a vital and a molding one. Administrators, he said, are generally picked from this department because the nature of their work brings close contact with the student. Young instructors hate freshman English, he said, but there is no better training for teachers of creative literature. He recalled how Matthew Arnold emptied Sanders Theatre by reading from his poems. No one could hear him. Afterward he took lessons and improved.

CHAPTER XVII

American Literature Since 1870

*A*s a subject in college curriculums American literature came late, almost yesterday as college history runs.

When attempted at all, it concerned itself only with what may be called the Big Ten: Irving, Cooper, Bryant, Emerson, Hawthorne, Longfellow, Whittier, Poe, Holmes, and Lowell. Thoreau and Mrs. Stowe might also be treated. But not even these were mentioned in many colleges. Princeton as late as 1924 had taught no American literature in class rooms once attended by Philip Freneau, and that same year Katharine Lee Bates of Wellesley wrote me, "The college has not risen to the view that American literature is anything more than a branch of English literature."

Few college instructors were so bold as to suggest a course in *current* American literature. I had started a course at Penn State as early as 1894 and had been allowed to continue it year after year with small classes of Liberal Arts seniors, but it had been no easy task. There was no text-book in the subject, there was little data in print as to the lives of the still-living authors, and little had been said concerning the influences that had affected their varied writings. The more I taught the course, the more it became evident to me that the Civil War had cut a canyon through American history and that a new and distinctive literary flora had sprung up on the hither side of the gulf. The Civil War henceforth, it seemed to me, would have to be the bench-mark for future surveys. Its end had been a beginning, the opening of a new period, and now, a generation later, that period was coming to a close. I had always insisted in my classes that a literary period is a generation, 30 years on the average, three periods each century.

It was time for a history of this period, a pioneer study with the available materials, a foundation upon which later historians and critics with more data might build with permanence. My plan already was made. I had access to the files of *The Critic*, *The Atlantic Monthly*, *The Nation*, *The Chicago Dial*, and most of the other standard magazines where I could find reviews and sketches. The Library of Congress sent me, in care of the college library, any books I might need, a marvellous help in my work. But even with these helps, I was greatly handicapped. The materials I needed were non-existent. There were no biographies of contemporary writers and few reliable biographical sketches. I must look to the authors themselves. Not one of the prominent living writers but sooner or later was either interviewed by me or else induced by me to write letters about themselves and their work.

271

To cite but a single instance of my methods, I wished to get the real facts concerning the literary evolution of Hamlin Garland whose earliest Middle Border tales had greatly impressed me during my senior year at Dartmouth. In answer to my letter he wrote me:

> I am to be in Philadelphia on the 13th and 14th of January, [1914] and if you should chance to be in the city at that time we could talk it all over at the Franklin Inn Club . . . I date my own fictional awakening from 1887, but I was at work on the problem you have in mind for two years. I disagree with Burroughs. I think our real American literature began after 1870. Ibsen, Kipling, Tolstoi, Hardy, and Maupassant were the new influences. But write me at the Players and we'll talk the personal side of this.

As a result I dropped everything, made the long trip to Philadelphia, took lunch with Garland at the Franklin Inn Club, and then, securing a room upstairs, interviewed him during the entire afternoon. Little there is in his *A Son of the Middle Border*, published in later years, that he did not touch upon in this memorable afternoon talk, I as fast as possible taking down his words.

When my volume, *American Literature Since 1870*, came out Garland approved of my report of him and incidentally he approved of my book as a whole, though accounting for its goodness by the material of his own that he alleged to have found in it, material he said that was in his *Crumbling Idols*, which at that time I had never read. Moreover he was quick to say that he could give me no help in floating the book. This he wrote me:

December 4, 1915

Dear Prof. Pattee:

I am rereading your book with minute care, and on the whole I agree with it. I think I see bits of "Crumbling Idols" scattered through it, so it is no wonder it suits me. As you know, I correlated that "Local Color" movement in "Crumbling Idols,"—not as completely as you have done, but I saw it and wrote of it, I think in the *Forum* when Page had it. My publishers told me that nearly a thousand editorials were penned in opposition to my poor little book which was addressed to creative men, as you remember. It did not sell and its message was distorted into an opposition to culture. Hope your book gets adopted as a text book for on the whole it is just, and certainly it is American. If you had not spoken so well of me I could write an article in praise of it but as it is I can only commend it in private.

I still think your Riley chapter is unjust and also that on Howells is not quite adequate. His work is so varied and of such a high general level that it must always stand for the best of its period.

I again express my sincere appreciation of your services to a true Americanism.

HAMLIN GARLAND

This was my reply:

State College, Pa.
December 6, 1915

My Dear Garland:

Again is it borne home to me that the truthful man pays a penalty for his truthfulness. You wrote that if I had not spoken so well of you, you might have written an article in praise of my book. Think of what might have been had I known this earlier, for who would not omit all mention even of Hamlin Garland from his book if as a reward he might have an article, even a damnatory one, from the pen that wrote *Main Travelled Roads?* I am always loaded with wisdom the day afterwards.

It impresses me with the vast change that 25 years have wrought in America when you speak of those thousand editorials which condemned your "Crumbling Idols." My book is fully as radical as yours and it even dares at times to speak lightly of the land of the sacred codfish, yet on the whole the press of the country has been inclined to agree with its ver-

ta, Ga, on the local staff of *The Constitution* began writing negro sketches using "Old Si" or "Uncle Si" as his vehicle, and soon made the character famous. Small, however, was very dissipated and frequently the Sunday morning Old Si contribution failed to appear. Joel Chandler Harris, the paragrapher for the *Constitution* as he had been for the Savannah *News*, was called on to supply something in place of the missing "Si" sketches and began with "Uncle Remus." His first contributions were not folk lore, but local. He soon drifted into the folk lore, however, and recognizing the beauty and perfection of his work, people generally, who remembered the stories of their childhood, wrote out for him the main points and sent them. I, myself, contributed probably a dozen of the adventures of Brer Rabbit as I had heard them. This service he afterwards acknowledged in a graceful card of thanks. Uncle Remus became, soon, the mouthpiece of the generation, so far as the animal legends are concerned, and I do not recall that any of us ever intruded on Harris' chosen field, tho' many of the newspaper men were writing sketches.

Then came the splendid stories of Thos. Nelson Page. I recall distinctly my delight in reading "Marse Chan," "Meh Lady" and "Uncle Edinboro's Drownin." I had been plunging around to find a field, and these stories were my guides and inspirations. I began with "Elder Brown's Backslide" in Harpers (1886) and followed it up with "Two Runaways," "Old Miss & Sweetheart" &c &c. To the success of Page's stories, Harris' and my own, coming at the same time and given a splendid advertisement by the southern press, I attribute the sudden development of the literary spirit in Georgia. In this, however, I should not neglect the fine spiritual influence of Henry Grady. His generous encouragement was behind us all, and he was the personal friend of all. Had he chosen literature instead of journalism and politics, I believe he must have led all, for his ability to seize and combine was marvellous. I used to tell him that if he had lived in the Florentine age he would have been the greatest maker of mosaic tables in the world. But he would have been great anywhere.

Since 1886 there have been developed many writers of stories in Georgia and the southeast. I haven't been able or inclined to keep up with the movement: for my profession never has been literature. As far as I know we all deal with a basis of fact in our stories and the product perhaps should be classed as romantic realism. But there is one big fact behind all of this that has never been touched on.

In the late 30s—1839 to be exact, Wesleyan Female College came into being at Macon,—the first chartered College for women in the world, and soon began to turn out large classes of highly educated and accomplished graduates. The majority of these came from Georgia, but the whole South has always been represented in Wesleyan. Without going into this subject, I wish to state as my personal opinion that Georgia's literary development, which is undoubtedly more extensive than that of other southern states, is due to the intellectual and spiritual soil or environment produced by this College in the 50 years of its existence previous to 1890. You will understand how this can be true tho' the mothers of the State's best known writers may not have been graduates. In my youth, every girl associate I had was of this college. Its atmosphere was everywhere apparent. Today its graduates lead all over the State.

This is a rambling letter and you'll have to pick out from it what you need,—if it is there. I can't venture to name from memory the "Georgia school of literature." Suppose you go to the extensive work on "Southern Literature" gotten out several years ago by the University of Va. It seems very complete.

In conclusion:- my Father died in 1861 while the Sumter guns were busy. His genius was smothered under adverse conditions and in the great break up, forgotten. I shall be glad to bring one or two of his poems,—formerly found in class books,—to your attention if the idea is within the scope of your proposed work.

Sincerely,

HARRY STILLWELL EDWARDS

William Dean Howells never liked my book. He shied away from it even before it was written:

Dear Mr. Pattee:

It *does* seem a little odd to me that you should ask me these questions, but since you ask them I do not mind saying that I thought it to my advantage to change from a Boston to a New York publisher, and it was finally natural that I should go to live in New York. Whatever were the effects on my fiction, I cannot see that these personal facts have properly anything to do with a literary story of the period, and I had no psychological motive in the affair.

Yours sincerely,

W. D. HOWELLS

James Lane Allen's very popular stories dealt with the blue grass region of Kentucky.

166 West 78th Street
New York City
18 February, 1915

My dear Mr. Pattee,

I am sending a brief reply to inquiries made in your letter of 26 December.

(1) I do not think any "influences led me to take up the writing of fiction." I should say that I began to write and have continued to write from natural impulses.

(2) I suppose that the first stories I wrote were written in some measure under the influence, as examples, of the best American work of the time both Northern and Southern, all of which had local color; but aside from local color, American local color, I think my work has always in essential ways been more in conformity with English and French fiction. Because of this allegiance to the great older models—which no new models can ever displace in actual literature—my work is everywhere regarded as not quite belonging to any American group, or school. For that reason, also, all the historians of American literature with whose work I am familiar, when they come to treat it and interpret it, do so with uncertainty as to classification. And this uncertainty is doubtless increased by the fact, that what I have written has been written in entire independence and sincerity—without the least aim of bringing it into likeness to some already recognized type. Typical historians are inclined to slight what they cannot classify—as though classification could possibly mean anything but—so far —the death of originality.

I have no opinion as to "the relative value" of my books.

Sincerely yours,

JAMES LANE ALLEN

Grace King well represents the attitude of Creoles toward the "outsider," G. W. Cable.

1749 Coliseum Place, N. O.
19 January 1915

Professor Fred Lewis Pattee

My dear Sir:

I am distressed at leaving your letter of Dec. 27th so long unanswered. But frankly, I have been too busy to give you the answer you asked. And even now, I am obliged to refer you to the World's Best Literature, for the dates you need.

Monsieur Motte appeared first in the New Princeton Review. (I really forget the date).

I was inspired to write by my love for the South and the feeling that justice was not being done here in the current literature of the country. Cable doubtless gave a true picture of the Creoles as he knew them (mostly quadroons). I have always considered his works a libel on the Creoles I knew. However, he pleased the audience he wrote for, and he has made money. Harris and Page of course wrote from a different standpoint, that of the white *gentleman* as I write from the standpoint of a white lady. Charles Gayarre influenced me in my writing, and so did Lafcadio Hearn, but no one else.

I am not a romanticist, I am a realist a la mode de la Nouvelle Orleans. I have never written a line that was not realistic, but our life, our circumstances, the heroism of the men and women that surrounded my early horizon—all that was romantic. I had a mind very sensitive to romantic impressions, but critical as to their expression.

My "New Orleans the Place and the People" I consider my best work,—I may say the one work I have accomplished. My "Balcony Stories" are valuable for the light they throw on social conditions in New Orleans after the Reconstruction.

Hoping that I have written you something that may be of use to you.

Sincerely yours,

GRACE KING

The Canadian, E. Thompson Seton, now neglected, once rivaled Kipling in popularity.

My earliest wild animal story was written in 1880 [when he was 20] and is not yet published.

In 1885 to 1890 I wrote many others which appeared in St. Nicholas, including the story of a little gray rabbit which I later expanded into "Molly Cottontail." In January, '94, I wrote the story of Lobo. So far as I know, all of these were written before London, White, Roberts, or Kipling had entered the field. I have a letter from Kipling acknowledging having read 'Molly Cottontail' before he wrote the Jungle Books. Jack London and Stewart Edward White were late arrivals in the field. I mean they came in 1900 and later. I do not think Kipling had any influence on my books. I had already written my things before I ever heard of him, and in any case, his humanizing animals by giving them full measure of speech was, to me, a discordant note.

Yours sincerely,

ERNEST THOMPSON SETON

Among the letters that came to me unsolicited after the book was published none pleased me more than that from Thomas Sergeant Perry, the scholarly critic who added so much of value to Boston magazines and literary culture.

November 5, 1915

Dear Sir:

You must let me tell you with what great pleasure I have just read your admirable book on American literature since 1870. Books on that subject I have generally left unread because I have found them unreadable—and as for their number, there have been more books about than in American literature, but yours is very different. I am extremely grateful to you for it.

I won't enumerate the different good qualities of the book, but will only thank you for presenting the subject in so many wise ways. Of course I do not always agree with you, though the moments of difference are few, but always I admire and respect your exposition. After all, what two men ever agree wholly about anything? I beg leave to congratulate you on so good a book.

Yours faithfully,

Thomas S. Perry

Another unsolicited testimonial was sent not to me but to the President of the Century Company, publishers of the book, by Margaret Deland, who wrote pleasant stories of her native Pittsburgh region.

Dear Mr. Ellsworth:

Mr. Pattee's History of American Literature, is like a spring in the "great and terrible land of wilderness and drought"—formed by the war books. I am so grateful to you for sending it to me, for probably (I am so deep in the "terrible land") I should not have been moved to read it. It seems to me a most important book—written with insight and humor and sympathy; and, as one of our little Jews at the Camp said of a girl who was both good *and* pretty—"My God, what more do you want?" Insight, humor, and understanding! They make the perfect critic. It has been a great refreshment to me.

If you come to Boston this winter, don't confine *all* your attention to Gail Coolidge, but come knock at our door!

Cordially and gratefully,

Margaret Deland

November 28th, 1915
35 Newbury St.
Boston, Mass.

From the sheaf of letters received from college men who have used the book none perhaps pleased me more than that from Edwin D. Chubb, Dean of Ohio University:

> I received your "A History of American Literature Since 1870" yesterday and dipped into it at once. I enjoyed reading what little I have read very much. I expect to read a great deal more in it. What I especially enjoyed is your fresh treatment of recent writers. I read, for example, your comment on O. Henry, Agnes Repplier, Richard Harding Davis, Hamlin Garland, and Paul Elmer More. I greatly enjoyed the information and criticism concerning these writers. Perhaps the highest praise I can give after my brief examination is that I feel it is just such a book as I wish I had been able to write myself. I feel pretty sure that I shall introduce this book of yours in a course which I intend to give during the first semester of the coming year.
>
> A book of this sort, giving me so much information and bright criticism concerning writers of our own epoch, will do much to make our students feel that literature does not deal only with the antiquities of the past but that it is something fresh and vital. I am sure our college students will enjoy a work of this sort very much.

The book has had a steady sale now for more than 25 years, one generation, and is still selling.

CHAPTER XVIII

Recording the New England Decline

ℳARY E. WILKINS, more than any other of the New England interpreters, was the voice of my generation, the fifth after the Revolution. We were born within a few months of each other. What she had seen and experienced had been a part also of my own early life. From the same angle and at the same time we had watched the break-up of a regime involving five generations, and had stood among the wreckage with open note-books. My paper in *Sidelights on American Literature* entitled "On the Terminal Moraine of New England Puritanism," an analysis of the work of Miss Wilkins, could be used as a chapter in my own autobiography.

The biographical backgrounds of the different studies I made of her were furnished by her own pen. This she wrote me in September, 1919:

> Certainly here are the 'Few Leading Facts.' Born in Massachusetts: straight American, with a legend of French lineage generations back. My family moved to Vermont when I was still of tender age, and naturally I went too. We lived in Brattleboro, Vermont. Sometimes I wonder if the marvellous beauty of that locality was not largely instrumental in making me try to achieve anything. I lived there until my parents and only sister died, when I was little more than a girl. Then I returned to Randolph, Mass., and made my home with friends. I was forced to work for my mere living, and of course continued writing which I had already begun, although when my father, the last of my family, died I had earned very little. I had written only three stories, that is, real stories for adults. One was a prize story, $50, the others were accepted by Harper & Brothers. I wrote and stories were accepted. I wrote novels, with fair success. I never wrote a 'best seller,' but I am entirely satisfied without that. Most of my work has been done in Randolph, Mass., and here where I came to live when I married Dr. Charles M. Freeman of Metuchen, N. J. I still write.
>
> In answer to your question concerning any influence of other writers which may have formed my style, it may seem

egotistical, but there was none. I did, however, strange as it may seem, stand entirely alone. As a matter of fact, I would read nothing which I thought might influence me. I had not read the French short stories and I had not read Miss Jewett's stories. I read a great deal, but very little fiction except the Classics. Of course I read Dickens and Thackeray and Poe, and some translations of heavy German novels, and translations of Goethe. I also read translations from the Greek. I remember being delighted at a very early age, with some of the Greek philosophers, I cannot remember which. I was on very intimate terms with mythological people. I read Ossian, I read a lot of poetry. But it is quite true that I read nothing which could be said even remotely to influence me. If I had been influenced, I should have written very differently because most of my work is not really the kind I myself like. I want more symbolism, more mysticism. I left that out, because it struck me people did not want it, and I was forced to consider selling qualities. Of course I tried to make my work good along its own lines. I would not have written for money alone. You ask 'what directed you toward the short story?' I think the answer is very simple. The short story did not take so long to write; it was easier, and of course I was not *sure* of my own ability to write even the short story, much less a novel.

I do consider the art of the novel as a very different affair from that of the short story. The latter can be a simple little melody; the other can be grand opera.

I am very glad that 'The Revolt of Mother' has succeeded. I thank you very much for the honor you do me by including me in your Century Readings and I congratulate you upon the success of the work.

I will add, that although I have repeatedly heard that I was founded on Jane Austen, I have never read one of her works.

MARY E. WILKINS FREEMAN

In answer to a series of questions came at once the following disjointed items:

Mr. Kipling went to Brattleboro soon after I went away. I met him there. I had not read any of his stories when I began to write mine, in fact, I do not think he had written those which made him famous.

The name of the prize story was 'A Shadow Family.'

The two stories first sent to the Harpers were 'Two Old Lovers' published in *Harper's Bazaar*, and 'A Humble Romance' in *Harper's Magazine*. I cannot remember the dates.

I wrote no mere *vers de societe*, no more 'Cherries in Blossom.' My dear Sir, do you remember I wrote you that I had to earn my living? I did not write this, but I also had an aunt to support. How could I have accomplished these absolutely necessary feats on poetry?

No 'realistic rush,' no 'Kipling freshness' swept me along in spite of myself. Pen and ink and paper involved slight capital and were most obviously at hand. I sat down and wrote my little stories about the types I knew. They sold. That is really all. Very simple.

You may be right. Given perfect freedom of choice, which I was not given, I might have been a lyrist, but the notes would certainly have been 'intense.' I do not know if I am 'akin to Hawthorne.' I do not care for him as I do for Tolstoi and Hardy. You understand. I have never bothered to analyze myself and fear I cannot. I will, however, state one thing: I do know, and have always known, my accomplished work is not the best work of which I am capable. But it is too late now.

I went to Mount Holyoke one year. Could not remain longer. Was not well enough. Afterwards I went as day pupil to a girls' boarding school in West Brattleboro.

On another page I answer your questions as best I am able. It is difficult for me to reply truthfully to some, as if they did not concern me at all. If I have attempted self-analysis, and of course I must have occasionally, like most people, I have met problems, half remembered powers, half remembered achievements, which might not be even real, but just mythical for we all can invent myths, that I have given up.

As I wrote, I am convinced that the form of expression I have used, is not the best for me, but was forced upon me by my New England conscience, which is about all of New England I own.

Circumstances seemed to make it imperative for me to do one thing and no other. I did not at the time think much about the choice. I think more now. As I wrote, it is too late to consider another choice. I may have years of life left for the purpose, but I am not strong enough for very hard work, have had too many severe colds. Writing is very hard work, as you know, although nobody among the laboring ranks, or the resting ranks, thinks authors labor. I thank you for writing me as you did. I need encouragement as much as when I began. I doubt always results although I never doubt power if rightly used. So you cheer me very much, make me feel quite somebody. You may not believe this. It is true.

My reply was immediate:

>   Your very enlightening and very human letter reached me
> yesterday, and again I thank you for your aid. I think perhaps
> you did not understand me when I said you were caught in the
> current of the realistic rush of your time. I meant that just
> when you found yourself called to support yourself with your
> pen the market called loudest for the kind of work that you
> finally did. Localized studies of real life were accepted more
> surely by the magazines than anything else, and so, like a
> sensible person, you wrote what you could most surely sell. I
> see no reason why 15 or 20 of your short stories are not up to
> your highest powers, and I do not think you need be concerned
> about what you might have done under happier circumstances.
> Personally I consider your New England studies some of the
> strongest work of their period.
>
>   I was born in New England from a Puritan line, even as
> you, and as a result I know the people of your stories as well
> as you do. You, a writer with a Puritan conscience, have writ-
> ten the tragedy of the Puritan conscience, as it may be seen,
> often in distorted form, in the decadent remnants of the Puri-
> tans, and one of them turns critic—that's me—and says that
> your work is well done. I am frank when I tell you that aside
> from *Pembroke*, which is a series of episodes of short story
> quality, you have written no novel that comes anywhere near
> your early short stories. But these are enough. They are
> stronger than Miss Jewett's work, though not so beautifully
> written, stronger than Rose Terry Cooke's, stronger than Gar-
> land's Middle West tales.

2

Note first of all the materials she made use of, the human
derelicts left after the ice age of the Civil War, the industrial
revolution, and the westward migrations; a nondescript miscellany on a terminal moraine: village Lears, abnormalities of conscience, freedom of will become narrow wilfulness, unswerving
allegiance to inherited faith degenerated into balkiness, frugali-
ty engendered by a scanty soil warped into a Silas-Berry meanness of soul, sensitiveness born of isolated environment become
the very essence of sullen pride and egotism, and last, but not
least, a patriarchal sense of masculine superiority and household
headship based on narrow interpretations of the Old Testament
scriptures, which resulted in a type of womanhood often so individual and so peculiar as to be termed unique.

Her characters are predominantly unmarried women—
"old maids." Of the central figures in the 24 stories of *A New
England Nun*, 19 are unmarried females and all but five of them
are past middle age. When the westward exodus came the
father refused to leave the old home or else the mother was too
feeble to go, and a daughter remained to care for them, with
her marriage, while they lived, impossible.

The Wilkins style is Puritanic, even, so to speak, Ver-
montic. It is as bare and as disjointed as a scenario. She usually
concentrates on four persons and a situation and she presents
her material intensely with no more thought of ornamentation
than had her Puritan ancestors with their burning convictions
of sin and salvation. Every coloring adjective is primly removed.

In my study of her in my edition of the volume *A New
England Nun* I painted the Northern New England of my generation and hers. As she depicted it in her tales, so I saw it and
lived it. This was my analysis:

> Her characters are like plants that have sprung up from
> a sterile soil. As subjects for fiction, in the older interpretations
> of fiction, they seem impossible: tillers of rocky hillsides, their
> natures warped by their poverty-stricken environment; old
> maids, prim and angular, who have erected a secret shrine in
> their hearts in commemoration of a moment in the long ago to
> which a more sophisticated maiden would never have given a
> second thought; work-house inmates, forlorn children, practi-
> cal-minded women whom generations of repression have ren-
> dered sexless—the descendants of come-outers, nonconformists,
> dissenters, sons and daughters of the men who survived the
> earlier regime with its blue-laws, its interminable dialectic,
> its grim bareness, and added to all this, generations of solitude
> on hillside farms tilled in the face of nature's protest. The re-
> sult was survivals not of the fittest, but of the weaker elements.
> The young and the adventurous went West.
>
> In these tales we see not the New England of Mrs. Stowe,
> the New England of the high tide era, nor that of Miss Jewett,
> the New England of the transition. In Miss Wilkins' pastels
> we see the New England of the swift decline and the final
> wreckage, the distorted fragments of what once had been glor-
> ious. It is the fifth act of the Puritan drama. A half century
> before, the minister would have been the central figure of a
> New England village picture; in *A New England Nun* there
> are only four ministers mentioned, all of them minor figures,
> spineless and effeminate.

How did this young girl of 25 know of all this human wreckage, of all these grim and desolate lives, of all these abnormalities of soul? There are pages in her work as remorselessly gripping as can be found in modern realism. One might gather them into a New England *Spoon River Anthology*—pictures of senility almost terrifying as in "Louisa"; of the parish workhouse as depressing as Zola, in "Sister Liddy"; of human cruelty as harrowing as Balzac's *Pere Goriot*, in "A Village Lear."

She has answered the question herself. In 1900 when I was editing studies in the *Booklover's Reading Courses*, it fell to me to handle a critique on *Wuthering Heights* written by Miss Wilkins. It has never been republished. In accounting for Emily Brontë she accounted for herself. She wrote:

Hedged about by great spaces of loneliness and unsuperable barriers of religion, in an isolated parsonage with more of the dead than the living for neighbors . . . how she ever came to comprehend the the primitive brutalities and passions, and the great truth of life that sanctifies them, is a mystery. The knowledge could not have come from any actual experience. The book is not the result of any personal stress. She had given to her a light for the hidden darkness of human nature, irrespective of her own emotions. A lamp was set to her feet in the beginning. If a girl of 28 could write a novel like *Wuthering Heights*, no other conclusion is possible.

It was for my generation to see both the glacier that rolled over the generation before me and the terminal moraine that came as a result.

3

New England life as it was lived during the nineteenth century and beyond has been recorded largely by feminine pens. The high tide era lives in the work of Mrs. Stowe and Rose Terry Cooke; the transition period in the stories of Sarah Orne Jewett; and the deserted farm era in the writings of Mary E. Wilkins and Alice Brown.

Of these last recorders Miss Wilkins was the genius. Concentrating with intense soul upon the human elements involved, she worked with dramatic culminations as a Maupassant would have done. Miss Brown, working with the same materials, has been a more kindly observer. She has found spring blossoms on the terminal moraine, "love among the ruins," humor even, and hope.

I have often wished some inspired social science worker could put Alexandria, the township of my youth, into his test tubes and make an analysis of the precipitate. This Miss Brown attempted to do with her Tiverton township tales and what she recorded will live as history and not alone as fiction.

She was a part of the materials which she used. Born in rural New Hampshire, near my own birth date, educated in a small town school house and in a "female seminary," she became at length perforce a school teacher. Literature, as in the case of Miss Wilkins, was seemingly the only avenue of escape, and she tested it at every point. She was nearly 40 when recognition came. *Meadow Grass* was published in 1895. At last she had found the key to the literary times—actuality, human souls laid bare, but always humor as a saving condiment.

She lived with her materials summer after summer. She had bought a worn-out farm on Murray Hill, near Bristol, five miles from my Sabine farm. A neighborhood of abandoned farms on a sightly hillside had been turned into a distinctive summer colony. The old farm-house she had remodeled, the long hen-house across the road she had made into a study, and congenial souls came as visitors, chief among them Louise Imogen Guiney.

Her analysis of herself and of her fellow workers in New England contemporary life has in it revelations. This she wrote me some years after *Tiverton Tales:*

> I am the worst person in the world to formulate anything connected with myself. So far as I know, everything connected with my beginnings 'just growed' like Topsy. (You see you have conjured up Mrs. Stowe and therefore Topsy.) It is almost impossible, I should say, to trace the genesis of one's own work. All I can formulate about mine is that I should have chosen, if I had had enough to live on, to do nothing but verse and plays. I frankly don't know what I think about Mrs. Stowe's influence. I know I read her books when I was quite little, and that I haven't since. I feel that Miss Wilkins's work is the *truest* that has been done about New England. Miss

Jewett's, beautiful as it is, always suggests the library. She writes, I feel, like an observer, while Miss Wilkins calls the very person into the room and makes him talk. I think her first series of stories—Miss Wilkins's—perfection and nothing less.

Need you say anything about *Fools of Nature?* It's no good—the artificial claptrap of a 'prentice. And as to *Meadow Grass*, I suppose I wrote the stories rather fast just before 1895, for I think that must have been when they were published. (But I've no copies of the two books, I own.) I don't really think much of my long stories, and as to the short ones, I like the sophisticated ones far better than dialect! You see I am dropping into this miserable candor to excuse myself for not having anything worth while to say. If you include poetry, do drop a heavy laurel crown on Louise Guiney. She is an immortal—and what a pity we're not all saying it.

ALICE BROWN

One letter more: She has sold her farm on the hill. Sickness in her Boston home had required her continued presence there.

October 19, 1927

Dear Prof. Pattee:

How delightful you have been to deal with, and how the book, sent me by the Century Company, repays your care over it! I am pleased to be in such good company, thank you! and shall enjoy it very much. And you were so good to send me the very faithful picture of my house. It will be the more valued because I have just sold the place and have been up to take away my personal loot, and that chapter is closed. It would have been harder still if the purchaser—a young friend of Kenneth Murdock and altogether delightful—had not seemed, as he does, the very person for the place. He is a business man whose real heart is in music, and I hope he is going to have a piano in the Forge, across the road, where I liked to write.

I was so very sorry to see in the *Boston Herald* that your going back to begin your college year was so sad. What things they do to us, the invisible ministers of life!

Always sincerely yours,

ALICE BROWN

My wife, Anna Plumer, had died near her old home, and mine, September 13, 1927, after a long illness.

To realize what had happened to New England during the years of my generation, compare the work of Miss Wilkins with a feminine novelist born one generation earlier (the same year as my mother)—Harriet Prescott Spofford. She had sought to support herself by writing fiction precisely as Miss Wilkins was to do a generation later. And she had succeeded like few others of her time. Lowell hesitated about publishing her early work: it was too brilliantly written to have come from the pen of an American. Elizabeth Stuart Phelps declared that her *The Amber Gods* made upon her an indelible impression. And yet in the period following the war, the author of the weird classic lost her literary market and was forgotten. Her autobiographical sketch in a letter to me in 1914 is a vital paragraph in the history of later American literature:

> In reply to your inquiry, I may say that at the time I began to write, the great short-story writers, like Poe and others, were no longer living, or like Hawthorne, were silent. I think Mrs. Stowe had not begun her short stories, and Rose Terry had just begun. I think no successor has ever surpassed the best of her romantic or dialect stories. It was some years later that Sarah Orne Jewett with her delicate and delightful art, and Mary E. Wilkins and Alice Brown came with their quaintness and humor. At the time of my beginning, which was in the second year of the Atlantic Monthly, all literature had a high tone, and much that is now a commonplace, would not have been allowed. With the problem and sex novels taste has deteriorated. But I dare say my grandmother would have said the same thing of Dr. Young and Jane Taylor and Hannah More, etc. Possibly the strong emotions of the Civil War had been so strenuous, something that did not require thought, the flippant, was needed to lighten them, and war had made the violent and dramatic seem natural.
>
> You wonder why I did not continue in the vein of "The Amber Gods." I suppose because the public taste changed. With the coming of Mr. Howells, as editor of the Atlantic, and his influence, the realistic arrived. I doubt if anything I wrote in those days would be accepted by any magazine now. A volume of such stories as, "The Godmothers," "A Sacrifice," "Dark Ways," "The Story of the Green," has failed to find a publisher. But I had great happiness when writing on those lines. But I have had pleasure when writing my stories of

homely life, such as those about the elder, and Miss Mahala &c, in their settlement. A Telephone Company asked permission to use one of them, "A Rural Telephone," as an advertisement. And although I like to write stories like these last, yet I cannot say that I am entirely in sympathy with any realism that excludes the poetic and romantic. But I like to read Mr. Howells and Arnold Bennett, while detesting the work of certain of the English women which seems to me degrading both to literature and to humanity.

You ask what I think I have chiefly accomplished. I don't think I have accomplished *anything*, except to have made some hours pass pleasantly perhaps to some readers,—not very many. I have enjoyed writing my *verse*, and Professor Bradley, Professor of Poetry to the University, (Oxford) has given it generous commendation. But I doubt if either of the volumes has come to a second edition. Do not think all this very egotistic? It is in answer to your questions.

I append a list of such books as I remember,—not having them all in my possession I give the dates of those I recall.

May I ask your acceptance of a volume of prose and another of verse,—being all I have by me. I have been told that the story called "The Wages of Sin" has done missionary work.

Very cordially,

Harriet Prescott Spofford

Again she wrote me, this time from her "winter quarters" at the Ludlow, Copley Square, Boston:

Although knowing its faults I have had a kindness for the "Amber Gods,"—partly on account of an incident, more interesting to me perhaps than to another. The story was printed in the first number of the Atlantic after its purchase by Messrs. Ticknor and Fields, and the magazine was sent to Mr. Fields in Florence. He lent it to Robert Browning, who was enthusiastic in praise of the story. When the next number came, (the story had been divided into two parts,) that also was lent to Mr. Browning. The next morning, before breakfast, he came running to Mr. Fields, crying "Oh, Fields, Fields, I hope you didn't think I knew what was coming when I so praised this story!" What was coming was the quotation of passages from his own work. You see it is *nothing*;—but "Did you once see Shelley plain?" It is so long ago that I seem to have nothing to do with it when I remember with what an acclaim that second part of that story was received.

When "Sir Rohan's Ghost" was published there was a critic who read into it all sorts of esoteric meanings that I never dreamed of. I am afraid you have found more in the

"Amber Gods" than I really meant. I was only telling a story. I was quite young, and had been watching a great deal with a person dying of cancer. She had had a career as a beauty, and my whole thought was of too luxurious beauty, pursued to its end, coming to rank decay. "Fruits of the fig-tree, rathe-ripe, rotten rich." I did not know at the time, as I have since been told, that the name of the heroine was, in rabbinical or Cabalistic lore, the symbol of womankind. I wonder if Shelley knew it in his 'Ione,'—to speak of lesser things in the same breath with great. But I am shamed to have said so much of my small wares.

Mrs. Spofford was nearly 80 when she wrote this and was making her home for the most of the year on a small island estate near Newburyport, Massachusetts.

Many have followed these early depictors of the New England decline, but none with the fidelity of the two fifth-generation recorders—Mary Wilkins and Miss Brown who were a part of their own materials. They saw and recorded. Now one later-born can only philosophize. The New England realist now must deal with the foreign elements that have seeped into the Puritan commonwealth, Joe Lincoln, for instance, who has presented the latest chapter in the story of Cape Cod. I who read the first edition of *Cape Cod Folks* and lived through the storm raised by the Cape Codders who thought they had been caricatured, hardly thought I should live to see fiction in which the Cape Codder was represented as a "Portygee."

CHAPTER XIX

Of Hyacinth and of Brimstone*

A N OLD BOOK-REVIEWER, heavy with experience, once said, "Speak softly in your reviews and you will dine in many happy flats," which explains, perhaps, why I have dined in flats so few. One can deal as one will with the books and the authors of early days and make no enemies, but touch the living author's work with unfavorable criticism, no matter how impersonal your approach and how sound your reasoning, and you have made an enemy. Review in caustic terms a man's new book, no matter how worthless it may be, and he will review your own next book in hypercaustics. I have samples.

A generation ago when I issued my first histories of American literature, it seemed to me that literary America was one colossal sore toe and that one could not move without stepping on it. I was showered with letters of protest, the most of them emotional. I had overemphasized Yankee New England, I had belittled Indiana, I had neglected the South, I had mentioned no Negro poet, I had overpraised Mrs. Stowe, I had left out prominent Catholics, and dozens of authors, mentioned in long lists, I had forgotten to notice. As a sample, this from poet Father Egan:

> I approve very much of Prof. Pattee's method in writing his history of American Literature, but I regret that he has not included certain names which Mr. Stedman mentions with honor:—Mr. John Boyle O'Reilly's or Mr. Charles Warren Stoddard's, for instance, or even my own, as a careful writer of sonnets.
>
> MAURICE FRANCIS EGAN

Certainly the church affiliation of an author never once influenced me. The letter from St. Benedict's College, Atchison, Kansas, I present here as a curiosity in literary criticism. It was sent to my publishers:

---

*Revelations 9:17.

Gentlemen:

Pattee's English literature has been handed me for review by Rev. Leo Aaron, whose place as Prof. of English Literature I now hold at St. Benedict's College. For evident reasons, this text-book will never be introduced into Catholic Colleges —neither should it. Let me in all kindness say, that a man who totally ignores all our claims, merits no recognition at Catholic hands. To the 10,000,000 Catholics of these U. S. there are Catholic writers whose names are near and dear names that have left the impress of their greatness. Either Prof. Pattee knows nothing of these writers, or he is not fair enough to mention them, either of which facts is sufficient to disqualify him for the work he has undertaken. What of Brownson, Shea, Brother Azarius, Hecker, Spalding, Hughes, England, John B. O'Reilly, Ryan, the poet priest, whose name is dear to every southern heart, McMaster, Hiskey? To names of less importance, early scribblers, he has devoted pages. Otherwise, the text-book contains good things. But this unfairness is enough to bar it from every Catholic College. Let us hope that the days of narrow prejudice and unfairness are fast passing away.

Respectfully yours,

(Rev.) Aloysius Bradley, O.S.B.
Prof. of Literary Criticism

More noteworthy was the reaction of the Kentucky novelist, James Lane Allen. I had taken especial pains with the seven pages of analysis of his work that I published in my history, parts of it commendatory, and this had been my conclusion:

His work on the whole is the product of a follower rather than a leader. He learned his art deliberately impelled not by a voice within which demanded expression, but by a love for beautiful things and a dogged determination to win in the field he had chosen for his life work. By interminable toil and patience, and by alertness to seize upon every new development in his art, he made himself at last a craftsman of marvellous skill, even of brilliancy. He was not a voice in the period; rather was he an artisan with a sure hand, a craftsman with exquisite skill.

Then had come this letter from Allen, written July 30, 1917.

My dear Professor Pattee:

You, in your History of American Literature, on page 372, writing of the several years ago as of one whose life was was ended and whose record was closed, summed me up and dismissed me to the posterity to which you addressed yourself in these words of total annihilation—in effect:

He was moved by no impulse to express anything within him.

He had nothing in him to express ("not a voice of the period.")

He, by hard work and by the use of tools put in his hands by other writers, was at last enabled to make of himself a successful artisan.

I now have a letter from you in which, wishing me a pleasant summer, you ask me to choose and place at your disposal some selections from my writings to be used by you in a volume to be published and sold for your benefit.

My dear Professor Pattee, I simply cannot understand you, either in your book or in your letter.

I am very truly yours,

JAMES LANE ALLEN

The letter I wrote him in reply, I reproduce here because it defines my position as a critic and because it answers dozens of similar letters received by me after reviews, or critical summaries in my various anthologies, or literary analyses in my various histories:

My dear Mr. Allen:

No letter which I have received in recent years has surprised me more than the letter the Century Company has forwarded me from you. Really I hope it was the hot weather that dictated it. Should I speak slightingly of the members of a man's family circle,—his parents, his wife, his children,— I should be meddling with what was none of my concern and very justly I should be reckoned by that man as an enemy. When, however, a man has published a book, he has deliberately challenged the world; he has forced his creation upon a public that did not ask him for it, and, when once it has been published, it has, except in the very unimportant commercial sense (and that only for a brief period), ceased to be his. The brief lifetime of the author is only an episode in the life of a book. Sooner or later an author must become a mere set of books.

I did what every critic must do if he is to be worthy of the name critic: I told precisely what I thought of your books. I approached them absolutely without prejudice, or, if I had prejudice, it was wholly in your favor. I told what I honestly thought of these books, without a thought of pleasing you or anybody else. You have a perfect right to condemn my standards of criticism, you can lament my lack of judgment, but, my dear sir, you do wrong to expect me to go against my best judgment because it is going to hurt somebody's feelings. God knows we have had all too little of honest, fearless literary criticism in this country. To write me that you simply cannot understand why I should even feel like wishing you a pleasant summer is to imply that I wrote my review of you wholly from my emotions.

As to the truth of what I have concluded concerning your work, that of course time must settle. I have done my honest best after a careful study of every word you have written. I will say this however: my book has passed into the hands of nearly every person in the country whose judgment is worth heeding. It is now in its fourth printing. I have received letters by the hundreds, literally by the hundreds, concerning almost every part of it and there have been reviews by all the prominent magazines and periodicals. In all this mass there has not been a single criticism of my treatment of your work. On the contrary not two weeks ago a review in New York singled out among other verdicts in the book my summing up of you and termed it "an acute study."

When I asked permission to use in my *Century Readings* a selection from *Flute and Violin*,—a book that in my literature I compared even with Hawthorne's best—I had not the slightest idea that I should be considered as having asked you "to place at your disposal some selections from my writings to be used by you in a volume to be published and sold for your benefit." The benefit would have been more yours than mine. *Century Readings in American Literature* is to be a book for schools and will have a very wide circulation since it is to be the companion to the widely used *Century Readings in English Literature*. If you do not care to have yourself represented in a book dealing with the American writers it is immaterial to me. It will make not the slightest difference with the sale of the book one way or another.

I remember at a dinner in May, 1924, Professor Stuart P. Sherman suddenly turned to me with: "What's become of James Lane Allen? He seems to have dropped out completely. I wonder why? We had high hopes of him once." Nine months later, February 15, 1925, Allen died. A generation has gone since that review that so disturbed him, but were I to estimate the man's work now with the 25 years' verdict to help me, I should change it not at all.

Most attacks upon my criticism were winged with emotion or prejudice rather than knowledge of facts. For instance after the death of Muir, I wrote an appreciation of his work and life for the *Century Magazine*. In it occurred this sentence: "Unlike Burroughs, he had named all the birds without a gun." Instantly came letters from women charging me with ignorance concerning "the dear man who in his whole life never killed anything but woodchucks and flies and mosquitoes." In vain I quoted from Burroughs' own writings. In his *Wake Robin* there is much bird shooting. In the article entitled "In the Hemlocks" he records that he heard in the tree-top "a very fine insect-like warble," but the bird eluded him. "It is for just such emergencies I have brought my gun. A bird in hand is worth half a dozen in the bush." And the bird was soon in his hand. On the next page he records the shooting of another bird. Clara Barrus, secretary and friend of Burroughs, was critical but was willing to compromise:

> I have known him 14 years and know that long before I knew him he had said in print that the time had long since passed when he could kill things. Still I know in the first years of his ornithological studies he did kill them, and speaks of so doing in his books. And yet in a fair estimate of the man what has been true of him for the greater part of his life, is unquestionably the thing you would want to emphasize. Of this I feel sure even from my hasty reading of your appreciation of our beloved 'John of the Mountains.'
>
> I had the privilege of being with Mr. Burroughs and Mr. Muir in 1909, through the Southwest and on the Pacific Coast and I know how well you did your work in that Century article.

Once I surrendered, and suffered myself to go into complete reverse. The attacking forces were my own publishers and the *casus belli* was Mrs. Burnett, famous for *Little Lord Fauntleroy*. Let William Fayal Clarke state the case for the prosecution; he was editor of *St. Nicholas*, published by the Century Company:

I venture to register an earnest protest against the comments upon Mrs. Burnett's work which appear on page 388 of the proofsheets of 'American Literature since 1870.' Aside from the fact that these few sentences seem a very inadequate estimate of an author who undeniably has won a place in the fore-front of the writers of to-day, do they not convey a very superficial view of her work as a whole. Certainly I should be disposed to challenge this criticism as altogether too sweeping, and to question every one of its statements; and I believe that this feeling would be shared by every unprejudiced reader of her books. Instead of saying that the "Lass o' Lowrie's" 'had in it elements of promise which never came to fruition,' would you not regard it as one of the greatest initial successes of modern literature? That its author's trend in subsequent writings veered toward a more romantic view of life does not— in the opinion of many critics—imply a lessening of her powers, but on the contrary should be taken as a proof of her versatility. It must be remembered, moreover, that 'Little Lord Fauntleroy' was written originally as a story for children, and surely in this field romance has its proper place. It was, in truth, like many another romance, a 'fairy tale of real life,' and, if it was as here declared a 'failure,' then Heaven send us more such! The majority of readers and of critics, I believe, would predict a longer lease of life for it than for any of E. P. Roe's novels, and quite as 'wholesome' an influence.

Both from long personal acquaintance with her, and a familiarity with nearly all her writings, I would declare, unreservedly, that no author of to-day cherishes a higher ideal of her art, nor strives more loyally to impress the loftiest ideals upon her readers. She has a searching knowledge of the human heart; her characters live for her, and she makes them live in the printed page. Moreover, she knows her England and America as thoroughly as her Lancashire; her instinct for the dramatic is sure and unfailing; she has a rich fund of humor, and her command of dialect and characterization is unsurpassed.

William W. Ellsworth, president of the company, seemed to defend her for her best-selling qualities. It would be poor business to criticise one of the company's "sure-to-sell" artists:

We all feel that your estimate of Mrs. Burnett is not just. I have asked Mr. Clarke, editor of *St. Nicholas*, to write me about it and I enclose his letter. Mr. Clarke has known Mrs. Burnett intimately for 30 odd years. He was on St. Nicholas when it printed what was probably its most successful serial, 'Little Lord Fauntleroy.' Her books are always written on the principle of fairy stories and she does it conscientiously and

she has a right to. 'The Secret Garden' is an exquisite piece of work. 'Little Lord Fauntleroy' has delighted two generations of children and has been made into a very successful play. The 'Century' has printed 'The Shuttle' and 'T. Tembarom' as serials within the past few years, and both stories have been liked far beyond the ordinary,—each has sold in book form over one hundred thousand copies. If it is true that the chief evidence of life in a novel is that it lives, I am sure that 'Little Lord Fauntleroy' is very much alive,—and I hardly think that can be said of any of E. P. Roe's books. This great sale of 1,400,000 which you speak of was brought about by editions of his books issued as paper pamphlets, 100,000 each, and sold at very low prices. We all hope that you will feel like making some change in your estimate of Mrs. Burnett.

As a result, I toned down my estimate until it satisfied the publishers, but I did it largely by the excision of such phrases as 'over-sentimentalism' and 'lack of restraint.' My final estimate I did not change: "She has been exceedingly popular, but she cannot be counted among the original forces of the period."

Criticism that can render its verdicts like a judge on the bench, unmindful of the personal feelings of the author or friends or agents and unswayed by the critic's own prejudices, is somewhat rare. Mr. Ellsworth, always most considerate and kindly in his dealings and judgments, seemed to rate the final value of an author by his book sales. He urged me to include in my fiction chapter "Frances Little" (Mrs. Fanny C. Macauley) "whose *The Lady of the Decoration* was a tremendous success."

Many things militate against the honest critic. Professor Henry Beers once told me that his biography of Willis was not at all what it would have been had the Willis family not threatened suit if he told what he knew.

From the files of the Century Company I was able to settle finally one of the literary mysteries of the early '70s—the authorship of the "Saxe Holm Stories" published in *Scribner's Monthly* and then issued in two series in book form. Helen Hunt Jackson had denied vehemently that she wrote the stories, and had even published a positive denial in the New York *Tribune*. As a result of this signed denial the publishers kept silent their knowledge and the affair died down. However, the entire correspondence has been in my hands. Two letters are enough:

Dear Mr. Seymour:

I shall have the next Saxe Holm finished by a week from to-day. I have been at work on it for three months and I do very much hope that it is the best one I have yet written. It will be about 700 pages of my Mss.—or about 80 pages of Scribner's. There are 12 poems in the story, some long and some short. Reckoning the story at 80 pages—it will be worth $960—and the 12 poems I will reckon at $10 each although they would bring me $15 to $20 each if printed under my own signature. That makes $1080 for the whole. I hope it will be worth that much to the magazine. Now would you be willing to send me $800 at once on account of this story?—The remainder whatever it may be—(the pages may be a little over my estimate or a little under)—to be paid on the completion of the story in the Mag. I expect to start for the East on the 10th of June—and if I can have that money now, it will enable me to carry out a project which I much want to accomplish before I leave.—I know I am asking a favor, but the manuscript will be in your hands by the time the money reaches me, unless some accident intervenes;—and I shall willingly wait for the remainder, till the last no. is printed.—The title of the story is "Mercy Philbrick's Choice"—and it is a story which I have been thinking over for a long time. Mr. Jackson says it is far the best of them all: but I suppose he is not an important judge.

I propose also, if you approve, to send you at the same time, a short and graphic account of the "Claimants" to the S. H. Stories—the letters of Mrs. Burleigh & Miss Katharine Gray to the Woman's Journal & the Commonwealth—Saxe Holm's replies to them—their singular silence—&c.—the young woman in New York also ought to come in. & her patron the Jeweller.—this whole can now be signed sealed and delivered by *Saxe Holm* himself, herself, itself—themselves— & published under the authority of Messrs. Scribner.—It is really time to put a stop to that Ruth Ellis business & the rest. I have had half a notion to go and see Ruth Ellis. She is the worst liar of them all. It is certainly the most inexplicable thing I ever knew. Three women in different parts of the country all claiming to be the author of stories they never wrote! You would know best how this "History of the Claimants" should be published. I think in the N. York Tribune—all the papers would copy it: and I think it would be *huge* fun, besides advertising the new story splendidly.—I hope Dr. Holland will be able to begin the publication of the story soon—It will take seven nos. —two chapters a no.:—I would like to bring out the volume next spring:—this and the other two stories already printed.

yours truly

HELEN JACKSON

Dear Dr. Holland,

Perhaps Saxe Holm has been a little spoiled.

Then in charity recollect that he she or it has been again and again in the course of the last year and a half by both Editors and Publishers asked to write another story.

This is a little excuse for his her or its being so sure that the story as soon as done would be welcome. Secondly:—as to the "prepayment."—The Scribners have always paid "on acceptance." The manuscript would have crossed the money on its way had the money been sent as requested: and about one third the price of the story was not to be paid for some months. Therefore the proposed arrangement does not seem to me a "pre-payment." Mr. Seymour (or Smith) sent me the money for one of the other stories, in the same way, when I wanted money for some special purpose: the check was mailed the same day I mailed the manuscript.

So much by way of explanation and apology. By this time you will have perhaps read the story and have decided whether you wish to use it, and how.

Of course it has, for me, a present and intrinsic market value, and I am sure I need not say that I should be extremely sorry to have you feel the slightest hesitancy about declining it if it does not please you.

I should be glad to know as soon as possible what your decision is. With many thanks for your kind letter, I am

yours truly

HELEN JACKSON

It is interesting to know that *Mercy Philbrick's Choice* was published in the autumn of 1876, not in Dr. Holland's magazine as she had wished, but anonymously by Roberts Brothers of Boston in their "No Name Series."

2

The jittery period of the 1920s and early 30s was rendered sensational and picturesque by H. L. Mencken, who found the language lacking in superlatives and who wrote criticism with a bludgeon. His motto, so he announced, was "Stir the animals up!" Who the animals were he explained in his "Free Lance" column in a Baltimore newspaper: "General aim: to combat,

chiefly by ridicule, American piety, stupidity, tin-pot morality, cheap Chauvinism in all their forms. Attacked moralists, progressives, boomers, patriots, reformers, and finally Methodists, etc., by name."

His weapons were words of his own invention, outrageous barbarism, wholly new. In his own exposition of his art, he said: "Invented many new words and terms. e.g., chemical purity, osseocaput, Baltimoralist, smut-hound, honorary pall-bearer, snoutery, Boy Scout snoutism, snouteuse, boose-hound, malignant morality,—some of which got into circulation."

Indeed they did. They struck the English departments of the colleges like a flu epidemic. Themes came in now written in Menckenese. A literary revival struck Penn State which to that time had been a "Sahara of the bozart."

Having studied his early work, his *Book of Prefaces*, his *Damn—a Book of Calumny*, and the files of his magazine, I made a study of the man, based wholly upon his writings, and I published it in my *Sidelights on American Literature*, 1922, with the title "A Critic in C Major." In the article I had said: "I finished the book [Prefaces] with gusto though its ram's-horn roared against every wall I ever had stood upon. I am of the Puritans for five generations, I am a Methodist, I am a college professor: imagine the massacre of this book in a future number of *The Smart Set*."

There was no massacre. Instead there came this letter:

Dear Dr. Pattee:-

    I have just read "Sidelights on American Literature": the first book to greet me on my return from Europe. Your treatise upon my own crimes and misdemeanors seems to me to be a very excellent piece of work—well thought out, and competently and persuasively done. I incline to think, indeed, that it is quite as close to the fundamental truth as criticism ever comes. I have only two caveats to file. First, you greatly overpraise my early verse, which was chiefly done when I was 16 or 17 years old and is plain mush. Secondly, you assume erroneously that I have (or, rather ought to have) a cultural purpose. Unless I am badly self-deluded, I actually have no such purpose. My only conscious aim in writing is to get relief from internal pressure. In some obscure and unintelligible way I get satisfaction out of formulating ideas, putting them into words, discharging them upon the air. The thing is not unrelated, I suspect, to the physiological satisfaction that follows emptying the bladder. And there is equal lack of interest in the subsequent fate of the irritant discharged. So far as I know, I have never tried to convert anyone to anything, nor have I any sense of public duty.

On page 159, in your capital chapter on Jack London, you argue that the late war proved the falsity of the doctrine of force. This position puzzles me greatly. It seems to me that if anything in this world is clear it is that the war proved the exact contrary. If the Germans had won, they would have forced their peculiar delusions upon the whole of Europe. Having lost, they are forced to accept, at least formally, the peculiar delusions of their conquerors. Certainly you do not hold that the doctrine of force is not in full effect along the Rhine, and in such places as Silesia. I am just back from Germany. Not one educated German in 50 actually believes in democracy. Yet brute force compels him to act, at least temporarily, as if he did.

Which brings me to a small piece of business. The Amerika-Institut (Universitatsstr. 8, Berlin N.W. 7) wants your book, "A History of American Literature Since 1870" and simply can't afford to buy it. Would you care to send it? If so, have it addressed to Dr. Georg Kartzke. I am sure he'll be delighted to have the "Sidelights" also. All the German universities are woefully short of books. To remedy that lack Kartzke and his associates are trying to maintain at least one centre where the chief current American books may be consulted. It is astonishing how, in the face of incredible difficulties, German scholars keep up their enthusiasm.

Meanwhile, my congratulations on a very good piece of work. I had long had in mind a plan for a full-length essay on O. Henry. Now you have done it, and better than I could have done it.

Sincerely yours,

H. L. Mencken

His reference to his poetry delighted me. I had after long search resurrected a copy of his *Ventures into Verse*, a youthful venture, which he considered extinct, since he had bought or stolen every volume of it he could locate. Curiously enough he forgot that the copyright law demands two copies for the Library of Congress and he had secured only one of these. The other I borrowed and reviewed in my volume at length, largely to irritate him. But in it I actually found some distinctive lyrics from one of which I quoted this stanza addressed to Kipling:

Sing us again in rhymes that ring,
    In Master-Voice that lives and thrills;
Sing us again of wind and wing,
    Of temple bells and jungle trills:
    And if your Pegasus ever wills
To lead you down some other way,
    Go bind him in his older thills—
Sing us again of Mandalay.

Master, regard the plaint we bring,
    And hearken to our prayer, we pray,
Lay down your law and sermoning—
    Sing us again of Mandalay.

That was the beginning of a delightful long-distance friendship which still continues. Many times he invited me to Baltimore:

> Now that you have got in motion you must put down Baltimore as your next port of call. My cellar would make an archbishop break down and weep. It even includes absinthe. Also, some capital malt liquor. My private physician will keep watch on you. It is too bad that I was not in New York when you were there.
>
> After writing you, I discovered a fearful howler in your essay. I refuse absolutely to tell you what it is. Wait and suffer! The exposure of it, to be made anon in our great family and moral periodical, will rock the nation. If you do not commit suicide it is because you are shameless.
>
> I agree with you fully about the war. The amazing thing in Europe is the extent to which the United States is hated to-day. In England it is especially visible. The cause lies in the feeling that the United States made a large money profit out of the war. I incline to think that this is true. In any case, the English are full of bile, and the Continentals seem to be but little behind them. The American tourists who swarmed everywhere the past summer, flashing their dollars, completed the business. Their doings were inconceivably gross and irritating.
>
> I came back with the firm conviction that another war is not far off, and that it will be of extraordinary fury—one bad enough to make the last look like a debate before a Chautauqua.

In due time I learned that I had quoted from the column jointly edited by Mencken and Nathan a paragraph written by Nathan and had quoted it as written by Mencken. I wrote at once:

Some time ago you wrote me that you had found a 'howler' in my critique. I find now that this 'howler' consisted of a quotation from Nathan attributed to you. This quotation I took from your hermaphroditic column in the Smart Set. To have a quotation from Nathan attributed to a fellow is not a 'howler': it is a tragedy. The peculiar awfulness of the thing grows upon me. I advise suicide, and at once. F. L. P.

Mencken agreed and suggested a plan:

I make you a fair proposal. Let us go to Naples together, fill up on the excellent Lacrimae Christi there on tap, and then jump into the crater of Vesuvius. My knees begin to crack every time I try to walk. Please don't suggest that we take C along. He deserves no such noble finish. Let him be taken out to the Jersey marshes and shoved in.

It is years since I last spoke to a poet. They used to hang around my office, picking up cigar stumps, but I had them chased away by the Polizei. Lindsay was a decent fellow in his early days, when he worked for the Chicago Street Railways as a curve greaser.

You were far too gentle with Garland. He needs the ax.

Once in great glee he sent me a clipping. I had been interviewed, and he had clipped this paragraph from the published interview in the New York *Herald Tribune*, July 13, 1924:

"Dr. Pattee is a rather tall man with sandy hair, now tinged with gray, and a drooping mustache of the same color. His features are rather irregular, but are quite forgotten in conversation. He talks in a pleasantly modulated tone, with expressive facial movements and gestures of the hands. He does not monopolize the conversation, and has an admirable habit of stopping with a questioning look at the end of each remark, which may reasonably provoke reply from his listener. In fact, he has none of the dictatorial or oracular habits of mind and expression. What he does say is spiced with humor, which arises as much from his gestures as from his words, and it is often pointed, although never malicious."

Pasted on it was Mencken's comment:

Dear Pattee:

Thank God, you are a handsome man! Why don't you come down here some time and give the cuties a debauch? I have a can of Frank Harris' moustache dye, if you want it. It produces a superb gun-metal finish. My cellar is holding out beautifully.

Have you composed anything of late that would fit into the American Mercury? I surely hope so.

Send me your portrait. Let me have it at once. There is a place for it on my wall, between Coolidge and Lillian Gish.

In exchange he sent a photograph of himself taken when he was five months old. I asked for a photograph of the bronze bust of H. L. Mencken, made by Annett Rosenshine, at the Neuman Print Rooms, and got this:

I'd send you a copy of the bust at once, but unluckily the original has been acquired by Bishop Manning for the Cathedral of St. John the Divine, and he refuses to authorize copies. Perhaps it may be possible, after the thing has been put up in the Guggenheim chapel, to sneak up some night and make a cast. A number of beautiful women have applied for copies.

It will stand in the Cathedral between the busts of Henry Morgenthau and Otto Kahn. They are very strict, High Church Episcopalians, as I am.

The clipping bureau deluges me with notices of your book. I note with great satisfaction and renewed faith in God that it is getting some rough and waspish notices. That is your just punishment for attacking me so foully. I believe in retribution. The end is not yet. You will be in jail for bootlegging before you hear the finish of it.

What have you in hand or in mind that would fit into the American Mercury? Isn't there something to follow the excellent Cooper chapter? . . . I am listing you in the March Mercury among men who ought to be put to death. It is in a book review.

No editor ever accepted manuscripts with more heartening words than he. A letter like this brings "Life's brightest moment" to a much rejected author:

Dear Pattee:

I have been in New York all week and did not receive your MS. until last night. This morning I staid home from church in order to read it, despite the fact that five converted bootleggers were to be baptised. I like it immensely and am sending it to Nathan at once. It is, in fact, very high-toned stuff. I think it will fit into our great moral perodical admirably. My best thanks for the chance at it. But the title, I fear, is too long. We can set only one line, and our limit is about 32 letters and spaces. Will you change it?

Constantly I received from him calls for copy:

> It is a very long time since you last adorned our great
> family magazine. Have you anything in hand? If so I certainly
> hope you will give me a chance at it. The Melville was superb.
> I am at work on a book—of an idealistic tendency.

Earlier he refused an article of mine on Garland:

> Garland is such an obnoxious fellow that I don't want to
> mention him at all if I can help it. His conduct in the Dreiser
> case seemed to me to be not only silly but also downright dis-
> honorable. He is, in brief, a cad and a jackass, or I misjudge
> him sadly.
>
> Haven't you something else for our great moral periodi-
> cal? I surely hope so. It seems to be doing very well. We have
> had to reprint the second number as well as the first and sub-
> scriptions are pouring in. We'll probably go beyond the 25,000
> circulation in the third number. In a year the *Atlantic Month-
> ly* will be busted and Sedgwick will be in the poorhouse. It
> pains me to think of it; he is an old friend.

Years later, May, 1937, it was, at a dinner party given by
Mrs. Clinton Scollard, Richard Burton, then a professor at
Rollins, flashed angrily at the mention of Hamlin Garland who
had once served with him on a committee of award. "He would
always come to the committee meeting," he said, "all agog over
a totally impossible candidate and he would argue for the man
till he tired everybody out. Once Garland agreed to a committee
meeting to be held at three o'clock. Garland did not come; no
final business could be transacted without his vote. The committee waited and the man arrived one hour and a half late. Asked
if he did not know that the meeting was to be at three, he defended himself with the excuse that when he had agreed on that
hour he had forgotten a previous engagement with a school girl,
and of course he could not break an engagement like that. 'But
the committee meeting,' they had chimed, 'why hold us here an
hour and a half, a whole committee, for one school girl?' Garland had looked at them in surprise. 'But just think,' he had said,
'what it is going to mean to that girl all the rest of her life, that
hour all alone with me. Oh no, I couldn't deprive her of that.' "

Mencken was constantly suggesting subjects for me to
treat in articles for *The Mercury*.

What have you in your lockers? Does this suggest anything to you: in every decade there are men and women who make great successes and who are hailed as geniuses, and who then disappear completely. Why not an article on those who did so in the '80s. Howells must have discovered and hymned at least 40 head of them. You have all of the material. I name a few: H. C. Bunner, E. A. Uffington Valentine (poet), Charles G. D. Roberts, Lloyd Mifflin, Julia Magruder, Harry Thurston Peck (really a clever fellow), Bertha Runkel.

And again:

So far as I know, no one has ever thought to make a scientific examination of what might be called the writers of the second table: for example, Opie Read, Harold Bell Wright, the Rev. Charles Sheldon, Julia Magruder, Miss Braddon, Mrs. E. D. E. N. Southworth, etc. I have glanced at them, but not gone further. All the histories of literature are silent about them, and yet some of them have exerted immense influence. Think of Edgar A. Guest and Dr. Frank Crane, not to mention Brisbane. They are sneered at by the intelligentzia, but they are read. I throw out the suggestion.

And again:

Haven't you something in mind that would fit into the Mercury? I make no suggestions because I don't know how your ideas are running. In general, we want to stick to living men and living issues—always American. No Dial translations and importations of ideas! Amerika ueber alles! The treatise on literature under democracy looks very interesting. When will you complete it?

A kindly soul with a wicked pen, with his many cheery letters he brought picturesqueness and laughter and often wisdom into the monotonous life of a mountain teacher and writer.

CHAPTER XX

New England Moves West

THE SUCCESS OF MY *American Literature since 1870* volume brought many summer school offers, and hardly a summer for the next 20 years but found me at some college or other. My first summer school had been at Dartmouth College in 1905, where I had given three courses, three teaching hours each day. For several years I taught in the Penn State summer school, and in one of my classes there I actually brought down the house. I was presenting Timrod and was reading his lyric "The Cotton Boll." Into the poet's final petition I put considerable force:

> Oh help us, Lord! to roll the crimson flood
> Back on its course, and while our banners wing
> Northward, strike with us! till the Goth shall cling
> To his own blasted altar stones, and crave
> Mercy; and we shall grant it, and dictate
> The lenient future of his fate
> There, where some rotting ships and crumbling quays
> Shall mark the Port that ruled the Western seas!

And at this precise moment the entire plastering at the top of the room fell with a crash upon the 30 teachers who were taking notes as if a prophet were speaking. Screams and sobs and a dense cloud of dust filled the room, but, by a miracle seemingly, no one was seriously injured.

Beginning with 1917 for two summers I taught in the University of Illinois under the direction of Stuart P. Sherman, Chairman of the English Department. To be in the Middle West was to me a new sensation. Never before had I been west of the Alleghenies, and the vast sweep of the corn fields to the horizon took my breath away, especially so when the summer hot wave smote the cornfields. I had known heat in Philadelphia and New York City, but this had additional horrors. The growing corn exhaled a humidity that is indescribable. The natives, however, seemed to enjoy it. Hot as it was I managed a limerick:

I remember one sizzling morn
How I wished I had never been born,
  And how all shook their head,
  And quite witheringly said,
"Don't you know it is good for the corn?"

To this a bright colleague on the teaching force added a foot-
note: "They pray for Hell that they may have hogs."

The college I found highly enjoyable. First, there was
Stuart Sherman, vigorous shoot from the old Harvard stump
transplanted in the corn loam, but sending down no taproot.
With him in the English Department I found Ernest Bernbaum
who boasted that never in his life had he written a rhetoric; and
Jacob Zeitlin, profound scholar but yet human; and old Professor Dodge, authority on Lincoln, who, asked at one time to
coin a slogan for a dinner that was to be given certain old
members of his order, wrote this, "The Old Guard dines but
never surrenders." Dean Babcock, too, was a dean one could
admire and even love. My classes were mostly girls, better
always in literature than boys.

During my second summer at Illinois, the war summer of
1918, my wife and daughter were with me. College closed in
April at Penn State and most of the male students went into
war work. That was a summer greatly different. For the first
time in my life I became conscious of geography even to the
extreme of joining a summer school course dealing with the
physical geography of Europe. President James told me that
academic specialists in the subject of geography were rare. He
knew of but seven of highest rank in the whole world and three
of these had recently been killed in battle. He had for a long
time, he said, been trying to find an adequate professor of geography for the university, but so far in vain.

The atmosphere at Champaign and Urbana during this
battle summer of 1918 had been described for me before I arrived for my work. Mervin J. Curl of the English Department
had written me in May:

> We are fairly swamped with war lectures and movies and
> Red Cross sessions, and talks at fraternity houses, and beat-
> ings of the bushes for stray German rumors, and trying, to the

utmost of our powers, to make the good people of Illinois see that there is not a drop of Germanity in us! Oh, the duties of a State University! But I reckon we'll pull through, for Prexy is a shrewd old customer.

"Prexy" was President James whose success in winning funds from the State Legislature had made him a national figure. The personality of the man, his ability to be all things to all men, to sit in hotel lobbies during legislative sessions and make himself the center of legislative and lobbyist groups which might have assembled about him as enemies but which dispersed always as friends, was the talk of the campus. The almost hypnotic power, the ingratiating charm of the man, I once felt to the full. I had not once thought of seeking a professorship in the university. Hamlin Garland had once deplored my isolation at Penn State,—isolation almost total from the literary world in which, he said, I should be taking an active part. Once he had written me, "I am sorry to have you settled there in State College. I want you to go on with the work which you are doing for American literature. No one is doing just the work you have in hand and few have your outlook. Whatever you do, do not fail to go on with your critical work." But at the age of 55 I considered myself located for life.

Dean Babcock, however, as later I was to learn, abetted by Professor Sherman, wished to offer me a professorship in the university, but professorships must have final approval by the president of the university. Accordingly, not knowing in the least what was in the wind, I was favored with a dinner invitation to the president's home. One other summer school professor from another institution was also invited. Neither of us had the slightest inkling of why we had been chosen for such a distinctive honor. The president gave us the impression that loneliness oppressed him in the home that had been desolated by the death of his wife and that he desired to relieve the tedium at times by inviting in congenial fellowship. The three of us made up the entire dinner party. No longer was our host the president of the great university. He was jovial beyond belief. He could even tell in highest spirits how as a student at Harvard he had ascertained by grapevine telegraph methods the name of the Greek classic that was to be used as text-book the coming session. This professor always changed his classic from term to term, taking only such texts as were not to be found in an English translation. Having learned, as he thought, what the coming classic was to be, young James had spent the summer translating it and having it printed for sale to the members of the coming class. On the opening day, however, the professor had announced a quite different classic.

The president seemed much interested in my residences in German universities, showered me with questions, and for a time made us relive with him his own German university days. He won us both completely, but neither of us apparently won him, for nothing was said to us about an Illinois professorship. My failure to win the German Ph.D. was undoubtedly the obstacle that debarred me.

2

The war in Europe was now at high tide, and I was eager to be in it. My boyhood days during which the great Civil War had seemed to me glorious and romantic beyond all expression were alive again, and again I was dreaming. My brother Charles was a "Y" secretary at Camp Devens and my daughter Sarah had taken a full course in automobile mechanics, working as a government apprentice, had passed the course, and was ready to go into service when called. I took my physical examination at Urbana, passed it easily, and on my return East was at three different times under inspection at the "Y" headquarters in Philadelphia and New York.

Always was there delay; always red tape. I would be given a date and an hour, and often I would be called into the office a full half-day after my appointed hour. The ante-rooms were always crowded with applicants, often a hundred or more.

Finally I was chosen. That I was a teacher of experience, that I had long served as a department head in the college, and that I could speak German and to some extent French, seemed to be my qualifications. I made all arrangements at the college, said my goodbys to all, including daughter and wife, and was ready to sail. Suddenly an error was discovered. My blood pressure had not been recorded on my medical inspection blank. It had been omitted by accident I knew, for I remembered distinctly that the doctor when he had taken it, had said it was fine. But the blank had to be filled and they sent me to the "Y" medical examiner who, to my consternation, refused to pass me. The armistice had come and the "Y" it seems was frantically cutting down its quota to be sent abroad. Undoubtedly I was not up to passing point at the moment the "Y" doctor examined me. I had been under emotional strain, I had not slept the preceding night, and to bolster me after saying goodby to my wife I had drunk two cups of strong coffee at the station restaurant. Then I had been examined. Two days later our family doctor found my blood pressure normal. I was bitter at first; I was angry for days; but soon I became reconciled. Now it seems to me as if the Hand of Providence had made that blank space on my medical record sheet.

3

Once again in 1923-24 I was to be at the University of Illinois, and this time as a professor in charge of graduate courses in American literature. Several elements had combined to bring this about. Ever since the issue of my *American Literature since 1870* volume I had put all of my efforts upon the field that it had opened. In 1919 I had published my *Century Readings in American Literature*, a text-book for schools with this introduction:

> The recent manifestation of American patriotism, the new discovery by Europe of the soul of America, and the new insistence on the teaching of Americanism in our schools and colleges, especially in those that for a time were under government control, has brought the study of American literature into the foreground as never before. More and more clearly is it seen now that the American soul, the American conception of democracy,—Americanism, should be made prominent in our school curriculums, as a guard against the rising spirit of experimental lawlessness which has followed the great war, and as a guide to the generation now molding for the future.

The book was adopted in a surprisingly large number of colleges and schools; three complete revisions have since been made of it, the last a totally new creation. After the first world war there had come an increasing demand for what in general were called "articles" for magazine publication. There was a growing demand that books worth reviewing at all should be given for review to the specialists best fitted to deal with them. Furthermore, it was more and more insisted upon that these reviews were to be paid for and signed with the reviewer's name. It was a tremendous step in advance. According to one critic it opened a new essay period: "the essay is coming back again." It greatly helped H. L. Mencken, soon in furious eruption, his volumes entitled *Prejudices* growing rapidly into a series. Stuart P. Sherman was also putting forth volume after volume of critical essays. In 1922 I gathered my own magazine articles to date and issued them as *Sidelights on American Literature*. Later I made another gathering, entitling it *Tradition and Jazz*. In 1923 I completed a *History of the American Short Story* which was issued by Harper and Brothers.

I had long had in mind a complete history of American literature of which my *Literature after 1870* was to be a unit. One volume at least would bring the history up to 1870 and a third would treat contemporary writers and movements. I had had an interview with Stuart Sherman and not only had outlined to him my plan, but had intimated that I might spend my delayed sabbatical year at Urbana since my daughter was there as instructor in the landscape department, and since the university library there was well equipped with materials I should need in my study. His reply to my suggestion was prompt:

Dear Mr. Pattee:

Having just finished reading 1400 pages of manuscript for my graduate class, I take up my pen to say that I am sorry on our account that you could not join us this coming summer—that is the staff, for I myself shall not be there. So far as you are concerned, I congratulate you on your decision to go up to the farm. After nine months with the young people, I am ready for three months with the *adults*, up in the Michigan woods; and if I had not three months to read and think and write, I should not think very highly of the academic job.

I have read your "Sidelights" (not a bad title, even if made by the publishers) with great interest and pleasure. I don't see quite how your Baltimore friend can charge you with the chief academic fault, after this—I mean the fault of being dead and unconscious of it. All the papers are very lively and provocative. It is interesting to read your confession of ennui with respect to the classics, and your relucting welcome to the heroes of our own times.

I can't think that you do quite justice to O. Henry, or that you apply to him the appropriate standards. He strikes me as a comic caricaturist, with the exuberance of comic perception proper to the type. And, on the whole, you have treated Mencken more leniently than O. Henry, though Mencken is essentially a caricaturist also. In the one case you have seen that the "true truth" is not the rod to measure by; but in the other case you have spoken with the severity of a stern realist judging Dickens.

I found the piece on Jack London especially instructive, for I have never got round to wading through many of the works which he poured forth after he discovered the way to turn himself into a book-factory. I also had the misfortune to hear him lecture for about two and three-quarters hours at the Harvard Union—on socialism. In that evening he showed himself so essentially feeble-minded and lacking in all sense of proportion that I lost nearly all the interest that "The Call of the Wild" and some of the earlier stories had wakened.

I am glad that you are planning to do that new book in American literature with Urbana as a base, and I hope that we may arrange to bring you in for some kind of course. I will write you later on this point when I have sounded out the probabilities.

With best regards,

February 4, 1923   STUART P. SHERMAN

That I might be given teaching work in the university had been a mere suggestion and had not influenced me at all. I had quite forgotten the matter when in the mid-summer— July 29, 1923—I received another letter from Professor Sherman:

I have just had word from Dean Babcock that the appropriation for the proposed seminar in American literature is available, the sum being $1500.

What I should like best to have from a departmental point of view is a course meeting twice a week through the year (or if you preferred, once a week for a two-hour period). This would be for graduate students only; and should consume one-fourth of all their time; the theory is that to such a course eight hours of work, in addition to the class period, are devoted.

What would best 'fill the bill' would be a course suitable for M.A.'s and Ph.D.'s. There is at least one Ph.D. candidate who would be delighted to write a thesis in American literature.

With best regards,

STUART P. SHERMAN

Beginning September 1, therefore, I began my work as "Visiting Professor of American Literature," to serve for 10 months. The class numbered 19 in all. It was a year of revisions and unforeseen climaxes.

The great midland university opened for me a new chapter in the story of American education. I was impressed first of all by the size of the institution. Everything seemed to center about the element of size. Corn in the rich prairie soil was sometimes 15 feet tall and on each stalk one and often two ears of corn the size of a rolling pin. Everything else in proportion. I remember as our automobile entered the corn lands I jotted this down in my note-book: "The moment you cross the Alleghenies you are in the land where constantly you are shown the greatest this and that in the world. In Columbus, Ohio, I was shown a city bank foyer, the tallest in the world. So everywhere here. It is the soil. Jack must have planted his beanstalk somewhere in the Middle West." Illinois was a land-grant college like Penn State, but rooted in the corn loam it bowed to corn as king just as the Pennsylvania college bowed to steel, and coal, and oil. Located midway between the two commanding cities of Chicago and the East St. Louis, the university had but one real weapon when it approached the state legislature for the funds it must needs have in colossal amounts: it had in its hands the balance of power, the farm vote.

I was impressed early by the palatial fraternity houses, some of them evidently erected at costs approaching the six-figure mark. Money given by fraternity alumni or else borrowed from them erected this city of palaces, so I was told. To me it was a newness though not for long, for all the colleges, even Penn State, were being infected. What college could resist such good fortune, abundance of adequate dormitories furnished and maintained with no expense to the university of the state?

I realized now that the land grant college was educating America in mass formations. Education was being regimented. The individual was lost in the vast lecture rooms. Numbers, always numbers. For a single example of numbers, the teaching force in the English Department at Illinois numbered 70. Young men and women by the thousands were gathered now from the corn-land farms, domiciled for four years in club houses furnished with all luxuries, amused with weekly house-parties and cocktail soirees, packed weekly in a mammoth colosseum to yell themselves voiceless over the physical exploits of highly paid gladiators. Studies seemed to be secondary—at least in most student minds.

The university seemed to be aware of its geographical deficiencies. Never for a moment confessed was the feeling in the hearts of the natives that culture lay in the East. I have never dared to write "On a Certain Inferiority Complex in Westerners." The Cary Sisters, and Howells and Garland, to cite no other names, had gone to New England as to a sort of Holy Land, as Irving had gone to England. Chicago was near but Chicago was not enough. With the help of Professor Sherman the Mountain was brought to Mohammed, culture was imported in quantities in the shape of artists, poets, lecturers, novelists, oratorio organizations, and dramatics. Even in Boston one could not have found more of entertainment and instruction. Even the student "frats" had their lecture courses.

Once at a Y.M.C.A. committee meeting I found myself in a corner with the Dean of Agriculture. I asked him why the farmers of the West were always in revolt, always sockless Jerry Simpsons, always pathetic growlers? And he said this: "The tiller of the soil in all ages has been a peasant and he has lived close to his acres on bare necessities. Take your English etymology: 'ox' is Saxon; 'beef' is Norman French; 'hog' is Saxon, 'pork' is Norman French; 'sheep' is Saxon, 'mutton' is Norman French. The only meat with a Saxon name is 'bacon.' Why? The Saxons who tilled the soil and raised the hogs and sheep and oxen, never shared in the products they raised. That's the farmer peasant. But here in America the peasant revolts and considers himself entitled to luxuries such as industrial workers receive, luxuries no farming class in the world ever dreamed of having before the advent of the American republic. The farmer's land cannot produce enough to supply these additions and therefore he revolts."

In December came Vachel Lindsay "under the auspices of the Theta Sigma Phi." For a week the town was pasted over with advertising centered about a dictum of Professor Bruce Weirick of the English Department: "The greatest popular poet, exciting as a house afire, and as lyrical as a new moon on a spring night." The house that night was full of students who cheered the poet and certainly got their money's worth. No reading of "The Congo" in whispers that vehement night. His new poem "Dr. Mohawk" he read with conviction and he told his audience that America had added one newness to the poetry of the world, a tremendous newness he believed, the college yell. And of all yells "the jay-hawk yell" was king, and he proceeded to give it like an Indian war whoop. Lung power it certainly demanded to read "The Calliope" as he rendered it. He was never still for a moment. Poetry he ruled was to be heard and not seen. The art originated long before the days of books when "scops yelled out the joys of fight" and travelling minstrels recited battle deeds to warriors who were wrought to frenzies of excitement. That was poetry, he thought. I dined with him next day and was astounded to have him say that he considered his poems secondary in importance to his drawings. He would be remembered, he felt sure, for his art, and he had with him specimens of his cubist drawings and seemed annoyed when I asked him to explain them.

Poetry in the lands adjoining Spoon River, as I now caught echoes of it, demanded dynamic elements. An ag student asked me one day, "Where can I get some of this new rough-neck poetry that has got a kick in it?" A poet of the north woods, Lew Sarett, came down to read to us from his *The Box of God* and lyrics from his new collection *Slow Smoke*. More realism I never heard put into poetry. Standing at the piano with hands and feet and voice in furious action he produced what seemed to the ear a veritable Indian war dance, suddenly breaking it to say, "I'll give $50 if Dean Babcock will come up and do this."

Carl Sandburg came with his guitar to the college and was amazed to find that Sherman was not a senile Yankee Puritan with a beard; Lorado Taft lectured often on sculpture; Frost recited his "Birches," and Heywood Broun sitting on the stage table dangled his legs and talked endlessly I have forgotten about what. The English novelist Frank Swinnerton also came, and was properly dined by Sherman's department.

My year at the university was a climactic one for Sherman. His attack upon Dreiser's work had brought upon him a torrent of criticism and abuse. Mencken had turned upon him his whole battery of adjectives. But Sherman, though living under the very shadow of Chicago, had never lowered his Harvard standards,—not in 1918 when I wrote him a letter congratulating him on a particularly clever hit. This he had written me:

> I thank you for your kind words about my irritating book. As for Dreiser, half the reviewers revile me for not giving him more respectful treatment and the other half revile me for treating him at all. This situation I find fairly satisfactory! One main reason for writing critical matters is to force a consideration of "what we are about in God's creation"; and there are always at least two views about that.

In that last sentence lies the weak point in the man's equipment as a critic. Brilliant, scholarly, saturated with the classics, in the long run he was a waverer. One could never feel that he stood changeless like a stone wall. I remember once after he had read to a select group, many of them ladies, a paper frankly discussing sex problems in current literature, his first word when he met me after the reading, his face an interrogation point, was "Too timid, wasn't it?"

On the whole Sherman fought cleanly and obeyed the rules, but the mosquito swarm that descended upon him from

Dear Pattee:

Your letter pleases me immensely of course. How could it fail to do so?—as a mere confidence between you and me, your side of our mutual good opinions! And I won't let it go any further.

But so far as I can predict on the basis of my present state of mind, I shall not be a candidate for any presidential office. If I don't fail in the vocation that now absorbs me, I do not expect to revert to the academic walks.

In a way, this job is harder than teaching. That is why I like it—one reason why. It may kill me in a year or so. In a sense I don't care very much if it does. So long as it lasts, and I last, I have a chance to *use* what I've got. What more can we ask for? It's a very interesting opportunity which I have now and my heart is thoroughly in it.

Along in November an article which I wrote last summer will appear in one of the magazines (Scribner's), expressing what I feel nowadays about what you call "the academic prison-house" versus 'the primrose way.'

When I look beyond the primrose way to other paths, they lead my eye toward the blue hills which I've never yet had leisure to explore. I may never reach them. But there are no Deans or Presidents on them.

Three months later I sent him a letter telling with what consternation his article "An Interview with a Newcomer in New York," published in the December *Scribners*, had been read on the Illinois campus. Mildly I protested and this was his reply:

Dear Pattee:

It is cheering to hear where you go for the holidays. Perhaps, if we had had any holiday, we might have turned the same way ourselves, except that we had been warned that there was some danger of assassination if I appeared on the campus.

I am sorry no one here found time to *read* that offending article, which so far as the 'U. of I.' was concerned was good 'publicity' and almost, if not quite, wholly complimentary. As I remember, the 'U. of I.' was put on a plane with the best universities anywhere in the country.

My one mistake was this. Among my list of homelike places I should have included 'The inside of the Illinois Central Station in Chicago.' I could have included that with good conscience. For whenever *I* was in, I always felt there ought to be a home somewhere around for a man to go.

If any one asks you what I meant by the piece, please say that I intended it to be understood as 'a sigh of relief heaved up out of the heart of the profession.' That will be understood at least by the 'stalwart few.'

I don't see how a man of your perfectly clear and sound principles can 'fall for' summer session. However, if you play in the winter, you have some palliation for the offense.

We hope Sarah has a good satisfactory 'man.' Best wishes for Mrs. Pattee's health and yours during the new year. Life treats us all pretty rough at times, but then, thank goodness we can stand a lot. That's the bright side of life.

Dec. 30, 1925

Six months later he was dead, drowned in a lake in the Northwest where he was spending his vacation. New York, I felt, had given him nothing and had taken from him everything. He wrote nothing worth while after leaving Urbana.

4

In December of this Illinois year I read a paper at the annual meeting of the Modern Language Association, held that year at the University of Michigan. Widely distributed, it brought me many letters, none of which pleased me more than one from the old Yale savant who once as fellow guest in the picturesque home of James Fenimore Cooper, II, at Cooperstown, had dubbed me "Zeitgenoss":

My dear Professor Pattee,

This is to thank you for the copy of your very thorough and interesting article on "American Literature in the College Curriculum." It must have cost you a prodigious amount of work—only people more or less conversant with the subject can guess how much. It revives for me many old memories. I knew Richardson quite well—knew him when he was a young fellow, just out of Dartmouth, and working on Henry C. Bowen's *Independent*. He came up to New Haven to see if I would give him a course in Anglo-Saxon, &c.; but the arrangement involved too much travelling back and forth between Brooklyn and New Haven, and so fell through. I also knew Kate Sanborn—enterprising old girl. She came within an ace of marrying my old friend Gordon Burnham then in *articulo mortis*. But he died before she quite perfected her plans, and left her $50,000. Also I knew Tyler slightly. His big book in four volumes is absurdly out of proportion to the importance of the writings which it discusses and doesn't really come down to the true beginnings of American literature. Had it reached its subject and continued on the same scale, it would have needed 20 volumes. Tyler had little critical sense. He was a worthy, hard working, but thoroughly second class man. He wasn't in it with Lounsbury, e.g.

A few months ago I read your History of American Literature with much pleasure and general agreement; tho' I care very little for Whitman and nothing at all for Joaquin Miller. *Arcades Ambo*—barbarians both. Oh, I have met Miller, with his sombrero and velvet coat and red neck-tie; and I used to quarrel about Whitman with my old friend John Burroughs and my young friend W. S. Kennedy, one of the bearers at Walt's funeral. Mark Twain was also a kind of barbarian but different. You mention very kindly my "Century of American Literature," but I am not at all proud of that compilation. Much better, I think, is my little Chautauqua book, originally publisht as "An Outline Sketch of American Literature" in 1887. But even in that I failed to do justice to Mark Twain, and was taken to task for it by Howells one evening when he dined here. Howells was right, of course, and yet I have never understood his unqualified admiration for Clemens. Mark was so vulgar and Howells so refined! It shows how little a man may notice what is going on right alongside of him, that I never knew, till I read it in your article, that my colleague Prof. Cook, had a course here in American literature. But as nobody elected his courses, it probably gave no boost to the subject.

Sincerely yours,

Henry A. Beers

CHAPTER XXI

Ten Summers in the Green Mountains

OT TILL I HAD SPENT MANY SUMMERS at the Bread Loaf Writers' Conferences did I understand the Vermontness of the Green Mountain hinterland that had been settled by the same impulse that created the New Hampshire hill towns. Only one thing had ever separated the two states—the Connecticut River. Both peoples have been evolved out of mountain environments, with a similarity of soil and vegetation and weather. Both states were settled by men of independence and robustness of soul, and yet the two sections were by no means identical twins. Strangely different are the two mountain ranges and just as different in personality and viewpoint have been the people who have inhabited the ranges. To have been born in Vermont, I found, even during my first summer at Bread Loaf, was to possess a Green Mountain tang, a uniqueness as unmistakable as that of maple sugar, one that no amount of residence elsewhere can erase. Perhaps no other state has so completely preserved its original homogeneousness. Even until today to say "Vermonter" is to say English stock long in America, Protestant, Republican, hardheaded philosopher, frugal spender, sly humorist, 100 per cent believer in Vermont. The stock, as in New Hampshire, has been savagely depleted, and is sadly on the wane, but the type persists in all the Vermont valleys and hillsides even yet. Doubtless it will be in the heart of the Green Mountains that centuries from now will be discovered the last specimens of the old Yankee-Puritan stock, then long supposed to be extinct, just as one finds even now specimens of the aboriginal Celts in the mountains of Wales and Cornwall.

But even if the last of the living specimens die, we shall still know intimately the Green Mountaineer as he was in his golden day, for one of the breed, himself as redolent of Vermont as John G. Saxe, as Senator Morrill, as "I do not choose," as

Rutland marble, has preserved, in living likeness, a hundred specimens—Rowland E. Robinson, born in mid-Vermont, not very far from the now famous Plymouth, just one year before Artemus Ward was born near Skowhegan, Maine, and two years before Mark Twain was born in the Pike town of Florida, Missouri.

Mary E. Wilkins, who lived for years in Vermont, found the natives not all of them lovely. Uncouth often they are, inflexible, prejudiced, but always kindly of soul. To Miss Wilkins a Vermonter was like a Morgan horse, that peculiar native breed, tough and patient, serviceable and kindly, yet liable after a certain amount of abuse to sudden balkiness that not even fire could remove, and tempestuous bursts of cantankerousness exceeding all equine records, or like the Winooski River, beautiful and kindly, yet when once on the rampage knowing no bounds to its wrath, bursting into the headlines of all the newspapers of the country.

2

To lecture in a vigorous summer school of college grade has always been to me an ideal vacation. To Professor Sherman six weeks more of teaching after a seemingly interminable year with immature minds was intolerable. But a summer school class—barring always make-up classes for undergraduates below grade—is not at all like a class of college students. I have dealt only with graduates, the most of them teachers, some of them with years of experience. No better class can be found anywhere. Each member of it is in deadly earnest, each has come for specific courses, and each, in order to be advanced in rank or salary in the home school, must give an account of his summer to his superintendent or principal. Moreover, surrounding a summer school is an atmosphere of congeniality, of joyousness in key with the season, of youth resurgent after repression—it keeps one young to be with them.

After my year at Illinois I went to Bread Loaf with my American literature and until 1938 I was enrolled as one of the faculty there. I gave only a week in 1925, and I was granted leave of absence in 1926 to lecture in the Columbia University summer school and again in 1927 when my wife died. From that date I missed no summer until 1936—eleven summers. No part of my teaching life do I look upon now with more satisfaction.

The location of the school could hardly be improved upon: a picturesque plateau surrounded closely by mountains, and back of it all a unique tradition. Joseph Battell, a frail, sickly boy of a wealthy family, had been sent to live in a farmer's family on this mountain farm in hopes that the out-of-doors life would bring health and vigor. The experiment succeeded: the boy grew into robust manhood. Moreover, he fell in love with the place and in due time, inheriting the family millions, bought not only the farm but everything that could be seen from the farm, including a high mountain 20 miles down the valley, and 30,000 acres of woodland, including large parts of several townships—a veritable dukedom. Here he had made his home. He had erected a great three-story hotel, enclosing within it without change the farmhouse in which he had spent his youth, built a chapel, four hotel-like cottages, farm houses and a barn for his stud of Morgan horses and his dairy herd. A unique character he was certainly. Though a county road ran through his estate he allowed to the last no automobile to run over it. He ran his hotel on a no-profit, and largely on a no-pay, basis, and during his regime some of the most famous Americans of the period were his guests. His book, *Ellen: or the Whisperings of an Old Pine*, in two thick volumes voluminously illustrated, is one of the curiosities of American literature. He never married, and at his death he willed his entire holdings to Middlebury College, 10 miles away. A white elephant it had seemed at first, but in 1920 the Bread Loaf School of English was started, the hotel and cottages seemed as if built for the purpose, and success came with a bound. By judicious forestry methods the 30,000 acres of virgin forest, though the will specified that certain large areas were never to be touched with the axe, have become a steady source of revenue for the college.

For hiking and camping purposes no summer school has had a more perfect area all its own.

The school was fortunate in its first Dean, Wilfred Davison, a man with the imagination and the personality and the business sense to make fullest use of the hotel set-up, the geography, and the traditions of the place. It was his dream to make the school distinctive because of a distinctive personnel, first in the faculty and then in the visiting lecturers. For the most part the students were teachers of English in schools and colleges, and the object of the school, in the words of the dean, was "To have something *real* going on at Bread Loaf, and then to have those high school teachers who have been at Bread Loaf go back to their schools and start something *real* there. We have no patience with that high school teaching which is mere cramming for college entrance examinations."

The roll of instructors with whom I worked for 10 or 12 years was a distinctive one. Among them were Grace Hazard Conkling, Sidney Cox, Kenneth B. Murdock, Edith R. Mirrielees, Grant Overton, Dallas Lore Sharp, George F. Whicher, Marguerite Wilkinson, James Southall Wilson, Hervey Allen, Walter Prichard Eaton, Theodore Morrison. The roll of visiting lecturers reads like the index to a history of contemporary literature. Indeed it was said that the best way to know the current literary group was to sit at Bread Loaf and wait till one by one they came.

In the earlier years the "teaching load" for each instructor was one hour a day—a single course. Later, in a few cases, it was increased to two courses. But class work was only an incident in the instructor's day. He was constantly with the students. After he mingled with them in hikes and ball games and picnics they completely lost their awe even of the most famous of the savants. Once each week there was a total shift in the dining room so that during the term, so far as was possible, each student might sit each week at a table presided over by a different instructor. Sometimes senior students were allowed for a meal to dine even in "Finger-bowl-alley" with distinguished visitors.

From the first Robert Frost was a regular visitor, often for a week, until at length he was hailed as "the Godfather of Bread Loaf." His talks in classes he was asked to visit were always inspiring and his yearly appearance in the lecture course was always considered an "event." As a lecturer he was often disappointing. Of his lecture in July, 1936, I made this note:

330

> Frost came at noon. He talked ramblingly and apparently extemporaneously to the school from four to six. Always a rambler in his lectures, today he surpassed himself in his rambles. Bits of value here and there kept one listening, as when he said that years ago he had heard of the poem 'Piers Plowman.' He could not read it and for years did not try to do so, but the title haunted him. It was what he termed a 'gatherer.' He had brooded on it—all that was connoted in that word. And the result at last was his poem 'The Death of the Hired Man.' When at last he read 'Piers Plowman,' he was surprised to find it religious propaganda.

Often there were flashes of criticism. In one lecture he said, "William Butler Yeats is a poser. He is a conscious worker: conscious always of his readers. He takes an aristocratic view of life, dividing humanity into three classes: the aristocrats, the middle class, the mob. He himself sprang from the middle class, but he poses as if he were royal born and looking down with a sneer."

He was best when reading his poems. Always he read "Mending Wall," "Birches," "A Winter Evening," "Two Roads," "The Pasture" and others similar, invariably reading each lyric twice. He said he had been compelled by circumstance to live his life and do his work in this little north-east corner of the map, but of late his grandchildren, scattered over the whole nation, had compelled him to live in the larger world. This larger world he was now, he said, putting into verse, and he was doing it with new methods. I felt as he read specimens of this later work that his career as a poet was nearing its end. His earlier poems are himself, and no man survives himself. His one book for me has always been *North of Boston*.

Often we dined with him at his table in "Finger-bowl-row."

Irrepressible, happy-go-lucky, unconventional, he was a lovable personage and a charming table companion. His stories for the most part were colored by the Vermont hills, prose bits from his own experience. He told of an old Green Mountain farmer, who, when asked concerning the depression, "Anyone suffering in your town?" drawled out, "No-o-o. I guess there ain't no destitution in our town. The poorest folks we've got are the Joneses, and I judge they are looking up a little bit lately. He's swapped his second-hand Ford for a second-hand Essex."

At Bread Loaf, only horse-and-buggy distance from the boyhood home of President Coolidge, no gathering was complete without a round of stories concerning him. At one such gathering Frost related a personal experience. Some one had remarked to the President that a word of commendation spoken by Theodore Roosevelt had made the hitherto neglected poet Edwin Arlington Robinson all of a sudden a leading figure in the American poetic choir, and he had added, "Now, Mr. Coolidge, why don't you honor your fellow Vermonter, Robert Frost, with an invitation to the White House and put his poetry into the blaze of the presidential lime-light?"

"Got one of my own," snapped the President.

Whereupon Coolidge invited an unknown rhymester who lived near his birthplace—Frost would not tell his name—and showered him with attention making sure that the press had full particulars. But the reporters agreed among themselves to keep the episode from the press and it was never recorded. The poetaster, however, did not fail to utilize the event. He became a fixture at the Coolidge birthplace and every summer sold there copies of his effusions, many of them laudatory of Coolidge. One of the week-end excursions from Bread Loaf always took in the famous farm, and the students came back with photographs of "The Poet Laureate of Vermont," so titled by the President, and his book of verses.

Personally I met Coolidge only once, and that years later. Dr. Holt got him to Rollins College once and made much of the visit. He came with the distinct understanding that he came as Dr. Holt's guest and was to make no speeches. When he arrived from Eustis, Florida, where he was spending the winter, Mrs. Holt asked Mrs. Coolidge how long they expected to stay. "Over night, I think," she replied. "I saw him put two shirts into his bag." The college gave the ex-President a rousing welcome. At a mass meeting of college and townspeople, he was greeted with college yells and songs. Irving Bacheller gave the welcoming address which from beginning to end was roaringly humorous, but Coolidge cracked not a smile. The students did stunts, the student orchestra did its best, but through it all the great ex-President sat like an image of Buddha.

Among the entertainers who were to be found on the summer program at Bread Loaf there appeared early in the '30s Percy MacKaye, booked to read from his own poetry. I noted in my journal that he was "something of a frost." The lighting of the stage had to be changed after the audience was in the hall—the work of more than half an hour. He insisted that nothing on the stage should stand distinct except his own face,—a weird effect, but too conspicuously emphasized to be what the poet intended. Interminably he read from one of his Kentucky Mountain effusions.

Robert Frost was to come next day, and "Cy," the summer school major domo, was to meet him at Middlebury. MacKaye begged to accompany him so as to give proper greeting to his fellow poet. When the bard emerged from the Pullman, Percy threw himself into his brother poet's arms enraptured with lyric joy. Then resounded a harsh awakening call: "All-l-l aboard!" The train was moving slowly down the track. Suddenly Frost awoke. "My baggage! My baggage is on it. Stop that train," he shouted, and eagerly he began to run down the platform, his arms extended. The conductor, who knew Frost, at once stopped the train by pulling the emergency cord, and with Frost and the Pullman porter made a search of the Pullman for the baggage. No baggage there. The train thereupon moved on and the poet much disturbed, rushed back to "Cy," shouting, "I've lost my baggage! I've lost my baggage." "Oh no," said Cy." I knew you'd leave it. You always do. So I went in and got it. Here it is in the car."

President Moody in his Sunday sermons at Bread Loaf always left suggestive and quotable fragments of wisdom for one's memory. I remember this: "Busy men are tempted by the devil, but an idle man tempts the devil." I remember a sermon preached from a passage in *Hebrews* describing Esau as a "profane man"—"a surprising adjective at first sight. *Profane*— outside the altar. Esau was an unfenced man, a man of the world, a man of the mere day. He was the Babbitt of his time. He lived in the moment. He lacked the sense of the unseen. Abraham sought a city that hath foundations; Moses endured as seeing him who is invisible; Esau saw only the moment, only himself, and he perished."

A jovial soul was President Moody, son of the revivalist Dwight L. Moody. In my day at Bread Loaf it was a joy when a student or an instructor group could "get him started." During his long stay in Vermont he had acquired Vermontness to the full. His stories were as redolent of the state as maple sugar. In any region where Green Mountains can be seen one hears no tales of "two Irishmen," or of a "tight old Scotchman." Vermont is sufficient for Vermont. I remember at a dinner at the cottage of Mr. Endicott, treasurer of Harvard, the President was at his best. He told of the old Vermont farmer who complained that one single cup of coffee "wan't more'n a skeeter bite" to him. When he drank coffee he *drank coffee*, never less than a whole coffee-pot-full.

"But don't so much coffee keep you awake?"

"Ye-s-s. It helps."

Another loyal Bread Loafer was Dorothy Canfield Fisher. At her home in Arlington, Vermont, we found her making a veritable profession of the conserving of the Vermontness of the town of her ancestors. Around her was gathered the whole town like a great family. When we were there she was directing a coming community play which was to be entitled "Tourists Accommodated." The whole town was writing the play, each one contributing an anecdote or an incident. That very morning a new item had been added to the play. A tourist had called at a farmhouse that bore the sign "Maple Sugar Bon-bons" and had ordered some that had less maple flavoring than the last they had bought. "If you haven't any now, make some maple-sugar candy with just a small amount of maple flavoring in it."

For several years Burges Johnson brought variety to the teaching force. Vermont born, he was completely at home in the Battell forests surrounding Bread Loaf and he shared his wood lore freely. He was, among many things, a poet with collections on his list like "Beastly Rhymes," and "Bashful Ballads," and his class-room was ruled by methods not conventional. For instance, this was the required lesson for one day: "Make a sonnet using these end-rhymes in the order given: *whole, sweet, greet, goal, roll, feet, neat, soul; sleep, pass, know, deep, alas, go*." I was not in his class, but I did the exercise with this result:

Not in Johnson's Dictionary

When Jonah by the whale was swallowed whole
   And in that awful belly far from sweet,
     Stripped of all hope the coming dawn to greet,
With gastric juice bedrenched and at the goal
Of newer deeps to come, while he did roll
   Now on his head, now on his useless feet,
     So my sweet Muse is swallowed, erst so neat,
As o'er these rhymes I sweat my inner soul.

Oh tell me, Muse, doth Johnson never sleep?
   Is there no path where he doth never pass?
     No dryad in a tree he doth not know,
And is not able by his magic deep
   To set it free; though once set free, alas,
     It haunts my dreams—O Johnson, let me go!

The literary happenings at Bread Loaf, if all were told, would make an entertaining book. Sinclair Lewis came,—but I forebear. Edwin Markham came and it is on record that he ate the largest meal ever consumed in "Finger-bowl-alley." I saw him eat it. At the reading later in the evening he presented with much enveloping frill poems few of us had ever read. Finally after repeated calls for "The Man with the Hoe," he read most effectively, but after the preliminary remark that he preferred reading his best poetry like the Lincoln Ode that had won a prize.

Willa Cather was a Bread Loafer, and Hamlin Garland, Carl Sandburg, Irving Bacheller, Henry S. Canby, John Livingston Lowes, Louis Untermeyer, William Lyon Phelps—who, indeed, did not come? Especially I enjoyed the visit of Ellen Glasgow who entertained most delightfully my class in Contemporary American Literature.

She told the class that *Barren Ground* was her best novel and that *Vein of Iron* contained her philosophy of life more fully than any of her other novels. She thought that the old philosopher in *The Virginia Comedians* was her best character. Questions came freely from the class. To Dr. James S. Wilson who remarked that *The Virginia Comedians* did not contain his favorite character, she flashed back, "Oh, James, of course he is not the character to appeal to a man of your type at all. You are a cross, you know, between Ariel and Sterne." She had once visited Hardy, she said, and was delighted with him. She also highly praised the work of Mary Johnston. Apropos of one of her remarks, Dr. Wilson told briefly the story of some strangers who exploring the grounds of the University of Virginia, where he held the chair of Poe Professor of English, asked a Negro who was mowing a lawn:

"Is that the Poe House?"

"No, no," said the Negro. "That ain't no po' house. That's the university."

5

One annual happening at Bread Loaf impressed me more deeply each year. Professor Harrington, hike leader, Professor of Philosophy at Middlebury, conductor of a summer class in Browning, read totally without notes the whole of the Caponsacchi section of *The Ring and The Book*, gave it dressed as a monk and with dramatic action. An hour long it took him to recite the intricate poem, a feat of memory that always seemed to me phenomenal.

Our two summers with Hervey Allen were most enjoyable. We saw much of him. He had come to Bread Loaf, we learned, to finish his new novel, but during the summer he wrote not a word on it. We took him for a week-end down to our Sabine Farm in New Hampshire and fed him with vegetables from our garden there and blueberry muffins, he picking the blueberries. He read to us from the manuscript of his novel. John Farrar, he told us, had "grub-staked" him for two years in Bermuda to write the novel and there he had finished two-thirds of it. The other third was still to do. It was to be issued in three large volumes to sell, he thought, at $5 for the three. The advice I gave him shows the quality of my critical judgment. I told him three large volumes at that price meant failure. The depression was at its height and people were not buying new novels at $5. He was overdoing the matter. He did not argue with me. Things, however, were soon to culminate. Farrar demanded the goods for which he had waited for two years and threatened to break the contract, and his wife also made her threats if he did not complete the work. As a result, perforce, he wrote volume three. And of the enormous success that followed the publication of *Anthony Adverse* it is needless to write. He was stampeded by the flood that came. He autographed 500 copies of the book in Wanamaker's basement in one day and nearly as many the next.

Dr. Wilson and Dean Gay defended the book. Both considered it a great work, but thought Hervey did not measure up to the novel he had attempted. It was my contention that the book petered out. The last third, done under pressure, is inferior, and he ended it as one ends a chicken—with the axe. Moreover I contended that the novel is a hodge-podge, that it lacks what I have called "soul," it has no upward look. Lyric passages there are and stirringly dramatic ones, but it lacks unity of the whole.

John Farrar came to lecture on current literature and we went out with him, a few of us, to view the blazing sunset. Marvellous it was. But Farrar detected flaws. "Now if the colors at the south were heightened a bit and that cloud at the north could be removed, that sunset would be perfect." "There you are," spoke up his wife. "Always editing. Now you are editing the sunset."

In his evening lecture he discussed book jackets. Critics are repelled, he said, if the jacket is lurid, but the reading public requires these colors. The first edition of *Anthony Adverse* was put into a plain jacket, but after it was found that the book was to be a success, a jacket was used that would attract the "low-brows."

Men like *Anthony Adverse*, Farrar maintained, because in the hero they see their own ideal of a man, one that they read about as if it were themselves who were doing the heroic deeds so graphically described. A novel, he believed, is successful only when its characters *live*. The reader must feel that these characters are true to actuality, are realities, not creations of fiction. The art of characterization cannot be learned; one has it or one has it not. Men read few novels. The bulk of all the current fiction is tinted with the feminine and is unattractive to the masculine taste.

When questions were called for, a lively debate ensued. Did not *Anthony Adverse* succeed because it was so sensationally advertised? All who were present remembered how widely and sensationally it was advertised that on a specified date "the greatest event in the whole history of American literature" was to take place. Daily this date was emphasized in black letters. A sensation was to be exploded like nothing else in the history of all literature. Everywhere a rising tide of curiosity. Then was disclosed the title of the book; then a pamphlet was sent as a flood over the country telling of the colossal literary event about to come. Then the book was published with full page advertisements in every journal. Was it not this that started the flood toward *Anthony Adverse?*

Farrar contended that it helped, of course, but did not made the book the best-seller it became. "Advertising," he said, "will increase the sales of a good book, but it will not put over a poor book."

The debate waxed hot but nothing was settled.

Sometimes I wonder when I listen to the miscellany found everywhere on my radio dial of an evening; when I hear the jazz music coming from juke boxes in restaurants and other places; when I attempt to read the current best sellers, especially the fiction; when I go to the movies, especially of a Saturday afternoon and see the "Western" put on to please the kiddies; I wonder if the feelings I have are simply the usual reactions of old age against the new world created by the new young generation now in control, or are American art and morals in rapid degeneration. As a very old man who has had his day and his world, I simply ask. The young leader who has just stepped into the place long occupied by an old maestro, rebalances at once the orchestra, changes the number of the horns and other instruments and puts newness into the old combination. It is as it should be. Each generation builds on the generations before it and each should build higher than the last, and perhaps an old maestro is not the best judge of the progress made.

In my classes of the current period I am impressed daily by the changes I find. Many of the boys, a majority let me say, are free to confess that they get no enjoyment at all from the poetry denominated good by their teacher. They read it only when compelled to do so as a punishment. The girls for the most part are still loyal to the poets. The short stories that delighted me in my college days, bore the students of today. When asked why the story has failed to move them, they reply, "Because the story does not move. It gets nowhere." To which I retort, "You are movie-minded. In a movie the movement is perpetual. You want your literature always at the speed limit." One student damned a novel he had read because "it is all littered up with background."

In one of my lectures I find this concerning the evolution that has brought our fiction step by step to its present condition. The transcendentalists as they wrote were concerned with the *unseen;* in a later period came the realists who dealt with the *seen;* now come the ultra-naturalists who deal with the *obscene.*

CHAPTER XXII

On Being a College Professor

ON FEBRUARY 11, 1912, died one of the dearest friends I have ever had, Benjamin Gill, Dean of the School of Language and Literature of Penn State, and College Chaplain. At the memorial service I said of him: "The services which Benjamin Gill rendered to the college were three-fold. First of all, he brought a genial personality, one that made friends easily and that inspired confidence quickly and held it permanently. His hearty laugh, his countenance beaming with fun, his inexhaustible store of wit and anecdotes made him welcome wherever he might go. Everybody knew him and everybody loved him. He was the prince of afterdinner speakers and the center always of social gatherings. It was this power of compelling confidence, of winning friendship, and of holding it, of radiating sympathy, of entering actively into the lives of others, that made his greatest impress upon the student body of the college."

Immediately two commissions were entrusted to me, both of them accepted by me with diffidence. I was to collect and edit and publish appropriately the leading sermons and addresses delivered by Professor Gill during his 16 years at the college, and I was to serve as acting chaplain until a successor to Professor Gill had been appointed. None was appointed, allow me to say, during the next 16 years. The memorial volume containing his addresses was issued in a distinctive edition in March, 1913.

As acting chaplain it became my duty to be in general charge of the daily chapel, to cooperate with the president in the securing of Sunday preachers, and to preside at the Sunday service. Attendance at chapel had from the earliest years of the college been a rigid requirement. To make the Sunday service worth going to, the most distinctive speakers possible were secured, speakers the students would be inclined to write to their homes about. The college, of course, is non-denominational; therefore it devolved upon us to secure leading representatives of the various churches, at least one representative of each of the major faiths, each year.

As I look back over my 16 years, certain features of the student chapel service stand still vivid, first of all,—illogically enough—dogs. Every fraternity had a specimen, the uglier the more highly prized, and despite the vigilance of the janitors, these dogs attended chapel. "Without are dogs" would be no fit text for a chapel sermon. One Sunday the sermon was interrupted by a dog-fight not far from the pulpit. Experience taught us early that it was poor policy to have the janitor try to remove a dog once he had entered. A dog is hard to capture and once caught is vocal *in extremis*. Once a grave old Beta mascot deliberately mounted the platform while the preacher was beginning his "fifthly" and sat dozily by the altar inspecting the audience. After a moment he gave a huge yawn audible in all parts of the room, and to this day the preacher does not know what he could have said that caused the boys to burst so suddenly into roars of laughter. It broke up the service.

The well-worn advice given by all college chaplains to preachers before the service that "no souls are saved after 20 minutes," usually slips from the preacher's memory the moment he begins his "firstly." I agree with Burges Johnson that public speaking of every variety is a form of self-hypnotism. Always I told the preachers, sometimes with emphasis, that they would be remembered by the students only as "longwinders" if the clock in the near tower struck 12 before they had finished. Nevertheless many exceeded the time limit, one at least by half an hour. No long-winder ever was invited back.

As chapel history allow me to record that one prominent Methodist bishop spoke at three different times during my term as chaplain and three times gave the same sermon. Another bishop preached the same sermon twice. Both of them, when I told them what they had done, seemed disturbed by the circumstance, one of them blaming his secretary for not keeping his schedule accurately, and both seemed uncomforted by my conciliatory remark that not a soul except myself remembered that they had heard the sermons once or twice before, and I should not have remembered had I not kept a diary.

In the war spring of 1918, when the senior class was graduated in April and the college was closed for no one could guess how long, a Sunday chapel preacher was the Reverend Hugh Black, then serving the Fifth Avenue Church in New York. No more fiery little particle ever lighted on the Penn State campus. His sermon had war in it without quarter. "Rather than be conquered by Germany," he shrilled, "we'll sink the blooming little island in the sea!"

I had been an early discoverer of Hugh Black. In Edinburgh in 1897 we had planned to take our breakfast in a restaurant, but a diligent search failed to find any eating place open. It was the Scotch Sabba' Day. Suddenly a chime of bells rang out with a volume of sound that seemingly filled the whole city. "Let's go in," I said, "and see a Scotch service," and we went in. Consulting a letter I wrote home that day, I find that the sermon was "preached from a tall pulpit by a very small man with a great mass of coal-black hair. He was well named—Hugh Black. His sermon was a rouser. Never heard a more dynamic speaker."

But compulsory chapel was everywhere under fire. From time to time the student body sent in petitions asking for its abolishment, the chief argument being that religion under compulsion was un-American. For a decade or more the fight continued and, one by one, colleges in various parts of the country either dropped the service or else made it optional with the student. It came with something of a shock to me when Dartmouth dropped compulsory chapel, but I recognized the logic of the opposition and said nothing. At Penn State, however, there were members of the Board of Trustees who were inflexible in their demand that compulsion be not dropped. Following an unusually vigorous protest against chapel by the student body, they asked me to take full charge of the week-day service and, if in anyway it was possible, to make the 15 minutes so attractive that the students would cease making complaints.

They increased my salary, provided at my request new hymnals with responsive services and gave me permission to do whatever I thought would make it attractive. For a year chapel leadership was my leading thought. I gave to it the best I had. One series of brief talks I issued through the Y.M.C.A. publishing house as a book with the title *Compelled Men* (1913). I altered the service so that the students did a large part of it, and from time to time I reviewed significant current books or had reviews made by selected students. No two services were to be alike. To some degree I succeeded. The senior class even presented me with a student lamp, but compulsory chapel was doomed.

On July 29, 1927, this letter from President Hetzel reached me at my summer home in New Hampshire:

Dear Doctor Pattee:

You will be interested to know that at the Special Meeting of the Board of Trustees held July 28, 1927, it was voted that the President of the College be directed to suspend compulsory week-day chapel and to substitute therefor such voluntary religious services as seem to him best designed to promote the religious interests of the student body. At a little later time, I trust you will allow me to counsel with you as to what further provision should be made in order to carry out the spirit of the action of the Board of Trustees.

When I hear a student say that a custom in the college comes down from antiquity, I recognize that he means it is more than four years old. A college professor gathers moss rapidly. Traditions of him start even in his mid-career. I remember buying a second-hand Horace at Dartmouth and finding after various passages the letter J. That meant "joke," so I was informed, and sure enough every joke came as marked.

Ten years after I had left the college Dean Warnock, in his *Half Column* contributed daily to a local paper, added this tradition to the lengthened string that 40 years had hung upon me:

In my earlier experience hereabouts I was a combination stage manager and ticket taker for the College morning chapel services. Pattee usually handled the devotional part of the program. One morning he opened the big chapel Bible and proceeded to read (as it appeared) one of the psalms. Because of boyhood experience in psalming I thought I detected a variation from the conventional phrasing as he read it. After the service I took a look into the Bible on the pulpit to check the point. Pattee saw the act and chuckled. "Did I miss something?" he asked. Then he explained: "I forgot my glasses and had to read from memory."

2

The death of Dr. Sparks, June 15, 1924, closed a chapter in the history of the college. Broken in health, he had retired from the presidency two years before, and almost immediately had been succeeded by Dr. John M. Thomas, formerly President of Middlebury College, Vermont. In many ways the Sparks administration had been distinctive. It had been a period of enlargement. The college had grown phenomenally. It had been a period of reorganization. Student self-government had been tried and found successful, faculty advisers for small groups of the freshmen had been appointed, and the faculty organizations in the various schools had been changed.

As one who had been in the faculty inner circle during the administration, however, I had noted fundamental weaknesses, to such a degree that at one time I had been on the point of leaving the institution. When the new president, feeling his way at the beginning of his administration, asked each of the department heads for advice concerning methods for strengthening the college and its work, I outlined in no spirit of grumbling or complaint, what I thought had been the leading weakness of the Sparks regime:

"You ask concerning 'definite lines of educational policy.' Here I can be more confident. The greatest failure of the college during the past few years has been at this point. You have seen much since you have been here, but one thing you have not yet seen,—the deplorable lack of morale among the teaching force. If you examine the faculty roll from year to year you will note that an unusual number resign at the close of each year. At the opening of the first semester last autumn something like 150 (the registrar will supply the exact figure) new men appeared for the first time upon the faculty roll. This was not caused by low salaries alone. The last administration exalted the student at the expense of the faculty. Again and again in faculty meeting we were told 'you are the hired men of the college: the college exists for the students.' In any question between faculty and student the faculty was not heard. I hesitate, Mr. President, about writing these things, but it is the truth that the teaching force here has been an angry, discontented, growling body on the whole and the spirit for 10 years has been: 'I'll stay here only as long as I have to stay.' I do not hear so much at the present moment about resignations: the force is eagerly watching you to see if they are to be treated as 'hired men' and be told if they complain, 'Oh, there are probably 50 men waiting for your job if you don't like it here.' Enough.

"We must keep our strong men for a term of years and we must keep them with a love for the college and a faith in the future of the college. A gathering of teachers should never be a gathering of angry men.

"The student body has been given too much freedom. The last administration seldom said *no* to a student. During the last 10 years ground has been yielded that never can be won back. We need a firm policy—not too firm—but one that does not temporize and one that is not always in deathly fear of what the students may do if they are in any way opposed.

"As to the student side: the fraternity situation needs to be handled with extreme care. Without dormitories, the college is peculiarly dependent upon them. At present they are united and harmonious and free from bad political tendencies. They have been given almost unlimited social privileges, however, and the time I feel has come when their house-parties and week-end dances should be supervised more carefully. There is dynamite in this suggestion however, and it must be handled with tact and not hastened. The boys, however, spend too much money and time and a limit should be set I feel. The last administration never set limits."

I wrote to Dr. Thomas, the new president, May 4, 1921, before my visiting professorship year at the University of Illinois, and that **Dr.** Thomas heeded my warning, his administration, which was peculiarly helpful for the teaching staff, fully shows. In May, 1924, he sent a letter to the alumni, a paragraph of which I am vain enough to reproduce:

Rumors have been current for some time that Professor Pattee is to leave our Faculty. I am glad to report that the statement is not true: Professor Pattee has definitely promised to return to us after his present year of leave which he is spending at the University of Illinois. But the facts which gave rise to this rumor concerning Professor Pattee are instructive as to the relations between the internal problems of the college, its main business of providing efficient instruction under inspiring teachers and great scientists, on the one hand, and on the other hand the problem of adequate financial support and of an informed public sentiment which makes such support possible. Professor Pattee was offered elsewhere a salary 33⅓% larger than the present maximum salary of a full professor at Penn State. He returns at that sacrifice, and with the great reputation which his recent writings have brought to him, to complete his life of service at Penn State, because of the love he bears your college, and because he appreciates the tragedy it would be to us were the author of "Alma Mater" to turn his back. That is but an incident—others are here because of loyalty and affection. Yet the college is standing by its teachers to the utmost. Buildings, equipment, even necessary repairs are sacrificed for them. Penn State is spending each year in educational activities more money than the entire cost of its plant. I know of no other college of which that is true. And this is the moral: It may impress some as materialistic when we talk of money and buildings, but the purpose is not glory or size, but a square deal to men like F. L. Pattee and the privilege of bringing more men like him into contact with Pennsylvania youth, so that the coming generations also may sing:-

> When we stood at boyhood's gate,
> Shapeless in the hands of Fate,
> Thou didst mould us, dear old State,
> Into men, into men.

Following his election to the presidency Dr. Thomas had addressed the faculty, the students and the townspeople in an open air meeting and his speech had been interrupted five times by dog fights. Smilingly he had said to me, "Do you think it is ominous?" Time proved that it was not. College and town approved of President Thomas. Some of his later difficulties came from his antagonism to the Pinchot administration at Harrisburg. A Vermont Bull Mooser, he unwisely fought against the governorship of the man who he believed had caused the split between President Taft and Theodore Roosevelt.

3

To be a senior professor involves one in labors manifold. One must head committees, make official reports, accept responsible assignments, edit publications. Following the first World War it devolved on me to compile after much research the military history of the college, with sketches of the men who had fallen in the struggle, and after the death of President Sparks I was made editor of the Sparks memorial volume.

But seniority brings delightful breaks in the academic monotony. I represented the college at the inauguration of several university presidents where nothing is required of one save dignity and academic attire, horribly uncomfortable during a June hot wave. When I received the Litt.D. degree at Dartmouth, the newly varnished chair arose when I got up to face the president, and John Drew, also a candidate, whispered behind me, "You sure are stuck on your college." He was right. No commissions ever pleased me more than the two that took me to Dartmouth as the representative of Penn State. The first visit was in 1904 at the corner-stone laying of the new Dartmouth Hall, the Earl of Dartmouth performing the ceremony.

The Earl certainly captured the college. His speeches flashed with humor to the delight of the students. His scholarship was evident too, he spoke perfect English with a literary finish, and he possessed a hearty, jovial personality. Contrary to all my expectations, I was much impressed by the man. The speech he made at the banquet could be used with effect at any English-American gathering at any time even in this era of the second World War.

I remember, he said, not very long ago a speech that was delivered by Mr. Joseph H. Choate, at a time when the relations between the two countries had been considerably improved. A good deal was said on that occasion. Mr. Choate gave a warning note. He said that 'no man could be an Englishman and an American at the same time.' I take it that he meant by that that where the interests of two countries come into conflict, whatever the sentiment may be, no country will allow its interests to suffer merely on the ground of sentiment. But what I believe and what I hope to be the case is, that by a better knowledge of each other, by mutual respect for each other's good qualities, which are many, and mutual forbearance with regard to each other's weaknesses which may exist, when the interests do clash, the governments of the two countries will be able to find a solution of those questions that will be mutually satisfactory.

Winston Churchill might have said this in his speech befor the American Congress in 1941.

And again:

Personally, descended as I am on the one side from the father of the first Lord Dartmouth, who was known among his contemporaries as 'Honest Will,' who was described by his sovereign, Charles the First, as the faithfullest servant that ever king had, and on the other from Elizabeth Washington, a great-grand-aunt of George Washington, who holds the world's record for truth and honor, I trust I shall not be blamed if at any rate I hope that there may be something in heredity.

I also represented the college when Dartmouth celebrated its one hundred and fiftieth anniversary in 1919. The pageant representing the history of the college was picturesque indeed. Especially I remember the representation of John Ledyard's entry into Hanover in an Uncle Sam rig, and riding on a one-horse shay hard to describe. Also I noted the emphasis put on the "five hundred gallons." As sung by Richard Hovey the story runs thus:

Oh, Eleazer Wheelock was a very pious man:
He went into the wilderness to teach the Indian,
With a gradus ad Parnassum, a Bible and a drum,
And five hundred gallons of New England rum.

On Sunday the service in the old white church where once I had Sunday after Sunday pumped the organ, was indeed impressive. Ozora Davis, a near friend of mine in college days, member of the class of 1889, preached the sermon from the text "Vox clamantis in deserto," a stirring and impressive effort, as Lee English, Warren F. Gregory, my classmates, and I all agreed.

The next morning I rode from Hanover to Danbury, N. H., on the train with Senator George H. Moses whom I had known for two years at the college. He was just from Washington where he had been a member of the "battalion of death" that had killed the League of Nations, so far as American entry was concerned. His hatred of Woodrow Wilson was vitriolic. "But," he said, "why should I interfere? God has laid his hand on him. He won't trouble us long now."

4

One other absence from the college I cannot neglect. In 1920 I had been for nearly 20 years the Superintendent of the State College Methodist Sunday School, had with the help of my wife organized the school with the new graded lessons, and had been one of the founders of the Wesley Foundation for the college students. As a result, the church insisted on submitting my name for lay delegate to the General Conference to be held in May at Des Moines, Iowa. It was my first experience as a candidate for office and my last. At the Lay Electoral Conference held that year at Altoona I was elected after vigorous electioneering by my friends and in due time spent the month of May with the conference, which was as large a body almost as the House of Representatives at Washington and was organized after much the same pattern.

For me it was a unique experience and I will add upsetting. It upset my churchliness almost completely. To be on the inside of a campaign for the election of bishops, to see ballot after ballot taken, with this man losing and that man gaining, to feel the rising excitement of the election, and to be conscious of the log-rolling, the bargains, the strategy, and the delegations of lobbyists rushed in from interested churches to sweep candidates in by waves of enthusiasm, was a disillusioning process.

While I was in college the Blaine-Logan campaign took place and four years later the Cleveland-Harrison campaign. Both were picturesque episodes with mud-slinging at its worst. In those days party affiliation was a matter of birth, like nationality. In a grand torch-light procession before one election I bore a torch. In assembling my outfit, consisting of cape and cap from the heap sent up from another Republican Club, I had difficulty in finding a cap large enough for me. Finding one at last, I was astonished to find my name in it: Fred Lewis Pattee. My *alter ego* it seemed lived at West Canaan, N. H., his father like mine was Lewis Pattee, he graduated at Exeter in 1888; I at Dartmouth in 1888. For years we ran into each other: I was showered with congratulations when he was married, and my wife received letters of condolence when Fred Lewis Pattee died. Booth Tarkington, an Exeter man, made a bet with another Exeter man that I was not the Exeter Pattee who was famous as a ball-player at the school. Tarkington wrote to me for information:

> Often when I have seen your name in print I have wondered if you went to Exeter and were there in the class of '88. There was a Pattee in that class and I think his name was Fred. Not long after I came to school he paused a moment in passing me one day, and said that the pipe I was smoking was a "great" one, leaving me immensely flattered.

I told Tarkington my story and under the date January 17, 1921, received this in reply:

> Your *doppelganger* was a very handsome youth. I had an awe of him, and I think his head, physically, was large. I am under the impression that it was in the Harrison-Cleveland campaign of '87 that we had torch light processions in which Pattee '88 marched and I also, at a considerable distance behind him.
>
> About your question: I recall that when I wrote "Monsieur Beaucaire" I thought that I was writing a short story and intended to write a short story. It ran out to 11,000 words and was instantly rejected by most of the magazines of that time. I think they no more than looked at its length, which was too great for one installment. I suppose it might be considered an 'intensive' romantic novel. Howells called me an 'intensivist,' and in my later talks with him I think he seemed to favor 'intensivism.' He seemed to have an idea that all that

was worth writing in a book was what an intelligent reader
was able to remember at a considerable time after reading it.
I got the impression that he thought the greater part of most
books wasted. I may be wrong in this impression of his meaning, gathered from casual and fragmentary talks.

5

To settle down to teaching as a profession is often to confess failure to realize early ambitions. Many who have failed as
teachers have immediately made a struggle for a Ph.D. degree,
hoping that with it they may be given a second chance. During
the Mencken era the professor became a synonym for the word
so often used by Theodore Roosevelt,—"mollycoddle." We who
have survived this era can almost from memory box the
Mencken compass of depreciation:

"Campus critics."

"College professors, alas, never learn anything."

"He sat in a professor's chair and caned sophomores for
throwing spitballs."

"Dr. Dewey went back to the insufferable dungeons of
Columbia."

"In the middle ground there is little save an indistinct herd
of intellectual eunuchs, chiefly professors."

"The professor is nothing if not a maker of card indexes;
he must classify or be damned. His masterpiece is the dictum,
that 'it is excellent but it is not a play.' "

I remember a story of the period of a gathering of men in
the smoking room of an Atlantic liner the first evening of the
voyage. To get acquainted with each other it was proposed
that each should introduce himself, naming his profession. One
was a lawyer, one a broker, one a manufacturer, and so on
around the circle, and at last the question came to a faded little
man with spectacles. "Well, I'm a college professor," he said.
"Now, damn you, laugh!"

One criticism of the profession comes often: "Who would
want to spend one's life always with inferior minds?" The professor does not live all his waking hours with his students. He has

more contacts with superior minds than most professions afford and there are always a few students in every class that the teacher feels are growing every day under his ministrations. A college is an intellectual center, a grouping of trained men, many of them leaders in their chosen field, and into the college circle come sooner or later many intellectual and artistic leaders of the period.

It must be confessed, however, that discouragement comes often to teachers of youth. Seemingly knowledge has to be stuffed into them by force as one feeds turkeys for the market. A college class is apathetic, seemingly enduring an ordeal, many of the students with minds, even during the teacher's lecture, far away on athletic field or coming house party. Only a small percentage are really touched. The examination period brings always to the teacher the thought of changing his profession. One instructor, not in my department however, in the midst of his lecture was interrupted by the closing bell. Up leaped the class heading for the door, but the professor peremptorily stopped them. "Just a moment, gentlemen," he said, "I want to cast before you one more pearl." The satire was wasted. Few students today are at all familiar with the Bible. Biblical allusions fall as unrecognized on their ears as do allusions to the Greek and Latin classics.

Professors there are who make collections of student blunders in examinations and themes, showing them around in high glee. Had I been a collector, I might have gathered enough for a Joe Miller jest book, howlers like these:

"Benjamin Franklin invented lightning."

"The Molly Maguires were not foreigners at all: they were Irishmen."

"Juno was God's wife. I forget who Cerberus was. Hymen is the three-headed dog that sits at the gates of hell."

But I get small joy laughing at youthful ignorance. I remember my own early days and the howlers that teachers undoubtedly found in my own written work. It makes me charitable when I look over the entries in my diaries, all the early ones of which I have burned.

Automobiling began with me June 1, 1904, when I was 41 years old. I find among my papers this note:

"Professor Foss has bought an automobile, the first one to be owned in the town. Just before six tonight he gave me my first ride in one of the things. I rode for nearly two miles at headlong speed, 15 miles an hour he estimated when he let it out once. As near flying as ever I expect to do. It is called a Stanley Steamer and it is beautiful. Horses all along the road snorted and kicked at the sight of it."

I'll close my chapter as Holmes did each of his Autocrat papers, with a poem. It is not from my own pen: it was written at a close of a summer school session at Bread Loaf, by one of my class of 52 members, Adelia Klum of Appleton, Wisconsin:

> You've made these writers come alive
> With anecdote and pictures clear;
> Your ways we lesser teachers strive
> To use but never come quite near.
>
> America has found, you say,
> Its own in poetry and prose—
> 'Tis Whitman who has led the way—
> The *Century Readings* volume shows.
>
> You've kept the right to change your mind,
> To understand each age anew;
> You've captured souls of human kind,
> These writers come alive through you.

CHAPTER XXIII

Escape to Florida

$\mathcal{G}$ HAVE BEEN TWICE TRANSPLANTED, once in 1894, and again in 1928 when I sought the Florida tropics. If one is to consider my life in terms of periods these are the two dates furnishing bench marks. In neither soil did I take root deeply, yet the three areas where I lived during my three periods each profoundly and differently influenced my work and my point of view.

I have had impulses at times to write a paper "On a Certain Condescension in New England Intellectuals." Lounsbury displayed it in his life of Cooper; Beers in his life of Willis; Warner in his life of Irving. William Vaughn Moody, writing from his "Sahara of the bozart," the city of Chicago, displayed it in his every letter. One finds it at Harvard and even at Yale. At my own college in the New Hampshire hills I never fail to hear when I arrive for class reunions, "Isn't it about time for you to end your academic exile and come back again into civilization?" At such times I have made use of Moody's drama title and have returned the "wise crack" that as seen from the halls of New England colleges, "The Great Divide" is the Hudson River, but I could assure them from actual explorations that even beyond this wild frontier there may be found traces of culture.

As I see it now, the climax of my life, the main summit reached, the cross-roads where all paths lead downward, came in the last years of the 1920s. It began with a shock that darkened for a time my whole horizon. In September 1927 came the death of my wife, Anna Plumer, who for nearly 40 years had been constantly with me, my companion and helper, sharer of my joys and sorrows. Never before had I realized what it meant to be alone. I was approaching 65, the retirement deadline, and no one can reach this exit gate without realizing that the break-up period of life has suddenly come into clear view. Then, little by little, addition will change to subtraction till all is gone. One can comfort oneself when the age of forced retirement has arrived by considering the thousands of splendid men at the summit of their powers who also have been displaced because of age and yet have turned to new work and have made abundantly good. Consider as an example Professor Wilbur L. Cross of Yale who when he had reached the deadline and was removed from his lifework, did not sit down discouraged to await the final counting out, but ran for Governor of Connecticut and was elected three times to the office. I have no complaint concerning the years of my retirement. After 1927 I wrote nine books and numbers of magazine articles and reviews, and for 13 years I taught a class, or classes, at Rollins.

After my wife's death I asked for a half-year's leave of absence and with my daughter and her husband, John M. Stetson, spent the winter in Florida. The following summer is remembered by me chiefly because I was offered during that summer three major jobs. On my way to Bread Loaf, I stopped at Woodstock, Vermont, where Dr. John Martin Thomas, late President of Penn State, was spending the summer. He had been elected President of Rutgers and he spent several hours trying to induce me to take a chair of English in the New Jersey institution. I begged for time to consider it. Later in the summer, President Moody of Middlebury College asked if I would carry on his work if he were to be called for a year on a mission he was considering. (Later he did not go.) Then in August Dr. Hamilton Holt came from his ancestral home at Woodstock, Vt. to offer me a professorship in Rollins College, Florida.

The offer seemed attractive. Because of the approaching age limit and because of growing ill health I already was contemplating Florida winters and then resignation from my Penn State professorship. After due consideration I told Dr. Holt that I would accept his offer, but with the provision that my work was to begin the following January first and be limited to a single class in American literature. He could make the salary fit the case. This he was willing to do. I was to learn that President Holt had a strong faculty because he had been able to secure many well-known scholars, who, like me, had reached the retirement age, while still at the height of their powers. He could induce them to come at a reduced salary because of the Florida climate which at their age would soon be prescribed for them by their physicians. September 4, 1928, I received from Dr. Holt the following letter, a characteristic document:

My dear Professor Pattee:

I have your letter and as we want to make Rollins a "Professor's Paradise," of course we shall fall in with your suggestion and give you only one subject, that is, for the winter term. If you care to take on two during the spring term, that can be decided on, but these matters, after all, come within the category of things I do not decide. As soon as I get to Winter Park, I will take up the question with the Department of English and will write you again.

I cannot tell you how much it has heartened me and my colleagues to know you will be with us in our circle next year.

Back in State College in the autumn I took up again my round of work. In October I sent my resignation to the President:

Dear President Hetzel:

I am presenting you herewith my resignation as Professor of American Literature in the Pennsylvania State College, the resignation to take effect at the end of the present semester.

I am asking for this release from a position that I have held since June, 1894. I make haste to assure you that it implies not in the slightest degree any criticism on my part of anything connected with the present regime of the college. My love for Penn State was never warmer than at this moment, and my dream for her glorious future in this transcendently beautiful location has never seemed nearer substantial reality than just now. I am in accord with heartiness, Mr. President, with all the policies of your vigorous new administration. I am with you and the trustees in all your plans and dreamings for the college, and could my youth, all its working years of which I have given to this college, be restored to me, it would be my highest joy to give again to the college the best that God made it possible for me to give. Dr. Atherton wrote 34 years ago in that spirit which put blood and iron and victory into all who came vitally near to him: "I am offering you at the Pennsylvania State College an opportunity which will satisfy your highest ambition as an educator." He was a true prophet.

But I have reached the age of retirement. I shall be 66 years old if I live till next March. I am withdrawing into what for me will be the late afternoon, the sunset, and the evening. I have much to do in the literary plans I have laid out for accomplishment, plans that forbid any save the smallest amount of the teaching of classes. I have found love and ideal comradeship for my declining days and I have found a home in a land whose climate is after my own heart.

Thanking you for your uniform kindness and sympathy and helpfulness, and assuring you of my willingness still to help in any ways that I am able, I remain

Yours most sincerely.

During the Thanksgiving recess I went to Florida, and on November 25, in her home in Coronado Beach, I was married to Grace Garee, six days my senior, a woman who for years had been Superintendent of Religious Education for the Presbyterian Church of three states with an office in Baltimore and another in Washington. A wedding reception was given us at Rollins College.

Back at Penn State, I finished my class work up to Christmas. Arrangements were made for me to end my work at the college with the beginning of the Christmas vacation. My packing was done and all was ready. No college ever sped a parting professor with words and ceremonies more complimentary or more winged with affection. At one farewell gathering I told them that all the week I had felt strangely embarrassed and out of place: I should be in a strongly-made box covered with calla lilies and not hearing a word of the funeral eulogies. The college paper had this news item:

> The past six days will probably go down in Penn State history as "Pattee week," for up to the time of his departure today for his winter home in Florida, Professor Pattee has received some special recognition each day since last Sunday.
>
> The most typical and outstanding of the Pattee tributes came Thursday night, when the college Senate presented the following resolution engrossed on parchment, and bordered with the scrolled words of the Penn State 'Alma Mater' song composed by Dr. Pattee in 1902:
>
> "The Pennsylvania State College, through its Senate, offers affectionate greeting and hearty congratulations to Professor Fred Lewis Pattee, M.A., Litt.D., upon the completion of 34 years of distinguished service. We rejoice in our association with him, in his preeminent success as a teacher, in the love

and loyalty of his students, and in his distinction as an author and a critic. We regret his withdrawal from the active service of the college; we wish him happiness and length of days; and we hope he may frequently return to the college and community that he has so long served with unselfish fidelity and notable devotion to high ideals."

The parchment was signed by a committee of ten senators, President R. D. Hetzel and Secretary W. S. Hoffman.

No college could have been more generous with its praises or more kindly with its farewells.

2

Of the many letters of congratulation that came to me at this multitudinous moment I single out one that came from Bread Loaf. Dean Davison, a rare soul, wrote it.

Dear Professor Pattee:

I have just read with great joy the excellently good news. If I knew Mrs. Garee, I'd congratulate her, though that might be a social error. But surely it will be quite all right to rejoice for you both. And we'll have another Breadloafer next summer; you must see to that, for important as the Southern work is, the bride must be introduced to Vermont hills. Bread Loaf, as you know, is already a famous honeymoon place, with John Farrar leading the procession. I had thought we'd have some walks next summer, the walks I hoped for last summer, but was not able to enjoy; but this is better—for you. Oh the news has all sorts of advantages!! But, seriously, you know I really am delighted. You so much need a home, and you so much deserve the happiest one possible. I think I'll go out and do a snake dance.

Arriving at Winter Park, I was impressed first of all, as are all visitors to Rollins College, by the beauty of its surroundings. Adjoining its campus is a chain of picturesque lakes, each landscaped by Nature with all the elements of Florida beauty. My second impression came from the fact that it is the oldest college in the state, a startling fact when one considers that it was founded in 1885, my freshman year at Dartmouth. I awoke to the fact that I was on the frontier: Florida even yet is frontier territory. Everywhere, I found, things were at the beginning point. The college had been founded in the missionary spirit as one starts Christian work in a heathen land. For years it was a church venture, supported almost wholly by funds from the North. Rex Beach, an early alumnus of Rollins, once defined it as "a decidedly churchly school in Florida." Perhaps it was so in his day. Until 1925 it had struggled on, and then its presidency had been given to Hamilton Holt who for 25 years had been connected with the editorial department of the *Independent* in New York City, finally becoming its editor. Without academic experience, he had entered on this Florida venture as one enters a crusade. He had embarked, as often he was to declare, upon a "great adventure." Quickly I found myself in educational territory as new to me as was the tropic land in which the venture was located.

The moment one struck the campus one heard of "the Rollins plan." There was nothing revolutionary about it. It was an editor's application of office methods to education. First, it was to be an eight-hour day in class rooms with no evening study-hour requirements. And second, no formal classroom lecturing was to be permitted. Each subject was given a two-hour period; classes were not to number over 20 members; and each class room was provided with a long table at the head of which sat the professor. Education by recitation was frowned upon. As one observer put it, it was "education by bull session." The students were there to study, to discuss the lesson, to help each other, to ask questions, and the teacher was to be their guide and director and friend. It was Plato's academy applied to undergraduates.

I agreed fully with Dr. Holt when it came to the failings of the lecture system. For students or anybody else to sit an hour like passive buckets trying to catch a rapid torrent of facts and conclusions accomplishes little so far as the students are concerned. With graduate students one can do more with the lecture than with undergraduates, for they are more mature and more prepared, but even with them there is great leakage. I was compelled to lecture in my later years at Penn State. No class that numbers over 30 can be conducted profitably with the recitation method, and my classes often contained over a hundred. I seated them in numbered seats, determined the vacancies as soon as the bell ceased ringing, called for one of the class to read the notes of the last lecture, and then poured out wisdom for the rest of the hour. Often I held quizzes, and at the close of the semester I required a written examination. The weakness of the system was evident in every written test. The ear knows only phonetic spelling, and mishearing while taking notes in frantic haste is an everpresent liability. Often I got such answers as this: "A leading pome of Lole is the Big Low Papers," perfectly right as to fact, but monstrous as it greets the eye. Undoubtedly that was the way the student's ear received the sentence from me.

I found the Rollins method as presented by Dr. Holt not greatly different from that which always I had used in the graduate seminars I had conducted at Penn State and at Illinois. With mature students, grounded in fundamentals, with a predetermined objective clearly in view, it worked perfectly, but with immature students it made for superficiality. One can talk and talk even in a class room and be ignorant. My own education I had got largely at night by hard work on hard lessons with no one to argue with and no one to help me.

But with Dr. Holt to explain the Rollins Plan, it always went over strong. His enthusiasm, his faith in it, his tireless advocacy of it even before many critical audiences in the North, were hard to resist. Once submerged in his plan he could see nothing else, would endure no criticism. A loveable man, a persuasive speaker, a dominating personality, a campaigner who brought funds to the college, he put the town on the Florida map as a place to visit and to linger. He was redolent of New England. With great glee he told us once that his grandmother, six removes back, had a sister who was executed as a witch. Cotton Mather had characterized her as "a vile hag gone to rule as Queen of Hell."

Rollins College had had touches of literary history before Dr. Holt's advent. Rex Beach had been a student there in 1891-96. In 1906 Vachel Lindsay on his tour of the South "spreading the gospel of beauty" had walked from Sanford over a primitive sand trail punctuated here and there with turpentine stills, and had lectured in Knowles Hall on the Pre-Raphaelites to an audience of 19 students. According to his biographer Masters, "Lindsay called it a glorious experience. He was ecstatic over the clear-eyed boys, the young gods, and the girls with kindly hearts and the sort of rapturous youth that departs when college days are ended."

With the advent of Dr. Holt, Winter Park more and more was referred to as "the literary center of Florida." His *Independent* editorship had made him many literary friends, who came to the college town to stay. The well-known author of *Eben Holden*, Irving Bacheller, established a beautiful home on Lake Maitland, buried in orange groves, one of the beauty spots of Florida. Authors came in numbers: Clinton Scollard and his poetic wife Jessie Rittenhouse, Ray Stannard Baker, Winston Churchill, Joseph Lincoln, Albert Shaw, Arthur Guiterman, Richard Burton, and many others.

Ray Stannard Baker we came to know early. His brother, Hugh P. Baker, had been in charge of the Forestry Department at Penn State and was in Germany working for his degree the year that I was at Göttingen. Ray Baker, who spent his winters at Winter Park, was working diligently upon his life of Woodrow Wilson. At his home at Amherst I had seen the extent of his preparations. For 10 years he had kept several secretaries at work and the mass of materials collected was astonishing. In reality the subject he had taken in hand was the history of the World War in its American bearings. What impressed me greatly was a card catalogue cabinet as extensive as that used by many libraries. Arranged chronologically in this cabinet were cards for every day and often for every hour of Woodrow Wilson's life from the time he took the presidency of Princeton. Every speech the President made and every interview was on a card and dated with notation where the report could be found. He told me that he was all but swamped by his materials. For them he had built a vault absolutely fire-proof in his basement and much of the materials he had stored in the new town library vaults.

Few men have, like Baker, played three totally different parts in the literary drama of their period. He had first won recognition as a writer of articles in the muckrake period. So successful was he that the reading public had him classified: he would go down to posterity, if he went down at all, as a muckraker. He rebelled, changed his signature to David Grayson, and wrote contentment books. For years no one suspected the change, so total was it. Then had come the World War and the life of Wilson, a work made possible only from the proceeds of the David Grayson volumes.

He will live as David Grayson. Often we have gone on fishing trips down the Indian River and it always was the David Grayson personality that made the trip unforgettable. He was an authority on bee keeping, on gardening, and small fruits, but always he was David Grayson, rural philosopher and preacher of contentment. For a dinner party at our home I wrote this card for his table place:

> With Wilson he's a clever Mason;
> The poet soul is David Grayson.

He died in 1946.

The extent of his fame was revealed to me in a curious way one summer at Blowing Rock, N. C. Time and again rumors reached us that David Grayson was summering in the region and was being entertained sometimes for a week, by wealthy summer people who had palatial residences in the mountains. We investigated at once and the man, evidently getting wind of it, disappeared into another section. He was an impostor of course, but he must have been a remarkable man. He went to receptions in his honor and was equal to the part. He gave a reading in the town of Blowing Rock, rendering a pathetic selection from *Adventures in Contentment* so feelingly that many ladies cried. For all of them he wrote his autograph. So well did he carry off his part that several aristocratic ladies who had entertained him refused to believe me when I pronounced him bogus. "We know," we said, "that Mr. Baker drinks no liquors, smokes no cigars, and has no daughters who exhibit at horse shows." The impostor had demanded at the houses where he was entertained a quart of whisky a day and a dozen choice cigars, and in at least two homes had got them. One prominent social leader would not believe the man a fraud until I showed her a dated letter from Baker saying he had not been out of Amherst for six weeks. She then was furious and set out to discover and destroy the man. But she never found him.

This man, or some other, had in an earlier summer, while Baker was in Europe, got another free summer in a western resort town and had finally married a school teacher there. The real David Grayson then got letters of congratulation from several western people. Baker being in Europe, Mrs. Baker opened the letters, and was startled.

When I arrived, Winter Park had become "The City of Homes"—distinctive homes—and also "the City of Lectures." Arthur Guiterman waxed poetic over this favorite Winter Park indoor sport:

> In many a town of lesser sort
> You hear a constant swishing-swashing,
> For people's means of self-support
> Is taking in each other's washing.

> But here where cultured folk reside—
> Or this my simple soul conjectures—
> We're almost wholly occupied
> In sitting through each other's lectures.

In February every year came "The Animated Magazine" which brought into the Winter Park area the authors wintering in Florida. In a two-hours' program authors read from their writings, each one for 10 minutes. During my years at the college over 100 authors appeared on this program, including such names as Jane Addams, James Branch Cabell, Zona Gale, Arthur Guiterman, Robert Herrick, Ed. Howe, Fannie Hurst, Maurice Maeterlinck, William Lyon Phelps, Opie Read, Cale Young Rice, Alice Hegan Rice, Marjorie Rawlings, Clinton Scollard, Carl Sandburg, and Countess Tolstoi.

Many, like Winston Churchill, Percy MacKaye, Ray Stannard Baker, Cora Harris, Albert Shaw, Joseph C. Lincoln, were with us the winter long. Always there was Irving Bacheller, the life of every gathering, older every day but always the youngest member in any college circle. Once at a lecture by Richard Burton my seat was beside Bacheller. The summer in the North had evidently agreed with him. I said, "How do you keep looking so young? What is your recipe?" And he said, "Go through a Florida boom, then go through a depression when all the banks break, and then go to work." Indeed he did work. I never saw him when he was not in the midst of a new novel. Sometimes I read the manuscripts, but never did he heed my suggestions.

3

We made our home at Coronado Beach, 50 miles from Winter Park, but when Rollins was in session we spent a part of each week there, either commuting by automobile or else living in rented apartments. For several years we spent our Rollins weeks in what in Europe would be called a *pension*, presided over by a delightful lady of the old school, Mrs. Pletchman. In another apartment lived for some years Richard Burton, poet and critic, and his wife Guthrie, later author of her autobiographical *Three Parts Scotch*. In the dining room Dr. Burton was Autocrat all three meals. Then came Ehrick Rossiter, architect, and wife; Major Ryan, retired, and wife; Mr. and Mrs. Barton, she the daughter of Charles A. Dana; and at times others, ourselves being included. The Autocrat was at his best at the dinner hour. We all agreed with his judgments, but when Professor George M. Whicher, Sr., of Amherst was a visitor at the table sparks sometime flew. O'Neill, recent winner of the Nobel prize, pleased the old professor not at all. O'Neill reminded him, he said, of the bishop in Browning's poem, "The Bishop Orders His Tomb":

> Saint Praxed in a glory, and one Pan
> Ready to twitch the Nymph's last garment off.

"O'Neill is a craftsman," he said, "and only a craftsman. He reads Euripides, who also was a craftsman but who works his characters into a climax where they must take one of two roads. Then he breaks them open and solves the problem by discovering the heart of the drama to be essentially religious, an illustration of an elemental truth. When O'Neill, however, at the crisis breaks open his characters, he discovers only a Freudian sex complex."

Dr. Burton's literary experience had been a remarkable one. Mark Twain and Mrs. Stowe had been near neighbors during his youth. He had shared rooms at Johns Hopkins with Woodrow Wilson, Albert Shaw, and Charles Wright, later professor at Middlebury. They had together bought *Huckleberry Finn*, just out, had read it with huge enjoyment, and then had cast lots to determine who was to possess the copy. It fell to Burton.

No man was more rich in anecdote. His friend, he said, Henry Bellows, had once published a book of poems entitled *The West Wind*. One reviewer did the book full justice in a review of two words, the shortest review on record: "Why *west?*"

He told how Dr. George Vincent once introduced Tyrone Power, who was booked to present single-handed Sheridan's *The Rivals:* "It is a pleasure to present one who has no rivals and so is forced to present Sheridan's."

Once, he said, he had determined to reread the major classics every seven years. In his early years he had greatly admired *The Vicar of Wakefield*. When he began his rereading of this classic and found it intolerable, he reversed his project and now his rule is never to reread a book that he has enjoyed in other years.

No table companion could be more enjoyable than the architect Rossiter. Literature to him had been an amusing avocation, but in an argument he could very often say the last word concerning an author. He told the story of Burroughs' father who considered writing for the papers mere waste of time. Once on a hunting trip his father shot the fox and John came back empty handed. His father got $5 for the fox skin, but John for an article describing the hunt got $50.

He quoted Stevenson who said, "He who loves the same books he loved 20 years before is an ass."

I countered with the information that I had planned a paper which I was to entitle "Saturations." One paragraph, I said, will concern R. L. S. It will be a long paper. In the earlier days of my reading when all there was of Stevenson was his own beautiful writings in their first editions, I loved him and read him with joy—doubtless adolescent joy. Now one can hardly open a current magazine or take up a list of new books without the fearful thought that it may contain more *R. L. S.-iana*. A jungle has arisen which now chokes and all but conceals the thin clear stream we once called "Stevenson." After all a man becomes at last a legend, and sometimes it occurs before he dies.

Burton then quoted from Henry Adams and added, "All through Stevenson, the 'Education' shows. His early associates were all second rate; he never seems by any chance to have come in contact with first-rate people, either men, women, or artists."

"Adams was a damned snob," came a voice in the direction of the major.

Sometimes the ladies joined in the chatter, but not often. I remember Mrs. Burton's definition of great poetry as "One step beyond." "The greater number of the poets," she said, "follow the old lane that all poets travel and finally they come to a locked gate. Few attempt to scale this obstacle. Sometimes a daring soul pushes through and takes a step out into the new field beyond. Only one step, and immediately all the fence is rebuilt to include this single step into the unknown."

"Yes," I agreed, "Whitman took that one step all right, but he wore seven league boots."

One morning, in defiance of the Rollins plan forbidding lecturing, I told the table that last night I had dreamed I was lecturing on current authors. I had told my dream audience that fame and permanence came only to rebels. Great genius—great rebel. I instanced Poe, Whitman, Emerson, Melville, Thoreau. Pausing at the newly-furbished-up career of Vachel Lindsay, I had added him also to the rebels. "He lives," I said, "and I believe he will live because he made something out of nothing: he made poetry out of college yells, chief of which was the demoniac jay-hawk yell of the University of Kansas. With his own jack knife he whittled out a saxophone and played it as if he were cheer leader at a game. To be heard one must invent, as Whitman did, one's own instrument. The telling music now is saxophonic, and the poetry set to it may be called saxophonics. The devil created the instrument during a depression in the Pit, and college students are able to wring from it infernal tones. I know, for I lived for years next door to a college frat." Then a cat in the yard had awakened me.

Especially delightful did I find old Professor Whicher who for years had rooms at the Bacheller Hotel. We agreed that his son, George F., was making too much of Emily Dickinson's verses. It seems that in Amherst you are either a Dickinsonian or you are not.

The old professor was versatile; he had written poetry I discovered and he presented me with his book with a delightful inscription. He long has been a neighbor of Robert Frost, who then was under contract at Amherst to give one-third of each school year to teaching in the college. He can do with his time, the professor explained, what he sees fit to do. His variety of teaching is like his variety of poetry. He is bare of ornament, bare of figure, bare of adjectives. Some years later Frost became poet in residence at Dartmouth.

4

Ten summers at Bread Loaf, as many Augusts on the farm of my childhood, now sold since advancing age has made it impossible to maintain, three short courses of lectures at Penn State,—the rest has been Florida. It was for me a harvest period. I completed my history of American literature which I had begun with the *American Literature Since 1870* volume, publishing volume three with the title *The New American Literature*, 1930, and volume one, *The First Century of American Literature* in 1935, and in 1940 *The Feminine Fifties*, an illus-

*Boyhood home and
study where F. L.
Pattee and family
spent summer
vacations after 1902
when he bought his
father's farm.*

*Professor and Mrs.
Pattee and daughter
Sarah Lewis in the
"horse-and-buggy
days."*

*Fred Lewis Pattee
swinging a scythe
on the farm.*

*The Breadloaf School of English near Middlebury, Vermont,
where Dr. Pattee taught for 10 summers.*

*Dr. and Mrs. Pattee at
Breadloaf School of English.*

Dr. Pattee lecturing at Rollins College, Winter Park, Florida, where he taught for 12 years after leaving Penn State.

Dr. and Mrs. Pattee at their home in Coronado Beach, Florida, 50 miles from Winter Park

trated volume dealing with the decade before the Civil War. Much other work I did, including editions of Mark Twain and of John Neal, and articles on Emily Dickinson, Constance Fenimore Woolson and others. I made also two highly publicised addresses, one on scholarship day at Penn State and the other a commencement address at Rollins College.

My exile in the South has prolonged my life. No harsher climate could I endure now. But not at all have I forgotten the New England from which I sprang, and I shall be laid away when the time comes under the maples and the northern pines I have always loved. My feelings sometimes overflow as in this lyric I lately wrote, published in the June number, 1941, of *The New Hampshire Troubadour:*

> Now it's lilac time in Old New Hampshire,
>   And all the North is drunken with the May;
> Now it's bobolink time in Old New Hampshire,
>   And here I am a thousand miles away.
>
> Oh, I'm sure the robin's in the dear old maple
>   To wake the morning with his brave bassoon,
> And I can all but hear the night hawks booming,
>   And whip-poor-wills complaining to the moon.
>
> And the bluebirds and the phoebes and the swallows
>   Are pouring out their love-lorn ecstacy,
> And the thrushes, and the ground-birds in the grasses,
>   And crazy grackles in the oil-nut tree.
>
> Oh, it's lilac time in Old New Hampshire,
>   And I'd give a year of life for just a day
> With the bobolinks and robins and the lilacs,
>   And here I'm bound a thousand miles away.

CHAPTER XXIV

Life's Armistice Years

THE ONE HUNDRED AND FIFTY YEARS of my family in the New England hill lands is a completed story now. The Pattee family of my branch is all but extinct. In the whole county that contains the once populous Pattee Hill there is not a single Pattee. Their farms are wilderness now. The story of my family is the story of a thousand families. I have used it as a type. It tells the whole story of a folk movement begun near the close of the Revolution. It is the story of the establishment of a vigorous Anglo-Saxon people in a new Scotland-like area that required for its clearing enormous toil. These folk-waves, after their arrival in the hills, organized themselves into small groupings called townships, each conducted as an absolute democracy. Across New Hampshire, Vermont, Maine, and the hill lands of Massachusetts this second wave of the New England settlement spread, and in its fourth generation it had become a veritable force, a democratic Scotland north of Boston.

The *Grapes of Wrath* complex dominates our literature today. To be in step with the times I should work this folk movement into a story of grisly tragedy, hardships all but unendurable suffered by uncouth peasants who were compelled to farm land that even the cliff-dwellers would have scorned. I have done nothing of the kind. A part of the great epic myself, an actual witness of the established hill-tillers in their prime, I write of it not as a tragedy, but as a vital force that entered American life. I saw the mountain towns as ideal nurseries of men, and I know now that the hardships of the frontier life they lived were a training school for the crisis in the national life that was soon to come. With their red school houses, their white churches, their town halls, their blacksmith shops, their country stores which were village forums, they developed centers of democracy which bred forces that were to be far reaching. As early as 1842, Miss Catharine M. Sedgwick had said, "The New England people are as yet but an extended family circle." She lived in the Berkshires, not in the Boston belt.

If the century and a half history of our family in America were to be written as a drama-history after the Shakespeare pattern, each of its five acts would cover a generation. The climax would come in the fourth act, and the fifth act would be catastrophe. My fifth generation saw the curtain fall after the final act.

Not alone was it the Civil War nor the westward movement that caused the abandonment of the hill farms and the depopulation of the rural villages. The economy that had ruled the four provincial generations, an economy dependent upon handwork to a degree that would have pleased even William Morris, yielded inevitably to the new industrial movement that had its centers in the large cities. The farms could not hold the young life which so prodigally they had produced. As a result my generation was a transplanted generation nowhere taking root, a scattered generation, a lost generation. Governor Rollins of New Hampshire at the opening of the present century dramatized the out-of-New-England movement in an act which he called Old Home Day, but it did little save to create sentimentalism and emphasize the tragedy.

Not wholly lost, however, has been the New England experiment, not wholly vanished even now those little democratic Edens, mountain shadowed, where freedom came as a divine right and liberty was as much taken for granted as the hill winds. Not entirely lost those small family-like neighborhoods with their white churches and town halls. The explosion did not annihilate: it only scattered. Over all the middle and the northern West rise now those same white church spires, and the democracy learned in the hill towns of New England still lives there and is potent in the nation's life.

But alas for the old mother hive. Old home day pilgrims from the distant West visiting after years the scenes of their youth seldom return for a second visit. They go back shocked and saddened. It is told that one of them returning after 50 years to his native Massachusetts was told that rum no more was made in a famous old distillery. Greatly shocked, he threw up his hands. "Close the Medford Rum distilleries!" he shouted. "My God! What would the old Pilgrim Fathers say if they should come back and hear that?"

The mills on the Merrimack, where my mother once worked as a loom tender, have either been moved to the South or else are now served by a foreign population. A great wave of French Canadians has swept down into New England. When the Amoskeag mills were in full operation more French was heard talked on the streets of Manchester than English. Other varieties of foreigners have come in, some in numbers. There is a colony of Finns or Russians in the town of my boyhood. They are bringing back into cultivation the abandoned areas south of Mount Cardigan, are honest and hard-working, a marvellous asset for the dwindling township. Everywhere these foreign settlers find in the woods the old stone fences that once had walled in cultivated fields, and here and there the cellar holes where buildings once had been, and they view them with wonder as travellers now view the abandonments in Mexico and Yucatan. What race, they ponder, could be so foolish as to build these hundreds of miles of stone walls in the utter woods?

My generation seems to have been a betwixt and between one. I was in the last wave of American students that matriculated in the German universities. I saw the growth of a land grant college in the days when industrial education was so new that there were no trained professors to be had in agricultural and industrial specialties. I have lived through the virtual abandonment of required Greek and then required Latin as the educational basis. I have seen American literature in college courses grow from practically nothing to its present degree of universal requirement. Everywhere in my life changes to the limits of revolution. When I left college it was announced that the frontier had vanished. There were no more public lands for public largess or "pork-barrel" distribution. Romance was lifting like a night mist from the west and one had to go to Alaska or the South Sea Islands to find it. I saw industry swiftly making new frontiers, doing miracles. With the thing right before my eyes, the airplane and the radio, I feel like saying with the old farmer, "there ain't no such animal."

Among the messages that came to me on my seventy-fifth birthday, none touched me more deeply than the one from the Penn State Board of Trustees. This was my reply:

> Coronado Beach, Florida
> March 25, 1938

President Hetzel and the Board of Trustees:

> The action of the Board of Trustees relative to my birthday touched me deeply. To be remembered in this headlong age after 10 long years of absence, and such a 10 years of growth and activity, is certainly a gratifying experience to the one remembered. Certainly it is not an experience that can come to one often. Accept my heartiest thanks and my heartiest wishes for the college we all love.
>
> I am living happily these latter years. My health is better now than it was 10 years ago. With my books and my writing I keep reasonably busy. I hereby send to you my prayer. It is from Horace: Car. I:xxxi. Your Latin, like mine I realize, is in a state of linguistic recession, so, in order to save your time in these arduous days, I am sending it in English. You will find *me* in it:
>
> 'O thou Son of Latona, grant me to enjoy my acquisitions, and to possess my health, together with an unimpaired understanding, I beseech thee, and that I may not lead a dishonorable old age, nor one bereft of the lyre.'

Masefield, the poet laureate, once wrote, "the things not touched with joy drop dead out of memory," and thereby demonstrated that he does not possess a New England conscience. I do possess one and it has added no comfort to my old age. I agree heartily with the Yankee philosopher who maintained that "the New England conscience does not prevent bad acts but it does prevent one from enjoying them after they are done." More and more as old age creeps on I am conscious of mistakes I made in earlier years and deeds I should have done and did not do. I often find myself brooding on these. It will be remembered that Mark Twain once remarked that his conscience did not awaken until he was 60 and then it never slept. Often, he said, he would find himself brooding on some little murder he had once committed and thought nothing of at the time. Mark could not have inherited a New England conscience; he must have acquired it during his residence in Hartford where always it has been epidemic and highly contagious. In my case it was inherited and certainly it is incurable.

Despite this one drawback old age has compensations so many and so valuable that one might wish to prolong it interminably. Many of these compensations are denied utterly to youth. For one thing the man in the seventies and the eighties is permitted to witness Time's revenges. Especially joyful is the critic whose prophecies have come true. Time is the final umpire; and after his verdict rendered in due time what joy like saying, "I told you so. I said that myself 50 years ago." And no one is alive to dispute you.

On some of my own prophecies Time has not ruled finally even yet. But on the judgments that were most hotly resented when made, Time has been for the most part with me. I note but a single instance. I was assailed savagely by many critics for my estimate of Richard Harding Davis in the sketch I wrote for the *Dictionary of American Biography* years ago. I had written this:

"In all his fiction Davis was essentially a journalist, quick to sense the demands of the larger public and working in the fashions of the hour. He dealt mainly with the surface of life, and even his best work will not endure. He was too facile, too headlong, too obsessed with contemporaneousness."

The day after Davis died in 1916, William Allen White in a passage later quoted in his autobiography, 1937, condemned most of his writings, but prophesied that a part was of classic quality: "All his clothes-model soldiers; all his pasteboard princes; all his addle-pated women will pass, but 'Gallagher' and 'Van Bibber' will carry Davis's baggage to a far posterity."

Republishing this 21 years later, White was forced to add this foot-note, "Alas, they seem to have dropped his bags less than a decade after he checked in. One of the lessons I have learned in a long and foolish life is that prophecy is the most futile of all blunders."

Enough. This is not an essay on old age. Cicero said the last word on the subject: why try to add to it? I have often wondered why *De Senectute* was prescribed for me to study intensely for three months when I was but a boy bubbling with adolescence. I got from it ablatives and accusatives of specification and a single sentence that clings brokenly in my memory: "Cato"—was it Cato?—"began the study of Greek at 80." A good suggestion: I am 80 and I think I shall try it.

And at 85, though bereft and again alone I have written,

> Old age is outer shell,
>   Inside is me
> Outside old age doth dwell,
>   Not in with me.
>
> When in my glass I stare,
>   Old age I see;
> Bowed back and whitened hair,
>   But that's not ME.
>
> Inside the soul is young,
>   As in its prime,
> When song was on my tongue,
>   Untouched by time.
>
> In chrysalis I lie
>   But soon shall be
> A bursting of the tie
>   And I'll be free.

Dr. Johnson is said to have had on his watch face the words, "The night cometh." My own night I realize is near, but

> I have loved the stars too fondly
> To be fearful of the night.

Postscript

A few additional facts will serve to complete the record of Dr. Pattee's life. His last years were saddened by the death of his second wife, Grace Garee Pattee, on April 30, 1946. Since his serious illness in 1935, when physicians gave him only three months to live, he had recovered a fair degree of health, but at times she had literally kept him alive by her constant care. Fortunately for him, after her death, her sister, Miss Ethel Gorrell, a social worker of St. Marys, West Virginia, served as his faithful nurse and housekeeper unselfishly and constantly until his death.

Another sort of grief occurred during the second world war. Publishers' plates of books no longer much in demand were scrapped and salvaged for the war effort, and many authors lost all hopes of securing new editions of their earlier works. Only one of Dr. Pattee's numerous books, *Century Readings in American Literature*, survived this destruction.

After the war Dr. Pattee continued to live in Florida most of the year but spent his summers at Miss Gorrell's home in St. Marys, from which he made two brief farewell trips to State College in 1946 and 1947. His last two years were spent mostly in hospitals; on his eighty-seventh birthday Penn State friends and alumni presented him with a purse of $1185 to help with hospital expenses.

He died on May 6, 1950 at Winter Park. Memorial services were held there on May 8 and in State College, May 10. He was buried on May 11, at Homeland Cemetery, a short distance from Bristol, New Hampshire, returned at last to the scenes of his youth, to the place he loved best.

W. L. W.

Bibliography

A list of books written or edited by Fred Lewis Pattee,
arranged in chronological order

Literature in the Public Schools. Teachers Co-operative Publishing Co., Cincinnati, Ohio, 1891.

Pasquaney: a Study. Musgrove Printing House, Bristol, 1893. Revised edition, 1929.

The Wine of May, and Other Lyrics. Republican Press Association, Concord, N. H., 1893.

A History of American Literature; with a View to the Fundamental Principles Underlying its Development; a textbook for schools and colleges. Silver Burdett & Co., Boston, 1896, 1903, 1909.

Reading Courses in American Literature. Silver Burdett & Co., 1897.

Wm. Shakespeare: *Tragedy of Macbeth.* Edited for school use. Silver Burdett & Co., 1897.

The Foundations of English Literature; a Study of the Development of English Thought and Expression from Beowulf to Milton. Silver Burdett & Co., 1899.

James Russell Lowell: *Conversations on Some of the Old Poets.* Edited with an introduction. T. Y. Crowell, New York, 1901.

Booklovers Reading Club series. Course IV, American Vacations in Europe. Course V, Six New England Classics. Course XIX, Out-of-Door Americans. Course XXII, Studies in American Literary Life. Editorial notes by F. L. P. The Booklovers Library, Philadelphia, 1901.

Poems of Philip Freneau, Poet of the American Revolution. Edited for the Princeton Historical Association, Princeton, N. J. Three volumes issued separately, 1902, 1903, 1909.

Mary Garvin; the Story of a New Hampshire Summer. Crowell, New York, 1902.

The Message of the West: an Ode, delivered June 16, 1903, at the dedication of the auditorium, The Pennsylvania State College. Seventy-five copies privately printed, 1903.

The House of the Black Ring; a Romance of the Seven Mountains. Henry Holt, New York, 1905. Reprinted, Mount Pleasant Press, Harrisburg, Pa., 1927.

Elements of Religious Pedagogy; a Course in Sunday School Teacher-Training. Eaton and Mains, 1909. Reprinted, Methodist Book Concern, New York, 1921.

The Breaking Point. A novel. Small, Maynard & Co., Boston, 1912.

Sermons and Addresses of Benjamin Gill. Edited for the College, State College, Pa., 1913.

Compelled Men. Association Press, 1913. Reprinted, 1930.

A History of American Literature Since 1870. Century Co., New York, 1915.

Century Readings in American Literature. (A college anthology.) Century Co., New York, 1919. Revised and reissued, 1922, 1926, 1932.

Mary E. Wilkins Freeman: *A New England Nun, and Other Stories.* Edited with introduction, Harper's Modern Classics series, Harper, New York, 1920.

Sidelights on American Literature. (Nine essays.) Century Co., New York, 1922.

The Development of the American Short Story; an historical survey. Harper & Bros., New York, 1923.

In Memoriam, Edwin Erle Sparks; President of The Pennsylvania State College, 1908-1920. Edited for the College, State College, 1925.

Tradition and Jazz. (Nine essays.) Century Co., New York, 1925.

American Short Stories. An anthology, edited with an introduction. Duffield & Co., New York, 1925. Reissued by Dodd, Mead & Co., 1939.

Charles Brockden Brown: *Wieland;* or the Transformation, together with the *Memoirs of Carwin the Biloquist,* a fragment. Edited with an introduction, American Authors series, Harcourt, Brace & Co., New York, 1926.

James Fenimore Cooper: *The Last of the Mohicans;* or a Narrative of 1757. Edited with an introduction, Modern Readers series, Macmillan, New York, 1927.

Century Readings in the American Short Story. (A college anthology.) Century Co., New York, 1927.

The New American Literature, 1890-1930. Century Co., New York, 1930.

Twenty-third Report of the Class of 1888, Dartmouth College. 1932.

Twenty-fourth Report of the Class of 1888, Dartmouth College. 1933.

Beyond the Sunset. (Poems.) Musgrove Printing House, Bristol, N. H., 1934.

The First Century of American Literature, 1770-1870. Appleton-Century Co., New York, 1935.

S. L. Clemens: *Representative Selections.* Edited with an introduction and bibliography, American Writers series, American Book Co., New York, 1935.

John Neal: *American Writers;* a series of papers contributed to *Blackwood's Magazine* (1824-1825). Edited with notes and bibliography. Duke University Press, Durham, N. C., 1937.

The Feminine Fifties. (Essays on literature and life in the 1850s.) Appleton-Century Co., New York, 1940.

A 22-page bibliography of all the writings of Dr. Pattee and all the writings about him is contained in *Fred Lewis Pattee: A Critical and Biographical Study,* a Master's Thesis in English, done at The Pennsylvania State College, 1951, by Major James F. Holly, U. S. A. (Available in the Pattee Library, The Pennsylvania State College, State College, Pennsylvania.)

Index of Persons

A

Typographical Data

The text of *Penn State Yankee* was set on the Linotype in 10 on 13 point *Monticello*, a distinctive early American type face, first cast about 1796 by Binney & Ronaldson in Philadelphia. In 1943, when Princeton University Press announced plans to publish the complete *Papers of Thomas Jefferson*, it was suggested that a version of this face would be suitable, since the prominent years of Jefferson's life coincided with the type's popularity. This face, recut by Linotype, was appropriately renamed *Monticello* and first appeared in book composition in Volume I of the *Papers*.

Penn State Yankee was composed and printed at The Carroll Press, Carrolltown, Pennsylvania, and bound at Arnold's Book Bindery, Inc., Reading, Pennsylvania. Wendell MacRae designed the volume and supervised production for the publication committee.